Yale Publications in American Studies, 7

DAVID HORNE, EDITOR

Published under the direction of the
American Studies Program

★ ★ ★ ★ ★ ★ ★

THE AMERICAN VISION

Actual and Ideal Society in
Nineteenth-Century Fiction

★ ★ ★ ★ ★ ★ ★

A. N. KAUL

NEW HAVEN AND LONDON

YALE UNIVERSITY PRESS

039206

Library of Congress catalog card number: 63–9309.
ISBN: 0–300–01377–9

Distributed in Great Britain, Europe, and
Africa by Yale University Press, Ltd., London;
in Canada by McGill-Queen's University Press,
Montreal; in Mexico by Centro Interamericano de
Libros Académicos, Mexico City; in Australasia
by Australia and New Zealand Book Co., Pty.,
Ltd., Artarmon, New South Wales; in India by
UBS Publishers' Distributors Pvt., Ltd., Delhi;
in Japan by John Weatherhill, Inc., Tokyo.

To my Father

PANDIT PREM NATH KAUL

Preface

This book seeks to give an account of the social theme of four nineteenth-century American novelists: James Fenimore Cooper, Nathaniel Hawthorne, Herman Melville, and Mark Twain. It is basically concerned with the manner in which these novelists confronted the society of the time, critically evaluating it and at the same time tending away from it to project, in their distinctive ways, the image of an ideal community or an ideal social order. The dialectic thus set up in their work has produced a complex theme in which the actual and the ideal function in a mutual critique.

This common theme, which unifies the studies of the individual novelists, is itself seen in two perspectives. On the one hand, the book analyzes the relation of the theme to an underlying cultural tradition handed down from early Puritan times and remarkably operative in the imagination of the nineteenth century. On the other hand, it considers the shaping influence of such a theme on the art of fiction displayed by the above novelists.

Quite obviously, my interpretation is indebted to the insights of the many critics who have written on the classic period of American literature from the time of D. H. Lawrence onward. But it takes the existing critical approaches for granted in an important sense, inasmuch as its essential purpose is to add the exploration of a somewhat neglected aspect of the subject to the cumulative understanding that is already available.

I must also point out that certain leading concepts that figure in my discussion—such as the concepts of actual society and ideal community—are used only as verbal equivalents of observed thematic elements. Their sole justification lies in the convenience with which they enable us to talk about the works of literature that suggested them in the first place. Accordingly I have made little attempt to define them in terms other than those warranted by the writers with whom I am concerned. To formulate their meaning more rigorously, or to offer a critique of their validity according to the standards of our own day, might have afforded some independent intellectual satisfaction; but such an exercise, it seemed to me, would also put an unjustifiable strain on the fiction to which the terms are primarily applied.

Finally, my study is limited to the historical period that came to an end with the Civil War—an event that Melville described as a "Sad arch between contrasted eras." I have contended that the war and its aftermath dislocated the vital tension of the theme that is examined here. But a theme so deeply rooted in a culture hardly ever disappears wholly from its literature. Mark Twain's *Huckleberry Finn* certainly recaptures it on the other side of the arch. One can even argue that the impulse continues into the present century and trace its operation in the later works of Henry James, in some novels of Edith Wharton, and in Fitzgerald's *The Great Gatsby*, not to mention the fiction of more recent writers. However, the techniques employed by the later novelists are so different and the social conditions they deal with so altered that the theme itself cannot be said to have remained unchanged. To pursue these developments would have made the book unwieldy and blurred its focus.

The book was undertaken as a doctoral dissertation at the

Graduate School of Yale University, where it won the John Addison Porter prize for 1962. It is with special pleasure, though with a sense of inadequacy, that I acknowledge my affectionate gratitude to the many friends and teachers at this university. I am particularly indebted to Norman Holmes Pearson, who supervised my work at every stage and helped and encouraged me in more ways than I can record here. R. W. B. Lewis, in whose seminars some of the ideas that have gone into this book first took shape, guided and stimulated me at several difficult turns. The suggestions made by these two teachers have greatly improved the result of my efforts. I have also profited by the advice of Edmund S. Morgan and Charles Feidelson, Jr., both of whom read the manuscript and were kind enough to comment on it. To David Horne, editor of Yale Publications in American Studies, I owe the benefit of expert editorial guidance.

I take this opportunity to thank the Institute of International Education which, by the award of a grant, enabled me to go to Yale in 1959–60. For the following two years I was the recipient of a Rockefeller fellowship, and I should like to express my gratitude to the Rockefeller Foundation and its officers—Chadbourne Gilpatric in particular—for their generous financial assistance.

And finally, I wish to acknowledge the debt I owe my wife, Mythili, for her many valuable suggestions, her help in the preparation of the manuscript, and her constant and cheerful encouragement.

New Delhi   A. N. KAUL
November 1962

Contents

Preface   vii

1. Cultural and Literary Background:
   The Type of American Experience   1

2. Nineteenth-Century Fiction:
   Themes and Patterns   45

3. James Fenimore Cooper:
   The History and the Myth of American Civilization   84

4. Nathaniel Hawthorne:
   Heir and Critic of the Puritan Tradition   139

5. Herman Melville:
   The New-World Voyageur   214

6. *Huckleberry Finn:*
   A Southwestern Statement   280

7. Concluding Note:
   Social Reality and the Form of American Fiction   305

References   325

Index   335

1. Cultural and Literary Background:

THE TYPE OF AMERICAN EXPERIENCE

> To derive a culture from a certain mythic ancestry, or
> ideal mythic type, is a way of stating that culture's
> essence in narrative terms.
>
> —Kenneth Burke, "Ideology and Myth"

The American novelists of the nineteenth century were concerned with many sides of human experience. As happens in
the case of other significant novelists of the world, the objects
of their concern included the society in which they lived.
Fenimore Cooper, Hawthorne, Melville, and Mark Twain
were all in their different ways preoccupied with certain
aspects of social life as it was shaping itself in the America of
their times. Of these four, Cooper and Twain were, in some of
their works, most directly concerned with the contemporary
scene. Though Hawthorne's and Melville's work is seldom
characterized by such directness of intention, it presents,
perhaps for that very reason, a subtler and more abiding
exploration of the very basis of social life and values.

It has always been difficult, however, to define the exact
nature of the relation between these novelists' greatest work

and the facts of American sociology as we know them. Nor
is the difficulty surmounted entirely by reminding ourselves
that their most significant themes were transcendent, engaging in but also going beyond the social aspect of life.
The works of many of their European contemporaries
(Dostoevsky and Balzac for example) also achieve a wider, if
not similar, concern for the more ultimate problems of
human destiny, and yet it has been comparatively easy to
make this correlation in the case of European fiction. If one
defines the novel as an art form entirely in terms of English
and continental fiction, works like *The Deerslayer*, *The
Scarlet Letter*, *Moby-Dick*, and *Huckleberry Finn* would
represent an achievement which easily measures up to the
requirements of great art but at the same time somehow
falls below the level of the good novel. This seeming paradox
has a great deal to do with the question of the relation
between American society and the American novel. Lionel
Trilling sees it when he observes in his essay on "Manners,
Morals, and the Novel":

> Now the novel as I have described it has never really
> established itself in America. Not that we have not had
> very great novels but that the novel in America diverges
> from its classic intention, which, as I have said, is the
> investigation of the problem of reality beginning in the
> social field. The fact is that American writers of genius
> have not turned their minds to society. . . . the reality
> they sought was only tangential to society.[1]

This perceptive formulation has a suggestiveness which
goes beyond the requirements of the context in which it
appears. Trilling has raised some important questions, and
he briefly touches upon at least one of them when he says in a

1. Lionel Trilling, *The Liberal Imagination* (New York, Viking Press,
1950), p. 212.

later essay that in America "the real basis of the novel has never existed—that is, the tension between a middle class and an aristocracy which brings manners into observable relief as the living representation of ideals and the living comment on ideas."[2]

To say that these observations are accurate but only negative is not to disparage Trilling, because his purpose is to provide certain fruitful comparisons rather than to argue why the American novel should not exist. It is true that some of the early American novelists themselves repeatedly evaluated their work in terms of the practice of their English contemporaries. Cooper started frankly as an imitator and perhaps never quite shook off the bad influence of Sir Walter Scott. Hawthorne admired Anthony Trollope and deprecated his own inability to write in the popular manner of the English novelists. Nevertheless, in their best work, the American novelists went their own way, and, if they felt uneasy about it, we must remember that they were creating a different kind of novel and did not enjoy our advantage of seeing it established in its own right as a vital and significant body of literature. Hence, whatever excursions we make into the realm of sociology must, in the last analysis, help our understanding of the primary fact of its enduring effectiveness. In the same way, a comparative study of the English and American novel of the nineteenth century can be useful only as a step toward a more positive account of the American novelists' concern with society and social values, even if such a comparison leads us finally to a revision of the accepted assumptions about social reality, the nature of the novelist's intention, and the relation between society and the novel.

One can thus proceed from Trilling's observations and ask: if the novel in America diverges from its "classic intention," what alternative intention do we find informing its best

2. Ibid., p. 260.

examples? If the American writers of genius did not turn their minds to social description, is it not necessary to examine their attitude to the whole question of "society"? In order to understand their genius, do we not need to look more closely at what constituted the social reality of nineteenth-century America? If "the reality they sought was only tangential to society," how far did this pursuit mirror the actual conditions of the time and how far did it lead them to imaginative constructs of a life and values which can be called "social" in the best sense of the term?

The problem of realism underlies most of these questions. It can be admitted readily that in comparison with the social solidity observable in the novels of Dickens and Balzac, Hawthorne's and Melville's approach to society would indeed seem attenuated and tangential. They, as well as Cooper and Twain, would face the charge of being escapists, allegorists, day-dreamers, wishful thinkers, fantasy-mongers, romancers —they would in fact be called anything but novelists. The matter of nomenclature is relatively unimportant. What we must consider, however, is that their best works do not strike us as fairy tales or transcendental tracts which have no relevance to human problems and values, including the problems and values of man as a social being. On the contrary, they seem to us less dated and more compelling than most English fiction of about the same time. In this connection it would be well to ask ourselves why, for example, a work like *The Gilded Age*, which achieves considerable density of social description, is not for that reason a greater novel than *Huckleberry Finn*, which is also concerned, though in a different way, with society and its problems.

The main object of this book is to show how these novelists were deeply concerned with both the society of their times and an ideal conception of social relationships, and how the consequent interplay between actual and ideal social values constitutes at least a partial source of their continuing vitality. The task of relating their work with the American social reality will involve a historical essay in the nature of that reality. At this stage I will only argue that the sort of social realism which we associate with European fiction constitutes one way of approaching reality but that there is no reason to assume that it is the only way. Realism, as Karl Mannheim has pointed out, "means different things in different contexts. In Europe it meant that sociology had to focus its attention on the very severe tension between the classes, whereas in America, where there was more free play in the economic realm, it was not so much the class problem which was considered as the 'real' centre of society but the problems of social technique and organization."[3] What is said here of American sociology may be applied, *mutatis mutandis*, to American fiction. The most significant American novelists of the first sixty years of the nineteenth century did not confine themselves wholly to the description or criticism of existing social conditions. They shared the general feeling that America was the land of social experimentation, and, while practical men battled over new political and economic institutions, they sought in their work the moral values necessary for the regeneration of human society. Exploration of existing society led them repeatedly to the theme of ideal community life.

It is against this background that we can approach those elements in the work of Cooper, Hawthorne, Melville, and Mark Twain which do not seem to fit our ordinary assumptions about the social realism of the novel. There is a way of regarding social reality which takes into account not only observable social facts but also various aspects of imaginative response to these facts; which considers such things as ideals, or mythic archetypes of thought, to be important if not

3. Karl Mannheim, *Ideology and Utopia*, tr. Louis Wirth and Edward Shils (London, Kegan Paul, Trench, Trübner, 1936), p. 228.

readily visible components of that reality. Such an approach is especially helpful when we are dealing with a complex body of imaginative literature. To quote Karl Mannheim again:

> Wishful thinking has always figured in human affairs. When the imagination finds no satisfaction in existing reality, it seeks refuge in wishfully constructed places and periods. Myths, fairy tales, other-worldly promises of religion, humanistic fantasies, travel romances, have been continually changing expressions of that which was lacking in actual life. They were more nearly complementary colours in the picture of the reality existing at the time than utopias working in opposition to the *status quo* and disintegrating it.[4]

If one accepts this statement, and if one remembers further that, according to Mannheim's unusual definition of terms, a "utopia" is an idea which is "situationally transcendant" but also realizable in actuality, one would conclude that Cooper's Leatherstocking Tales and Melville's *Typee* bear a closer relation to the social reality of nineteenth-century America than, let us say, the utopia of Jacksonian democracy which was materially working against and disintegrating the status quo of the time.

In reality, however, dissatisfaction with existing society did not make Cooper, Hawthorne, Melville, and even the Mark Twain of *Huckleberry Finn* wildly fanciful. They did not employ their imaginations in the construction of fairy tales or fantasies. As for other-worldly promises of religion, strictly speaking, these can be found only outside the work of the great novelists, in such fictions as Sylvester Judd's *Margaret: A Tale of the Real and Ideal, Blight and Bloom*. The four important novelists mentioned here derived their ideals from

4. Ibid., p. 184.

another source. In many different ways, they all leaned over backward and at some points achieved a sustaining contact with the great myth of America—the complex of ideas and ideals which had animated the beginnings of the experiment that had now grown into the social and moral world around them. Since it recognized the limitations as well as the promises of human existence, it was not altogether an expansive myth. Nor did its promise represent even to the most sanguine mind anything more than a possibility, a suggestion of potential reality.

I am aware that one of the many dangers implicit in this kind of discussion is that it is always possible to trace many myths in the past of a country, or, rather, a myth by its very nature permits a diversity of implications to be read into it. I might therefore say at once that I am concerned with those components of the American myth which have a bearing primarily on the social concerns of the classic American novel and which, it seems to me, will help to illuminate some of its problems. My contention is that, though this myth grew out of a definite sociohistorical moment and was eventually defeated by the historical development of its own paradoxical nature, some of its essential features remained for a long time operative in the American creative sensibility. Accordingly, the best account of the particular set of implications I see in it will be a historical one.

What imaginative men will say in critical times is often revelatory of certain aspects of the national sensibility which in more normal times remain hidden from common view. A good example of this fact is provided by *I'll Take My Stand*, the documentary response of twelve famous Southerners to the great economic crisis in America. Although the whole enterprise was conducted with the air of a political gesture, the document is interesting precisely because its contributors were not politicians but primarily writers, and it is interesting to speculate whether, during the depression years, it would have been possible in any other country of the Western world to collect under a similar banner an equally intelligent set of critics, poets, novelists, sociologists, and historians. To say the least, anywhere else the program and values they advocated would have been considered too impractical to deserve serious or systematic exposition, much less to receive any attention at all. And yet some of their values—such as the desire for an unencumbered existence, for an intimate contact with the earth, for direct personal relationships rather than elaborate social arrangements—have always figured somewhere in the substratum of the American mind. To take a concrete example, "A Statement of Principles" written most probably by John Crowe Ransom and appended to the volume as an introductory essay, has the sentence: "The responsibility of men is for their own welfare and that of their neighbors; not for the hypothetical welfare of some fabulous creature called society."[5]

Here we have in relatively simple form two important characteristics of the American sensibility: the insistence on the individual as the only proper unit of social calculus; and a definite feeling that what people generally call "society" is no more than an evil and chimerical invention that one can destroy by simply wishing it away. But this is not all. The statement contains a vague and barely perceptible reference to a third social category, for it makes one ask the simple question: Where exactly does neighborliness end and society begin? To ask such a question is to force into explicit statement an assumption concerning social values and organization that constitutes the third characteristic of the deeper American sensibility, but which has seldom, outside of certain

5. *I'll Take My Stand*, by Twelve Southerners (New York, Peter Smith, 1951), p. xviii.

reform movements in the nineteenth century, received rational
or systematic formulation. This may be described as the concept of community life. It has figured primarily as an unstated
ideal, a measuring rod rather than a blueprint for actuality.
It qualifies the concept of individual freedom and prevents it
from degenerating into an attitude of selfishness and irresponsibility. It postulates a set of values for relationship between individuals which, in their turn, provide a basis for the
criticism of actual society when it seems to become cold and
impersonal, or when its very foundations seem to rest on
cruelty, greed, and acquisitiveness, to the total disregard of
the claims of fellow human beings.

The career of this concept in America begins with the first
settlements of New England. John Winthrop had written in
"A Model of Christian Charity" which he composed during
his voyage on board the *Arabella* and delivered to his fellow
immigrants as an admonitory sermon on the life that lay before them:

> . . . we must be knit together in this work as one man.
> We must entertain each other in brotherly affection; we
> must be willing to abridge ourselves of our superfluities,
> for the supply of others' necessities; we must uphold a
> familiar commerce together in all meekness, gentleness,
> patience and liberality. We must delight in each other,
> make others' conditions our own, rejoice together,
> mourn together, labor and suffer together: always having
> before our eyes our commission and community in the
> work, our community as members of the same body.[6]

The sentiment expressed here had received a practical trial
almost a decade earlier in the short-lived cooperative land-
farming experiment of the *Mayflower* pilgrims. Although,

6. *The American Puritans*, ed. Perry Miller (New York, Doubleday,
Anchor Books, 1956), p. 83.

strictly speaking, Plymouth colony was never a communitarian settlement, it set an example for the long line of such settlements which followed it in America, and it is interesting to note the reasons for its failure as William Bradford gives them in his *History*:

> For this community (so far as it was) was found to breed much confusion and discontent and retard much employment that would have been to their benefit and comfort. For the young men, that were most able and fit for labour and service, did repine that they should spend their time and strength to work for other men's wives and children without any recompense. The strong, or man of parts, had no more in division of victuals and clothes than he that was weak and not able to do a quarter the other could; this was thought injustice. The aged and graver men to be ranked and equalized in labours and victuals, clothes, etc., with the meaner and younger sort, thought it some indignity and disrespect unto them. And for men's wives to be commanded to do service for other men, as dressing their meat, washing their clothes, etc., they deemed it a kind of slavery, neither could many husbands well brook it. [7]

If we compare this passage with the one quoted from Winthrop, we notice that the cause of the failure was precisely the nonobservance of the conduct Winthrop had enjoined: the abridgment of superfluities for the supply of others' necessities; upholding a familiar commerce together in all meekness, gentleness, patience, and liberality; and remembering always the commission and community in the work as members of the same body. The surprising thing then is not that

7. William Bradford, *Of Plymouth Plantation 1620–1647*, ed. Samuel Eliot Morison (New York, Knopf, 1959), p. 121. All references to Bradford are to this edition.

the communitarian experiment at Plymouth failed but that there should ever have been a hope of its success. Indeed, on their departure from Leyden, John Robinson, their minister, had warned the band of Puritans of this danger. "And, lastly," he wrote in a letter to "the whole company" which Bradford quotes in full, "your intended course of civil community will minister continual occasion of offence, and will be as fuel for that fire, except you diligently quench it with brotherly forbearance."[8] Winthrop and Robinson were speaking in terms of Christian social ideals, whereas Bradford, in his practical experiment, had to encounter the hard economic reality of the individual's self-interest.

These were indeed the two main drives behind the social movement which led to the settlement of America. It was a continuation of that historical moment in which religious fervor, as Mannheim says, "joined forces with the active demands of the oppressed strata of society."[9] Its animating energy had a dual purpose and a millennial character: "The impossible gives birth to the possible, and the absolute interferes with the world and conditions actual events. This fundamental and most radical form of the modern utopia was fashioned out of a singular material. It corresponded to the spiritual fermentation and physical excitement of the peasants, of a stratum living closest to the earth. It was at the same time robustly material and highly spiritual."[10]

The economic motivation, however, formed no part of the grand design as the Puritan leaders conceived it. It was there from the outset, but it was not acknowledged on the same terms as the religious aspect of the enterprise. Indeed, in the long line of communitarian colonies in America it was not until the nineteenth century that a colony was frankly organized as an economic experiment. Even Cotton Mather,

8. Ibid., pp. 51, 369.   9. Mannheim, p. 190.
10. Ibid., p. 192.

by whose time the original energy of religious dedication was already waning, believed firmly that the earlier colonizing attempts of the English in New England had failed because "the designs of those attempts being aimed no higher than the advancement of some *worldly interests*, a constant series of disasters has confounded them." It is after this observation that Mather relates the well-known story of a preacher of his who urged his congregation in the northeastern regions "to approve themselves a *religious* people" since otherwise "they would contradict the main end of planting this wilderness." Hereupon a well-known person stood up in the assembly and cried out: "Sir, you are mistaken: you think you are preaching to the people at the Bay; our *main end* was to *catch fish*." After suitably deprecating this attitude, Cotton Mather goes on to say how his own colony was "formed upon more glorious *aims*."[11]

In 1623 Bradford does not seem to have even noticed this Cod-God paradox, this discrepancy between Winthrop's high Christian ideals, which he shared, and the conduct of his fellow colonists. The economic side of the enterprise was important to him (indeed it takes up a great part of his narrative) but it was not allowed to figure in the providential design which had sent the pilgrims across the ocean. He was content to leave the economic predilections of man alone. His final comment on the breakdown of the communitarian experiment is perhaps significant in its farsightedness and definitely more shrewd than Cotton Mather's observations quoted above: "Let none object this is men's corruption," he says, "and nothing to the course itself. I answer, seeing all men have this corruption in them, God in His wisdom saw another course fitter for them."[12]

11. Cotton Mather, *Magnalia Christi Americana* (2 vols. Hartford, Silas Andrus, 1855), *1*, 65–66.
12. Bradford, p. 121.

The important thing to Bradford was the religious community, the "enjoying much sweet and delightful society and spiritual comfort together in the ways of God"[13] as he puts it in describing the Puritans' first settlement in Holland. Here also of course the individual was important; indeed he was the all-important moral integer. But he was bound by covenant both to God and to his fellow Christians in the Church. And on occasions the governor of Plymouth Colony was prepared, like the other Puritan governors of the later colonies, to enforce the requirements of the covenant by forceful exercise of civil authority and to preserve the community thus in a life of unalloyed moral purity.

The American settlement was only partially important to the Puritans as a way of improving their material fortunes. Its main importance was that here the covenanted church could be established and maintained without challenge, interference, or persecution by any outside authority. It has been argued often and for too long that frontier conditions lead to individualism. As recently as 1961 we find Edwin T. Bowden connecting the theme of "human isolation" in the American novel with "the frontier isolation," and vaguely confusing both with the historical force of individualism.[14] As a matter of fact, as we shall see, the theme of the nineteenth-century novelists was not physical isolation but moral alienation, or, as Emerson saw it, solitude in the midst of society. The movement toward individual freedom, as it is scarcely necessary to insist at this late day, was older and more extensive in origin. Like many other ideas which later blossomed in America, like Puritanism itself, its roots were in Europe. The difference lay in the fact that on this continent there was no older order, no constituted order at all, to hinder its growth. The only

13. Ibid., p. 17.
14. Edwin T. Bowden, *The Dungeon of the Heart: Human Isolation and the American Novel* (New York, Macmillan, 1961).

countervailing force was provided by ideals; like this first Puritan ideal of a commonwealth, a close-knit community of like-minded believers and worshipers.

By itself the frontier leads neither to an unfettered individualism nor to a restrictive society. The wilderness is by its very nature as much a temptation to capriciousness and irresponsibility as it is a force for social cohesion, for bringing people together in the face of a vast and unknown or hostile environment. If it provides an opportunity for the assertion of romantic individual freedom, it also inevitably brings about the less romantic but more necessary mutual self-help associations such as existed in all frontier stations. On the same scene the Indian way of life had for centuries enforced successfully a very severe tribal discipline without mass defection or desertion by individual members of the tribe. Thus the importance of the virgin continent lay precisely in the fact that, as far as society and civilization are concerned, it was a *tabula rasa*, an invitation to create and construct, a visible proof that ideals need not always end in starry-eyed idealism. It gave rise to Daniel Boone and the Western myth. But it also provided the theater for the practical enactment of hundreds of variously motivated experiments in communitarian living which began in the seventeenth century and continued well into the nineteenth. For their bearing on the American sensibility, both these facts are important. A common theme of the American imagination has been the problem of reconciling individual freedom with a mode of social life to which the individual can give his allegiance without danger of impairing his moral, spiritual, or psychological integrity. It is a theme of the utmost importance in our own day, and this may well be among the reasons why the nineteenth-century novelists' exploration of the values involved in the problem seems so vitally significant to the readers of the twentieth century.

To return to William Bradford, the most fascinating thing

about his history is the bold outline of its narrative. It stands as a sort of imaginative archetype of American experience even as it may be taken for the first statement of the American myth. Divested of its endless details about shipping costs, adventurers, beaver-skins, and such other things, the frame of the story presents an epic reference: the solemn exodus of a band of people from a corrupt world and their journey across the ocean to build a New Jerusalem upon a virgin land. The Christ and Virgil whom Cotton Mather later called upon to inspire his own history, combine with effortless ease in the narrative of this literal-minded Puritan to whom the past was represented mainly by the Bible and the future by a great hope. Like the ancient bards, he himself remains anonymous, while the hero of his tale is not man but men, the constant and strangely moving "They" of the narrative.

At the same time, the story is also the unfolding of a phase in the endless drama between God and Satan—the two invisible but primary actors. With this extension we have that supramundane reference, that metaphysical dimension, which, in one form or another, is always present in the great American novels of the nineteenth century but which rarely emerges from the more purely social preoccupation of European fiction. Bradford's history is set in motion by those "wars and oppositions [which] . . . Satan hath raised, maintained and continued against the Saints, from time to time, in one sort or other."[15] Oppressed in this manner, rather than submit to the machinations of Satan acting through his surrogates in a depraved society, the saints decide to separate themselves from such a society altogether and remove themselves to "some of those vast and unpeopled countries of America" which are "devoid of all civil inhabitants."[16] Once there, with "the mighty ocean which they had passed" separating them "from all the civil parts of the world," they can hope to find no

15. Bradford, p. 3.   16. Ibid., p. 25.

15

"friends to welcome them nor inns to entertain or refresh their weatherbeaten bodies; no houses or much less towns to repair to, to seek for succour."[17] All that can sustain the small community is the spirit of God and the inward conviction of the righteousness of their course.

Here we have, in terms of the language and outlook of the early seventeenth century, the basic pattern of the drama which, in other and varying terms, was to find recurrent expression in subsequent American imaginative literature. Put in a simplified form, it may be described as the theme of separation from an established society in search of a more satisfying community life. Society, the individual, and community—the main points of this triadic theme—were variously termed and defined by the various persons with whom I am chiefly concerned. Nevertheless, they figured in the imaginations of all of them. And together with this preoccupation went a brooding sense of forces beyond man's reach and of a reality which is not man-made but which man must take into account: what I have called the metaphysical dimension of their vision.

The first separation from Europe was not the end but only the beginning of a process which was to repeat itself endlessly in America. It is fitting therefore that Bradford, whose narrative began with the first Puritan community's removal to Holland, should describe toward the end of the book, in what is one of its most moving passages, the separation of the younger members from the parent church, not as individuals asserting their freedom but only "like children translated into other families"[18]—the old narrator preserving bravely the intimate imagery of communal feeling while the elegiac note of the passage indicates that its lack of basis in actual social relationships was already becoming apparent.

17. Ibid., pp. 61–62.
18. Ibid., p. 334.

16

"God in His wisdom," as Bradford says, had seen "another course fitter" for the Americans. This was the course of individualism, and it was not long before the covenanted community began to feel the strain of the paradox which lay at the center of its life, and the severe unity of the Puritan church itself was disturbed by dissension. By the time we come to Cotton Mather's history, after the turn of the century, the narrator has emerged from communal anonymity and assumed the first-person singular, and Bradford's collective biography has given place to a collection of individual biographies. The fragmentation is accompanied by an increasing relaxation of religious discipline, a process of secularization which leads us gradually from the world of the Puritans to the age of Enlightenment in the eighteenth century. Cotton Mather may be said to reflect the stage of transition. A Janus-like figure, he is inspired by the ideals of the past and disturbed by what he can see of the future. The voice that speaks to us in the *Magnalia* is unable either to recapture the simple serenity of Bradford or to achieve the self-possession and shrewd dignity of Franklin's *Autobiography*.

Benjamin Franklin himself represents the consummation of the shift to economic and political individualism in America. There is something almost symbolic in his departure from Boston to begin his career in Philadelphia, the capital of the frontier state which was also to provide the scene for the next important literary performance in America. Franklin marks a nearly complete disseverance from the past. He lives entirely in the present and looks only toward the future. In him God seems indeed to have rivaled Defoe's creative power and produced an individual who can be called the single-handed author of his own world. No mists of metaphysical doubt cloud his vision. The science of electricity and mechanics has banished the theology of sin and damnation. The doctrine of salvation has yielded to the principle of self-help, and in place of spiritual communion we now have philanthropic association.

Much of this would apply also to Crèvecoeur who, as a literary figure, is more interesting for my purpose. A friend of Benjamin Franklin and a true Franklinian character, this "American Farmer" seems to have played more adroitly than the sage Doctor himself the role that Europe expected of a backwoods settler. *Letters from an American Farmer* is, as the title makes clear, aimed directly at Europe. Especially intended for European consumption are, apart from the bold touches of incipient literary romanticism, such tales (related with a seemingly meticulous concern for literal truth) as the one about the American owl whose wings measured 5′3″ or the 171 bees which Crèvecoeur exhumed from the "craw" of a kingbird and laid out "on a blanket in the sun" only to witness that "54 returned to life, licked themselves clean, and joyfully went back to the hive; where they probably informed their companions of such an adventure and escape, as I believe had never happened before to American bees!"[19] However, if we remember Crèvecoeur today as more than a pleasant *raconteur* it is because, under all the romantic nonsense of his work, we discover a serious attempt at exploring the meaning of America in terms of the assumptions prevalent in his time. This attempt is not altogether a matter of rational social analysis. *Letters from an American Farmer* has another serious aspect, a more imaginative dimension which goes beyond the world of Benjamin Franklin and points toward Fenimore Cooper and the other novelists of the nineteenth century.

Of course, the Franklinian side of the work is more readily noticeable. The values which dominate the book are the same

19. The edition used for quotations from Crèvecoeur is Hector St. John de Crèvecoeur, *Letters from an American Farmer*, New York, Dutton, Everyman's Library, 1951.

that Franklin preached and practiced: individualism, industry, sobriety, and honesty. The individual is seen essentially in economic terms, and Crèvecoeur shares the enlightened view that human character is environmentally determined. Linked with this are his freedom from religious orthodoxy and the insistence on manners as the representative identity of man. If he is not entirely optimistic, he shows a consistent belief in the virtues of expanding civilization. Whether or not Crèvecoeur is to be regarded as an early Romantic, his book certainly does not celebrate the myth of the noble savage. He is far too decidedly a child of the eighteenth century to hold such a view. He firmly believes in the moral superiority of a settled agrarian life over that of wandering hunters, and he sees the lone pioneers of the forest as the most depraved class of American citizens. As an agrarian, though he values his closeness to nature immensely, the fact of decisive importance to him is his being a freeholder. Unlike Wordsworth, he has nothing but pity for the European farmers who live close to the earth but do not own it. And as for the primitive African, he is neither a noble nor an ignoble savage. In the South, where he is kept in bondage and ignorance, the slave is rude and depraved, while in the North, where he is trained in the ways of civilization, he is as decent a human being as his master. In the last letter, Crèvecoeur does not expound his scheme of going to live in an Indian tribe without expressing a hope that he may be able to civilize the savages, especially through the art of inoculation in which his wife possesses much skill.

The first eight of Crèvecoeur's twelve letters thus provide a discursive answer to his celebrated question ("What then is the American, this new man?") mainly in terms of the economic and political differences between Europe and America. The American, Crèvecoeur says, is a European or the descendant of a European "who, leaving behind him all his ancient prejudices and manners, receives new ones from the new mode of life he has embraced, the new government he obeys, and the new rank he holds." In the "great American asylum" the poor immigrant is freed from the oppression of a feudal society, from the taxation of landlord, church, and monarch, from "involuntary idleness, servile dependence, penury, and useless labour." "Here religion demands but little of him; a small voluntary salary to the minister, and gratitude to God; can he refuse these?" Be he a trader, farmer, craftsman, or a common laborer, he will be rewarded amply for his labor, so that in time he will cast off his servile timidity and acquire the dignity and self-confidence of a true human being. No wonder Crèvecoeur should exclaim: "We have no princes, for whom we toil, starve, and bleed: we are the most perfect society now existing in the world."

Here we have struck perhaps for the first time that note of conscious superiority of American over European social institutions, of pride in democratic equality and abundance of opportunity, which we hear again and again in the subsequent literature of the country, though with increasingly critical qualifications. Crèvecoeur's own book is far from lacking in critical reference. However, before considering this aspect of it, it would be well to remind ourselves of its contextual breadth by turning a century and a half backward to the pilgrims or about the same number of years forward to modern times. William Bradford had also spoken of Americans as Europeans escaping oppression, when, after describing their landing, he asked whether future generations ought not to remember that their "fathers were Englishmen which came over this great ocean, and were ready to perish in this wilderness" but the Lord "heard their voice" and "delivered them from the hand of the oppressor."[20] The sense of mission, however, the urgency of high idealism, which he intended to

20. Bradford, p. 63.

transmit with this appeal did not endure for long in the face of the ascendant power of economic individualism. It was an inevitable development, but also one with which the American imagination could never wholly reconcile itself. The tensions created by this uneasy sense of disequilibrium have tended to produce a variety of attitudes, ranging from an unreasoned but acute sense of betrayal to more thoughtful criticism. For example, to take a recent formulation, this is how Richard Hofstadter sums up the chief characteristics of American politics in the "Introduction" to his book *The American Political Tradition:*

> However much at odds on specific issues, the major political traditions have shared a belief in the rights of property, the philosophy of economic individualism, the value of competition; they have accepted the economic virtues of capitalist culture as necessary qualities of man. Even when some property right has been challenged—as it was by followers of Jefferson and Jackson—in the name of the rights of man or the rights of the community, the challenge, when translated into practical policy, has actually been urged on behalf of some other kind of property. . . . American traditions also show a strong bias in favor of equalitarian democracy, but it has been a democracy in cupidity rather than a democracy of fraternity.

Crèvecoeur's account of the advantages of democracy is in keeping with this tradition, especially when he is describing the economic benefits that the country offers to the prospective "new man": "Here the rewards of his industry follow with equal steps the progress of his labour; his labour is founded on the basis of nature, *self-interest;* can it want a stronger allurement?" In moral terms, this is a far cry from Winthrop's social ideal, which would require

21

men to labor to supply other people's necessities.

Crèvecoeur, however, experiences no misgivings as he continues his undaunted exposition of this theme in the next five letters. Having described the new man as an agrarian, he shifts the scene to the islands of Nantucket and Martha's Vineyard. The sea suggests to him no "romantic" or "metaphysical" associations; it is only a setting for the fishing industry and for trade. If the continental American labors on the land, the democratic man on these islands plows the sea. In either case the world presents an uncomplicated and hopeful prospect. Indeed it is not until the ninth letter that we find Crèvecoeur striking the first disturbed notes of a contrary and larger theme. The occasion is provided by his visit to Charleston and his witnessing of the "facts" of Negro slavery as it is practiced in the South. The question that he now asks is not "What then is the American, this new man?" but "What then is man; this being who boasts so much of the excellence and dignity of his nature, among that variety of unscrutable mysteries, of unsolvable problems, with which he is surrounded?" To this somewhat Melvillian question Crèvecoeur proceeds to give an answer with which Melville could easily sympathize. Though even Negroes have hearts in which "noble dispositions can grow," by and large, everywhere, and at all times, men have proved themselves to be little better than predatory animals. What does the history of the earth show us "but crimes of the most heinous nature, committed from one end of the world to the other? We observe avarice, rapine, and murder, equally prevailing in all parts." Perhaps we can flatter ourselves with the thought that a kindly nature has implanted in us a spirit of stoical endurance which enables us to reconcile ourselves to the severities of her dispensation. "Yet if we attentively view this globe, will it not appear rather a place of punishment, than of delight? . . . Famine, diseases, elementary convulsions, human feuds, dissensions, etc., are the produce of every climate; each climate produces besides, vices, and miseries peculiar to its latitude." The evil in human nature rivals the perversity of physical nature to such an extent that

> one would almost believe the principles of action in man, considered as the first agent of this planet, to be poisoned in their most essential parts. We certainly are not that class of beings which we vainly think ourselves to be; man an animal of prey, seems to have rapine and the love of bloodshed implanted in his heart . . . If Nature has given us a fruitful soil to inhabit, she has refused us such inclinations and propensities as would afford us the full enjoyment of it. Extensive as the surface of this planet is, not one half of it is yet cultivated, not half replenished; she created man, and placed him either in the woods or plains, and provided him with passions which must for ever oppose his happiness; everything is submitted to the power of the strongest; men, like the elements, are always at war; the weakest yield to the most potent; force, subtlety, and malice, always triumph over unguarded honesty and simplicity.

"Such," the passage concludes, "is the perverseness of human nature; who can describe it in all its latitude?"

This is a Crèvecoeur who is not often recognized and who seems to subscribe neither to the rational optimism of the eighteenth century nor to the "romantic" ideas of the essential goodness of man and nature. The imagination that lies behind this letter (as well as the last one) would reveal him rather as possessing a closer kinship with the novelists of the nineteenth century. The American farmer is no longer the unreserved celebrator of democratic man and economic competitiveness, for he sees that human beings share the predatory characteristics as well as the passions of cruelty and violence which, in previous letters, he had discovered everywhere in the animal kingdom. The law of mutual destructiveness, which governs the world of nature, provides also the key to the history of human society. Accordingly, where he had expressed a firm belief in the virtues of civilization, he now regards both society and the wilderness as morally equivocal:

> If from this general review of human nature, we descend to the examination of what is called civilised society; there the combination of every natural and artificial want, makes us pay very dear for what little share of political felicity we enjoy. It is a strange heterogeneous assemblage of vices and virtues, and of a variety of other principles, for ever at war, for ever jarring, for ever producing some dangerous, some distressing extreme. Where do you conceive then that nature intended we should be happy? Would you prefer the state of men in the woods, to that of men in a more improved situation? Evil preponderates in both; in the first they often eat each other for want of food, and in the other they often starve each other for want of room.

This passage, apart from its own significance, provides also the proper background for an understanding of the strange last letter, entitled "Distresses of a Frontier Man," which is in some ways the most interesting of the whole set, and which develops further the theme of "civilized society." In letter 9 immediately after the lines quoted above, Crèvecoeur had concluded that for his own part he thought that the vices and miseries to be found in civilization exceed those of the wilderness "in which real evil is more scarce, more supportable, and less enormous." Now, as the attributes of "society"—war, destruction, and pillage—invade his backwoods sanctuary, the paradox acquires the immediacy and urgency of a personal problem, so that he forms and expounds at length the scheme of abandoning his house and farm and seeking refuge in the less complicated life of an Indian tribe. "Yes," he declares, "I will cheerfully embrace that resource, it is an holy inspiration."

It would be easy to form out of this letter a neat little bridge for crossing over to Cooper's Leatherstocking Tales in the next century. It would be equally easy to dismiss it as a vulgar contraption of the romantic writer at his worst. Nevertheless, as I have tried to point out earlier, it is a mistake to regard Crèvecoeur as being altogether a literary showman of current attitudes. Not even the most liberal discounting of his obvious posturing for effect can wholly eliminate the imaginative core of his meaning, for, like Cooper after him, he shows a serious if unsophisticated concern for the values implicit in the drama of rival civilizations. Even in this letter he does not at any place suggest an unqualified approval of the primitive tribal life. On the contrary, he consistently maintains his earlier critical ambiguity. He is repeatedly worried by the fear that his young son may slip permanently from the higher agrarian life of his father into the savage hunting state. He insists that the family will maintain their own separate forms of worship under the wigwams. He even hopes that his influence may help the Indians to acquire certain aspects of civilization. And finally he presents his decision as an inevitable but perhaps only a temporary choice.

It is not important to inquire into the actual facts which lay behind the dramatization of this choice. To argue whether these reflections had their origin in the Indian raid on his house or in the conflict of loyalties he experienced during the Revolutionary War would be about as meaningful as to speculate whether Crèvecoeur could actually have encountered the caged Negro whose plight he describes with incredible flourishes of melodrama at the end of Letter 9. It is much more important to note that the sense of pervasive uneasiness that he had communicated in that letter, is now imaginatively recreated as a feeling of total betrayal. The society he had described as the most perfect "now existing in the world" and as being free of any laws except those of a lenient and protective nature has now become encumbered "either with voluminous laws, or contradictory codes, often galling the very necks of those whom they protect." And gone too is the early assurance in the value of absolute individualism: "Whichever way I look, nothing but the most frightful precipices present themselves to my view . . . what is man when no longer connected with society . . . He cannot live in solitude, he must belong to some community bound by some ties, however imperfect."

Here again is the enactment of the American drama of organized society and the individual who says: *Non serviam!* Speaking in a different context, Crèvecoeur had said of Europe in Letter 3: "There the plentiude of society confines many useful ideas, and often extinguishes the most laudable schemes which here ripen into maturity." The new world has freed the American from social enslavement, and yet, as we have seen here, his sense of individual freedom leads inevitably in the end to an equally strong desire to belong to a group larger than himself, an irresistible urge toward social community. "I resemble, methinks," Crèvecoeur goes on to say in memorable language, "one of the stones of a ruined arch, still retaining that pristine form that anciently fitted the place I occupied, but the centre is tumbled down; I can be nothing until I am replaced, either in the former circle, or in some stronger one."

If the new social circle of Crèvecoeur's choice turns out to be the Indian tribe, it is not altogether for the romantic reason that the primitive savages are "much more closely connected with nature than we are; they are her immediate children, the inhabitants of the woods are her undefiled off-spring: those of the plains are her degenerated breed, far, very far removed from her primitive laws, from her original design." Undoubtedly, there is a good deal of such reasoning, but Crèvecoeur also goes behind it to make more valid discriminations. The two main aspects of the Indian communal life which he considers especially valuable, and which he sees also as providing a commentary on the practices of the society he has decided to abandon, are its social cohesiveness and its freedom from avarice. In a passage that recalls with fine irony the dominant theme of the early letters—America as the promise of material prosperity—he says:

> Thus shall we metamorphose ourselves, from neat, decent, opulent planters . . . into a still simpler people divested of every thing beside hope, food, and the raiment of the woods: abandoning the large framed house, to dwell under the wigwam; and the featherbed, to lie on the mat, or bear's skin. There shall we sleep undisturbed by fruitful dreams and apprehensions.

But what Crèvecoeur admires more is the tribal social system which is "sufficiently complete to answer all the primary wants of man, and to constitute him a social being." There must be "in their social bond something singularly captivating, and far superior to anything to be boasted of among us," because, as Crèvecoeur maintains, drawing an unusually long bow, thousands of Europeans have become Indians whereas not a single Indian has adopted the white man's civilization. Discord and strife between members of the same community are unknown to them; although the white people have selfishly drawn them into their quarrels, "a civil division of a village or tribe, are events which have never been recorded in their traditions." Religion, which provides the cause for a hundred disputes in civilized society, is, among the Indians, only an agency of harmony and universal brotherhood. "Each worship with us, hath, you know, its peculiar political tendency," Crèvecoeur writes, explaining the salutary influence that he expects the simple Indian faith to exercise on his children; "there it has none but to inspire gratitude and truth: their tender minds shall receive no other idea of the Supreme Being, than that of the father of all men, who requires nothing more of us than what tends to make each other happy."

To ask whether such Indians existed anywhere outside of Crèvecoeur's imagination would be as irrelevant as to remember that he never went to live among their tribes. As an imaginative writer, and not unlike some novelists of the next century, his purpose in introducing this example of ideal community life is not to describe an actual people in a factual place but rather to create a set of values by means of which he can evaluate the society of his time.

The thousands of frontier men who succeeded Crèvecoeur on the American scene did not share his misgivings about the course America was taking. Individualism, as Ralph Gabriel has pointed out, was the most dominant force behind the developments of the nineteenth century. Its pressure was not only advancing men over the continent along an ever-extending frontier but also breaking down social institutions in the older settled areas. "Aristocracy," Tocqueville observed, "had made a chain of all the members of the community, from the peasant to the king; democracy breaks that chain and severs every link of it."[21] Even in religion there was a shift, as Gabriel points out, from Calvin's monarch-God to Horace Bushnell's conception of Jesus as the divine man, "American

21. Alexis de Tocqueville, *Democracy in America*, ed. Phillips Bradley (2 vols. New York, Knopf, 1956), *2*, 99. All references to Tocqueville are to this edition.

Christianity" emphasizing the individual and his emotions rather than institutional observances.[22]

Insofar as individualism represented an advance in human values, its virtues were recognized implicitly or overtly by all thoughtful Americans of the nineteenth century. But it was also creating an atomistic society of isolated human beings which lacked moral and social purpose as much as it did any principle of cohesiveness. Writing in the last decades of the century, Henry Adams reviewed the situation of 1800 in the following words:

> In the early days of colonization, every new settlement represented an idea and proclaimed a mission. . . . No such character belonged to the colonization of 1800. From Lake Erie to Florida, in long, unbroken line, pioneers were at work, cutting into the forests with the energy of so many beavers, and with no more express moral purpose than the beavers they drove away. The civilization they carried with them was rarely illumined by an idea; they sought room for no new truth, and aimed neither at creating, like the Puritans, a govern-ment of saints, nor, like the Quakers, one of love and peace; they left such experiments behind them, and wrestled only with the hardest problems of frontier life.

It is not surprising, Adams goes on to say, that foreign observers as well as the Americans of the sea coast did not admire this development, asserting that

> virtue and wisdom no longer guided the United States! What they saw was not encouraging. . . . Greed for wealth, lust for power, yearning for the blank void of savage freedom such as Indians and wolves delighted in,

22. Ralph Henry Gabriel, *The Course of American Democratic Thought* (New York, Ronald Press, 1956), p. 33.

—these were the fires that flamed under the caldron of American society, in which, as conservatives believed, the old, well-proven, conservative crust of religion, government, family, and even common respect for age, education, and experience was rapidly melting away, and was indeed already broken into fragments, swept about by the seething mass of scum ever rising in greater quantities to the surface.[23]

Not all Americans, certainly not the great novelists of the nineteenth century, who were acutely aware of the situation described by Adams, were by any means conservatives. They did not wish to see Tocqueville's hierarchic chain of aristocratic institutions reimposed upon their society. On the contrary, they wanted to preserve the gains of democracy and looked forward to the realization of social possibilities which they believed to be inherent in the democratic principle itself. Nor were many foreign observers necessarily antagonistic to American democracy just because they found themselves among its critics. If Dickens considered the Eastern Penitentiary in Philadelphia an inhuman institution, it was only after he had discovered that the inmates of the many asylums, poorhouses, hospitals, and prisons at South Boston "are surrounded by all reasonable means of comfort and happiness that their condition will admit of; are appealed to, as members of the great human family, however afflicted, indigent, or fallen; are ruled by the strong Heart, and not by the strong . . . Hand."[24] In "Concluding Remarks"—the last chapter of *American Notes*, in which he presents his view of "the general character of the American people, and the general character of their social system"—he begins by observing that Americans

23. Henry Adams, *History of the United States* (9 vols. New York, Scribner's, 1890–91), *I*, 177–78.

24. Charles Dickens, *American Notes and Pictures from Italy* (London, Oxford University Press, 1957), p. 53.

are "by nature, frank, brave, cordial, hospitable, and affectionate. Cultivation and refinement seem but to enhance their warmth of heart and ardent enthusiasm." He goes on to add, however, that these qualities are "sadly sapped and blighted in their growth among the mass" by that "great blemish in the popular mind of America . . . Universal Distrust." Linking this distrust itself with the American's "love of 'smart' dealing," he locates the ultimate root of the evil in "the national love of trade."[25] This diagnosis is paralleled by Emerson's criticism in "New England Reformers": "This whole business of Trade gives me to pause and think, as it constitutes false relations between men"[26] or again in "Man the Reformer":

> The ways of trade are grown selfish to the borders of theft, and supple to the borders (if not beyond the borders) of fraud. . . . I leave for those who have the knowledge the part of sifting the oaths of our customhouses; I will not inquire into the oppression of the sailors; I will not pry into the usages of our retail trade. I content myself with the fact that the general system of our trade (apart from the blacker trades, which, I hope, are exceptions denounced and unshared by all reputable men), is a system of selfishness; is not dictated by the high sentiments of human nature; is not measured by the exact law of reciprocity, much less by the sentiments of love and heroism, but is a system of distrust, of concealment, of superior keenness, not of giving but of taking advantage.

We can notice here how the principle of self-interest, which

25. Ibid., pp. 244–46.
26. The edition used for quotations from Emerson is *Emerson's Complete Works*, 12 vols. Boston, Houghton, Mifflin, Riverside Edition, 1888–93.

Crèvecoeur had recognized as the strongest allurement that America offers to the "new man," has degenerated into selfishness and mutual distrust. We must notice, too, that for Dickens, as well as for Emerson, these characteristics of a commercial culture are evil primarily because they warp natural feelings and destroy human relations, for this was also the main point of the ninteenth-century novelists' criticism of their society. And if Dickens' survey led him to conclude that the American people would be well advised to love "the Real less, and the Ideal somewhat more" and to encourage "a wider cultivation of what is beautiful without being eminently and directly useful,"[27] we must not forget that a few years later, in his story "The Artist of the Beautiful," Hawthorne attempted to give imaginative embodiment to precisely the same idea.

These men of imagination thus recognized the relation between economic forces and moral values. But, insofar as the emphasis falls on the moral consequences rather than the economic machinery of the system, they viewed the freedom of the individual as something real and meaningful. In the lecture on "New England Reformers," Emerson, by way of illustrating his concept of the sufficiency of the private man, relates the story of the individual who was excommunicated by his church on account of his connection with the antislavery movement and who thereupon promptly and boldly "excommunicated the church, in a public and formal process." Society thus presented the image of a body of men unfettered by any restrictive pressures, liberated from the restraints of religious, social, and economic institutions, enjoying a freedom of thought and action such as individuals had not known in any other place and time, and yet the world these men were creating was coming to rest increasingly on

27. Dickens, p. 248.

the foundations of selfishness, distrust, and crass materialism.

These products of individualism were not only falsifying
social relations but abstracting from them all human content,
so that the most alarming feature of this society was the
isolation of its members. Tocqueville observed that democratic equality "places men side by side, unconnected by any
common tie,"[28] and Emerson exclaimed in "Society and
Solitude": "But how insular and pathetically solitary are all
the people we know!" Emerson's position on this question of
insularity and social relatedness, as on so many other questions, is interesting partly because of his dialectical manner of
arguing both sides of a case. On the one hand, he seems undoubtedly to approve this tendency and to approximate
closely his popular image as the champion of the self-reliant
individual, of "the great Transcendental fallacy" as Daniel
Aaron calls it. Nevertheless, as Aaron points out: "He was
both the critic and the celebrator of his and subsequent
generations, the Yea-sayer and the Nay-sayer."[29] Many positive elements of his attitude were shared by his contemporaries, not excluding the novelists, because, if their awareness of
the limitations of individualism went beyond his, they, as
much as he, took individual freedom as their starting point.
If he seems to insist more on the individual's standing alone,
a part at least of his reason is the same as theirs, for, as he says
in his essay on "Friendship": "To stand in true relations with
men in a false age is worth a fit of insanity, is it not?" And
finally, if in "Society and Solitude" he talks of the "necessity
of isolation which genius feels," it is, as he goes on to say, a
"tragic necessity . . . irresistibly driving each adult soul as with
whips into the desert, and making our warm covenants

28. Tocqueville, 2, 102.
29. Daniel Aaron, *Men of Good Hope* (New York, Oxford University
Press, 1951), p. 7.

sentimental and momentary." A little later he adds, as though by way of a conscious comment on the other and better-known side of his own attitude: "But this banishment to the rocks and echoes no metaphysics can make right or tolerable. . . . A man must be clothed with society, or we shall feel a certain bareness and poverty, as of a displaced and unfurnished member."

Thus, while the practical-minded citizens of America were pushing forward to reap the benefits of unrestrained freedom, its philosophers, poets, and novelists were pondering the loss of moral and social values that went with the development. If the former lacked, as Adams said, all sense of moral purpose, the latter were deeply aware of the missionary tradition which had accompanied the settlement of America. No one doubted the necessity of destroying older social institutions. But what had happened to the expectations of a new society, the hope of a regenerated humanity, the vision of New Jerusalem? The American philosophers and poets felt that the process of democracy had defeated its promise.

A visionary conception of society provided more than the measuring rod of their criticism; from it came also their positive social values. In this sense the myth of America was still operative in the nineteenth century. An ideal society could be created as soon as the individuals concerned subscribed to the ideal principle which was to inform it. Since Americans were no longer the victims of old institutions but the prospective creators of new ones, the decisive factor was the moral regeneration of the individual. Emerson's answer to "this whole business of Trade" in "New England Reformers" was simple: "Let into it the new and renewing principle of love." For, as he had said in "Man the Reformer": "We must be lovers, and at once the impossible becomes possible." This was also Whitman's answer in 1864 when, after his disillusionment with the workings of practical democracy, he wrote in a characteristic vein: "The final meaning of Democracy through many transmigrations is to press on through all ridicules, arguments, and ostensible failures to put in practice the idea of the sovereignty, license, sacredness of the individual. This idea isolates, for reasons, each separate man and woman in the world;—while the idea of Love fuses and combines the whole. Out of the fusing of these twain, opposite as they are, I seek to make a homogeneous Song."[30]

The visionary aspect of the American tradition was not, however, monopolized by literary artists. The great type of American social experience—separation from a corrupt society to form an ideal community—was receiving practical enactment in the numerous experiments of the contemporary communitarians. The first colonies were settled in the second half of the seventeenth century by foreign sectarians such as the Dutch Mennonites and Labadists. During the eighteenth century the Moravians and the Shakers had great success with their Utopian settlements, illustrating, as Arthur Bestor has said, "the process that was repeated time after time in America in the seventeenth, eighteenth, and nineteenth centuries."[31] In the nineteenth century the movement was considerably accelerated and the number of utopian colonies increased to well beyond 200, the experiments exciting widespread interest, both critical and enthusiastic.

Though the seminal idea of these colonies was in all cases brought over from Europe, the schemes came to full flower only in the new world, showing how persistently America figured in people's imagination as the bright hope of Europe. If Europe represented the hard facts of social reality, America was seen as approximating the possibility of ideal community

30. *Walt Whitman's Workshop*, ed. C. J. Furness (Cambridge, Harvard University Press, 1928), pp. 127–28.

31. Arthur Eugene Bestor, Jr., *Backwoods Utopias* (Philadelphia, University of Pennsylvania Press, 1950), p. 26.

life. In the nineteenth century, however, the communitarian tradition registered certain developments which were more significant than the quantitative increase in the number of experiments. In the first place, it was no longer restricted to foreign immigrants or to groups which continued to regard themselves as alien. As general social conditions in America itself grew unsatisfactory, American intellectuals, artists, and reformers started experimenting with utopian colonies of their own. A more important development lay in the fact that, in keeping with the general tendency of the nineteenth century, the economic and social implications of the communitarian way of life began to supersede its earlier religious and theological inspiration. Even the older utopian groups regarded themselves increasingly as communitarians first and sectarians second. When the followers of Father Rapp established the third of their villages in 1825, they called it not Harmony, as on both previous occasions, but Economy. The apostles of this new phase of communitarianism were Fourier and Owen.

Nevertheless, in America, unlike Europe, there was a continuity of tradition between the secular communities of the nineteenth century and the religious fervor of the seventeenth. "In America, and America alone, the religious socialism of the seventeenth century evolved without a break into the secular socialism of the nineteenth."[32] This transmission of communitarian tradition is illustrated by Brook Farm. Two years and a half before its establishment, its founder, George Ripley, visited the German sectarian community at Zoar, and his wife wrote enthusiastically about its way of life. The first prospectus of Brook Farm made allusion to the Moravians, the Shakers, and the Rappites, while Hawthorne, who joined the community early in its career, had already shown interest in the Shakers by publishing two tales about them in the 1830s. "The communitarian tradition

32. Ibid., p. 38.

36

influenced Brook Farm," Mr. Bestor concludes, "and Brook Farm, in turn, passed the influence along. The Fruitlands experiment of Bronson Alcott . . . was in some measure its offshoot, for Alcott had participated in the original plans for Brook Farm, and inaugurated his own experiment only when convinced that the older community was 'not sufficiently ideal.'"[33]

Hawthorne, of course, had the strongest critical reservations about the whole communitarian enterprise, and their nature was such that they would be shared by many of his contemporaries who never made the experiment of actually living in a utopian community, or even paid much attention to the movement. But before taking this up, it would be well to note two aspects of communitarian thought which represent the nineteenth-century residuum of the American myth and which bear a certain resemblance to the pattern of social experience as revealed in American imaginative literature. The first of these is the idea of the complete regeneration of society that we find in the American Fourierites and Owenites as much as in Emerson, who says in "New England Reformers": "It is handsomer to remain in the establishment . . . than to make a sally against evil by some single improvement, without supporting it by a total regeneration." Closely linked with this are the communitarians' refusal to work within the established society and their habit of viewing the two principles, the social and the communitarian, as mutually exclusive. These two concepts were termed differently by different persons but always with this suggestion of mutual incompatibility: Fourier called them "society" and "association," the American Fourierist Albert Brisbane, "civilization" and "association," and the elder Henry James, "civilization" and "society." As is obvious, "civilization" had thus a special connotation. Albert Brisbane prefaced his very

33. Ibid., p. 51.

popular book *Social Destiny of Man*, published in 1840, with a chapter entitled "Explanation of Terms," where he defined civilization as "the social system in which we live, *as it now is*, with all its defects and the little good it may possess."[34] It is useful to remember this while approaching the long line of American fictional heroes who abandon "civilization" in one form or another, for their decision represents the rejection of a particular social order and not of the social principle itself. It does not lead them ultimately to absolute individual freedom; more often it marks the beginning of a search for true community life.

The elder Henry James also believed that man's destiny was social, though his discussion of the problem owed more to Swedenborgian inspiration than to Fourierist doctrine. In his effort to achieve a combination of the two we notice again that relating of the metaphysical to the social aspect of life which characterizes the great American novels of the nineteenth century. His position with regard to utopian social schemes would also be close to that of the novelists, so that, in these as in certain other respects, his thought provides a good sounding board for contemporary attitudes. Though primarily a theologian, he was a friend of many of the important literary figures of the time, and his career, which spanned the bulk of the century from 1811 to 1882, seemed always to hover on the borders of literature proper.

Henry James' thought does not constitute an elaborate philosophical system. It derives basically from his belief in the social nature of all true spirituality and the spiritual nature of all true society. Its direction—the curious blending of religion and sociology—was clearly indicated in his first acknowledged publication: *What Constitutes the State*. "THE STATE," he

34. Albert Brisbane, *Social Destiny of Man* (Philadelphia, C. F. Stollmeyer, 1840), p. xi.

declared in this pamphlet, "then means simply the social condition peculiar to man: a condition which makes his highest life to depend upon his relations to his fellows, or which limits his enjoyment of life within the limits of his love to his brother."[35] Anticipating Whitman, he saw the nineteenth century in America pointing toward a vision of universal brotherhood. "The drunkard, the pauper, the lunatic, the slave," he observed, "lie no longer the victims of a cold indifference, but are laid each on the heart of his fellowman, and there warmed back into newness of life." In the century's outward signs of progress—"our steamboats, our railroads, our magnetic telegraphs, which laugh to scorn the limitations of time and space"—he discerned the "throbbings wherewith dumb nature herself confesses the descent of that divine and universal spirit, which even now yearns to embrace all earth's offspring in the bonds of a mutual knowledge and a mutual love."[36]

Universal brotherhood and the necessary destruction of selfhood are the two ubiquitous ideas in James' writings. Under such names as "selfhood," "the selfish principle," and "proprium," he constantly attacked the latent dangers of individualism. For him it was the chief evil of human beings and social institutions, the "curse of mankind, that which keeps our manhood so little and so depraved."[37] "Selfishness to be sure," he declared, "is a much more potent, stubborn, and profound evil than worldliness, and far more hostile practically to human society or fellowship."[38] The principle of individualism lay at the heart of "civilization"—the term which James, like Fourier, used to denote the contemporary

35. Henry James, *What Constitutes the State* (New York, John Allen, 1846), p. 17.
36. Ibid., pp. 42–45.
37. Henry James, *Society the Redeemed Form of Man* (Boston, Houghton, Osgood, 1879), p. 47.
38. Ibid., p. 198.

Christian capitalistic order. Echoing Emerson, he declared that the "entire system of trade, as based upon what is called 'unlimited competition,' is a system of rapacity and robbery."[39] And as for the American church of his day, there was no hint of the "social gospel" in its preaching. "As at present constituted," he wrote in his *Letter to a Swedenborgian*, published in 1847, "it is the citadel and shield of individualism, or the selfish principle."[40] Thirty years later, in his last work, *Society the Redeemed Form of Man*, we find James repeating the charge with greater emphasis in tracing back to Protestant Christianity the "insane habit of regarding human life as PERSONALLY and not as SOCIALLY constituted."[41]

James believed that the true Church of Christ "has ever been coextensive with the human race. Whosoever lives a life of charity—I do not mean a life of alms-giving, nor a technically devout life, but a really humane life, by the conscientious avoidance of whatever wrongs the neighbour—is *ipso facto* a member of that church, though he himself have never heard the name of Christ."[42] And just as spiritual Christianity represented a state higher than "moralism," James envisioned a social state beyond "civilization" which he called "Socialism." By socialism he meant "not any special system of social organization, like that of Fourier, Owen, or St. Simon, but what is common to all these systems, namely, the idea of a perfect fellowship or society among men."[43] James, however, had the true nineteenth-century regard for the positive aspects of individualism, and there was as little room for "squalid conformity" in his thought as in Emerson's. His image for

39. Henry James, *Moralism and Christianity* (New York, Redfield, 1850), p. 33.

40. *Tracts for the New Times. No. 1. Letter to a Swedenborgian* (New York, John Allen, 1847), p. 4.

41. *Society the Redeemed Form of Man*, p. 183.

42. *Letter to a Swedenborgian*, p. 18.

43. *Moralism and Christianity*, p. 39.

the community of perfect fellowship was that of a harmony which is "grand or complete just in the degree that its elemental notes are relatively various and distinct. . . . So in human society, if each member be similar in genius, in taste, in action to every other, we have at best a dismal monotony, a mere mush of mutual deference and apology. But if each is distinctively himself, or sharply individualized from every other, then we have a grand choral life hymning the infinitely various graces of the divine unity."[44]

If Henry James was criticized by the Fourierists for limiting himself to social theory without suggesting a method for attaining his end, he considered the Fourierist program a mere instrumentality whereas he himself was concerned with the more important question of spiritual values and ideals. His main objection to such schemes, however, lay in his belief that they sought to "restore the lost Paradise not by the true method of purifying the human heart from its inordinate lusts . . . but by a direct appeal to man's self-love."[45] In other words, like most thinkers and artists of the nineteenth century, James located the primary source of all social evils precisely where he saw the possibility of society's regeneration: in the moral and spiritual being of the individual. He thought that the great mistake of Fourier and Owen lay in believing that human fellowship was a natural condition of human nature, whereas the whole history of civilization proved man to be a creature of selfishness, acquisitiveness, and other "inordinate lusts." For James, "Socialism," or "Society" as he called it after his controversy with the Fourierists, was something to be *achieved*. Fourier talked "of organizing society as glibly as you would talk of organizing a military company. *But,*" James asked, "*where is the society which is to be organized?* The very possibility of human

44. Ibid., pp. 108–09.
45. Letter to *The Harbinger*, 2 (May 23, 1846), 379.

society yet remains to be demonstrated."[46] Society was not the natural state of man, but rather the ultimate state, the Redeemed Form of Man, and accordingly the only way of achieving it was through the regeneration of the individual.

James considered democracy a step, though only a step, toward the attainment of his society of perfect fellowship. The great virtue of the democratic idea is that it "avouches the sole sacredness of humanity, and allows no sanctity to institutions underived from that source. . . . It allows no usage nor recorded statute whatever, any binding obligation which is underived from the instincts of the universal human heart."[47] American society is to be praised for that very human catholicity which James regarded as the hallmark of true Christianity. If Americans have any reason to be proud of their country, he observed, it is "not because it is *ours* simply; on the contrary, we are proud to belong to it, because it is the country of all mankind, because she opens her teeming lap to the exile of every land, and bares her hospitable breast to whatsoever wears the human form."[48] What James praised in democracy was not so much its achievements as the possibilities it had opened for the development of human society. The lecture "Democracy and Its Issues," which he delivered in New York in the winter of 1850–51, is devoted almost wholly to pointing out the negative character of the task democracy has accomplished hitherto—the destruction of the old restrictive institutions—and the anticipation of the positive role it will play when it changes its character and becomes a moral and social agency for the attainment of

46. "An American in Europe . . . III," *New York Daily Tribune* (September 22, 1855), p. 5.

47. Henry James, *Lectures and Miscellanies* (New York, Redfield, 1852), pp. 8–9.

48. Henry James, *The Social Significance of our Institutions* (Boston, Ticknor and Fields, 1861), p. 9.

human fellowship. "We are good," he observes, "by comparison, not by position. When compared with the polities of the Old World, we present the auroral beauty of the morning emerging from the thick night; but the glowing morning does not always ensure an unclouded noon."[49] The essential function of democracy, like that of John the Baptist, is preparatory: it goes "careering over the wilderness of old polities" announcing the true promise of the new world.[50] Since the republican form of political organization makes it impossible to realize "any more expansive form of merely instituted or enforced fellowship" among men, it will lead eventually "to a free spontaneous society, or a spiritual unforced fellowship of each and all men, as the supreme development of human destiny."[51] These being his expectations, it is not surprising that toward the end of his last work, James should use his rhetoric in a characteristic combination of mysticism and sociology to evoke the old myth of America's promise: "The sum of all I have been alleging," he says, "is that we as a community are fully launched at length upon that metaphysic sea of being whose mystic waters float the sapphire walls of the New Jerusalem, metropolis of earth and heaven."[52]

Notwithstanding James' Swedenborgianism, he seems to me a useful and representative figure in the immediate background of the nineteenth-century American novelists. He shared with them a critical attitude toward the actual society of the time on the one hand and a constant preoccupation with ideal community life on the other. Like them, he was disturbed by the dangers of democracy, and inspired by its promise of human fellowship, regarding, in the true spirit of

49. *Lectures and Miscellanies*, pp. 5–6.
50. Ibid., p. 43.
51. *Society the Redeemed Form of Man*, p. 306.
52. Ibid., p. 473.

the age, the individual as the moral key to both the dangers and the possibilities. And finally, as for the visionary cast of his mind, we may say of the novelists what Austin Warren, his biographer, has said of James—that his "contribution to American thought was not a program but a vision. Men need both; but programs and their constructors pass away when they have made their contribution to the emergencies of the hour. Because they read not the times but the eternities, the men of vision belong to the permanent treasure of mankind."[53]

53. Austin Warren, *The Elder Henry James* (New York, Macmillan, 1934), p. 226.

2. Nineteenth-Century Fiction:

THEMES AND PATTERNS

That Art in America will be modified by circumstances, we have no doubt, though it is impossible to predict the precise form of the molds into which it will run. New conditions of life will stimulate thought and give new forms to its expression.

—James Russell Lowell, "Nationality in Literature"

To turn from John Winthrop, Henry James, Sr., Albert Brisbane, and the founders of Brook Farm to the novels of the nineteenth century is to witness how certain ideas, not perhaps extraordinary in themselves, become vital as attitudes and values when they inspire the form and themes of imaginative literature. The central truth of a work of art, if paraphrased into a moral dictum, often turns out to be as commonplace and intellectually as naive as the ideals of Winthrop or the beliefs of the elder James. But works of art derive their effectiveness from a wholly different source. If the novels of Cooper, Hawthorne, Melville, and Twain retain their vitality for us at a time when John Winthrop's sermon possesses only a distant historical relevance, it is not because the novelists reveal more competent and useful truths. Considered as blue-prints for moral or social programs, their works are equally idealistic and inapplicable to concrete human exigencies. But a novel is neither a plan of action nor a treatise on sociology. Its aim is not to secure rational conviction. Addressed to human sensibility, it works on those strata of man's person-ality which are beyond the reach of intellectual argument. Its effectiveness derives from the realignment of sympathies which is caused by the experience of reading it. Its thematic content is not a matter of systematic and rational exposition of a problem, but is to be found rather in the pattern of aroused and redistributed sympathies which it creates. Thus, though the novel achieves all its effects through a concretely presented situation, its moral or social truth does not depend on the exactness of its correspondence with present or histori-cal facts. Insofar as the human sympathies it alters, extends, and creates achieve a wider reference, the novel itself acquires a more universal and enduring quality. It is therefore by appraising what I have called "the pattern of aroused and re-distributed sympathies" that we can judge rightly of a novel's truth or falsity, its penetration or superficiality, and its effec-tiveness or irrelevance. This pattern provides also the key for understanding its theme and form.

My purpose in this chapter is to attempt a general formu-lation of certain values, themes, and structural patterns which are observable in the classic American novel, recurring fre-quently, with obvious differences but also with striking similarities, in the work of the four novelists with whom I am primarily concerned. Since, by definition almost, generaliza-tions tend toward oversimplification and overemphasis of resemblance at the expense of diversity, they are offered here as provisional and partial statements to be com-pleted and corroborated only in the discussions of indi-vidual novelists which follow this chapter and for which, I hope, this outline will provide certain useful signposts.

A good way to define the distinctive character of the nine-teenth-century American novel is to approach it through the fiction which was produced contemporaneously in England. The comparison is particularly relevant, since the two countries were bound by ties of a common language and cultural heritage. What is more, in the first decades of the century, English and continental literature provided the models upon which American writers sought to fashion their own works. As a matter of fact, the dawn of the literary renaissance in America was heralded by many complaints against servile conformity to foreign literature and repeated demands for original creations. Writing on "American Literature" in 1846, Margaret Fuller felt that, though many books were written in America "worthy to be read, as any out of the first class in England," they were "most of them, except in their subject matter, English books."[1] In the same year William Gilmore Simms observed of his fellow American writers that "with very few exceptions, their writings might as well be European. They are European. The writers think after European models, draw their stimulus and provocation from European books, fashion themselves to European tastes, and look chiefly to the awards of European criticism."[2]

Notwithstanding these facts, however, the significant American novel of the century fashioned a radically different course for itself. One may begin an analysis of this difference by saying that whereas the English novel of the 1840s and 50s was predominantly reformist in intention, the American novel of the same period was rarely so. Dickens, Disraeli, Kingsley, and Mrs. Gaskell directed their critical intelligence to concrete

1. S. Margaret Fuller, *Papers on Literature and Art* (New York, Wiley and Putnam, 1846), Pt. II, pp. 126–27.
2. William Gilmore Simms, *Views and Reviews in American Literature*, First Series (New York, Wiley and Putnam, 1845), p. 1.

social issues, and their creative imagination was stimulated by particular evils like imprisonment for debt, sweatshops, legal malpractices, child labor, poorhouses, working
conditions in factories, slum life, and the consequences of
poverty and want generally. These novelists accepted society
as a.more or less permanently established arrangement, and,
insofar as they attacked it, their tendency was toward arousing
sympathy for the practical reform of the institutions they
exposed.

These two decades mark indeed the great age of the social
novel in England. Dickens' *Oliver Twist, The Old Curiosity
Shop, Bleak House,* and *David Copperfield;* Disraeli's Young
England trilogy; Kingsley's *Yeast* and *Alton Locke;* and
Mrs. Gaskell's *Mary Barton* and *North and South*—all these
works were extending the frontiers of fiction into previously
unexplored areas of society and focusing attention on a variety
of social problems. In the 1830s English fiction had been
dominated by the so-called silver-fork school, whose ex-
ponents, novelists like Bulwer, specialized in extravagant
portrayals of high life. But when numerous newspaper articles, the reports of the Royal Commissions on factory labor,
and the gathering momentum of the Chartist agitation drew
attention to the more seamy side of contemporary society, the
tide of popular fiction turned accordingly, and Bulwer, in
novels like *Paul Clifford* and *Eugene Aram,* sentimentalized
"low life" where formerly he had sentimentalized "high life."
These picturesque portrayals of poverty and crime were, however, frankly exploitative attempts to catch up with the altered
fashion in reading.

The authentic social novel of the 1840s distinguished itself
from this trend by the seriousness of its intention. Its purpose
went beyond that of accommodating the new taste. It sought
primarily to address itself to the public's newly aroused social
conscience. Dickens, who had parodied the silver-fork school

in an episode in *Nicholas Nickleby*, expressed his dissatisfaction with the fashionable "Newgate novel" also. In the 1841 introduction to *Oliver Twist* he made fun of the current fictional accounts of crime by saying that he "had read of thieves by scores—seductive fellows (amiable for the most part), faultless in dress, plump in pocket, choice in horseflesh, bold in bearing, fortunate in gallantry, great at a song, a bottle, pack of cards or dice-box, and fit companions for the bravest. But," he added, "I had never met (except in HOGARTH) with the miserable reality." In contrast to this, he saw his own realism closely linked with social purpose: "It appeared to me that to draw a knot of such associates in crime as really do exist; to paint them in all their deformity, in all their wretchedness, in all the squalid poverty of their lives; to show them as they really are . . . would be to attempt a something which was greatly needed, and which would be a service to society."

The social novelists did not claim to be pioneers of reform movements. For instance, as Humphry House has pointed out: "Imprisonment for debt, which Dickens hammered at for over twenty years, had been attacked before he was born . . . He was even rather behind the times."[3] The cry for reform was in the air everywhere, and these novelists decided simply to support it with their works. How effectively this support worked on the popular imagination can be gathered from the statement of the Nonconformist preacher who listed Dickens' work among the three chief sources of reformist sentiment: "There have been at work among us," he told his people, "three great social agencies: the London City Mission; the novels of Mr. Dickens; the cholera."[4] And yet Dickens was

3. Humphry House, *The Dickens World* (London, New York, Oxford University Press, 1941), p. 42.
4. Quoted by G. M. Young, *Victorian England: Portrait of an Age* (London, Oxford University Press, 1936), p. 55.

the least propagandistic of the four novelists I have mentioned. Disraeli's *Sybil*, Kingsley's *Yeast*, and Mrs. Gaskell's *Mary Barton* were more directly intended to open people's eyes to certain social evils of the time. Egremont, the hero of *Sybil*, which was subtitled "The Two Nations," is made to discover, for the benefit of his own class, the other, and to them unknown, nation: the slum-dwelling and savage poor of the manufacturing towns. In the same way, Lancelot Smith, the hero of *Yeast*, explores the poverty and wretchedness of agricultural districts. In *Alton Locke*, Charles Kingsley took for his hero a sensitive young man who is held in virtual slavery by the operators of tenement sweatshops. Mrs. Gaskell's theme in *Mary Barton* was industrial strife and violence, while in *North and South* she wrote of both the northern manufacturing towns and the southern agricultural areas.

This preoccupation with social questions was by no means confined to English fiction. The new and rapidly growing industrial-urban society, which, among other things, was responsible for the great boom in European fiction, also provided imaginative stimulus for continental novelists. When George Gissing, who was himself a latter-day social novelist, decided to devote a chapter of his book on Dickens to a search for those of the English novelist's "foreign contemporaries" who could be appropriately compared with him, the novelists he selected were Balzac, Dostoevsky, Victor Hugo, and Daudet, "writers of fiction who, like the English master, were preoccupied with social questions."[5] These names, together with that of Dickens, represent the important European novel of the mid-nineteenth century, and there is much to be said for Gissing's way of defining the nature of its realism. Gissing was also right in leaving out of his account all mention of

5. George Gissing, *Charles Dickens* (New York, Dodd, Mead, 1898), pp. 283–84. The chapter is entitled "Comparisons."

Dickens' American contemporaries, who hardly approached society in a similar manner and whose imagination responded to Scott rather than Dickens. The great American novels of this period were preoccupied neither with "social questions" nor with the reform of social institutions. Even *Huckleberry Finn*, which appeared much later in the century, is concerned not with the institution of slavery but with a fundamental social ethic which includes but also goes beyond the disapproval of slavery.

This difference between the English and the American novel cannot be explained away entirely in terms of the temperamental bias of the writers concerned. Nor was the social situation itself so radically different in the two countries. In both, the 1830s and 40s marked a period of social movement, change, and reform activity. In America the moral energy of the nation, liberated from old religious orthodoxy, was turning increasingly from the exploration of evil within the human being to the task of locating it in man's social environment. These years of ferment gave rise to numerous reform movements, to cultistic communities, spiritualism, vegetarianism, hypnotic healing, mesmerism, phrenology, as well as the various forms of socialism. If the more ridiculous aspects and pretensions of this activity were parodied by Emerson in the opening section of his essay on "New England Reformers" ("a society for the protection of ground-worms, slugs, and mosquitos was to be incorporated without delay"), English reform movements did not lack similar critics. J. S. Mill observed, for instance, that the "stream at present flows into a multitude of small channels. Societies for the protection of needlewomen, of governesses—associations to improve the buildings of the labouring classes, to provide them with baths, with parks and promenades have started into existence." He added that these schemes of benevolence were not looked upon simply as acts of ordinary charity but were "propounded as instalments of a great social reform."[6]

On the other hand, America lacked as little as England in genuine occasions and leaders of reform. Slavery and the race question, workingmen's condition and child labor, democratic equality and the widening of suffrage—these were weighty problems, which engaged the novelists' personal convictions as much as they aroused other intellectuals and leaders to think and act. Theodore Parker, for example, did not, unlike Alcott, cultivate vegetables at Fruitlands, nor did he join any utopian communities. He was a realistic and life-long reformer, and to get an idea of the questions on which popular sympathies needed to be aroused, one can turn to his ordination sermon on "The True Idea of a Christian Church," which he preached to Boston's Twenty-Eighth Congregational Society in 1846 and in which he enumerated such evils of the time as popular ignorance, pauperism, crime, war, and slavery. A novelist like Charles Dickens would have lost no time in supporting Parker with his works, as can be seen from his observations in *American Notes* on such subjects as the human suffering involved in slavery, the Eastern Penitentiary in Philadelphia, and the Negro slums of New York. And these works would be not journalistic tracts but profoundly moving masterpieces of fiction.

If practical reform was no part of the American novelist's conception of his function, it was not because he was less humane than Dickens or Mrs. Gaskell. Nor was he wholly at ease with social conditions around him. On the contrary, we recognize him among the most penetrating critics of his society at the same time we notice that his criticism rarely tends to arouse sympathy for the amelioration of existing institutions and evils. The explanation of this attitude is to be sought, not in the social reality of America but rather in the novelists' conception of it—a conception which exhibits a

6. Quoted by House, p. 48.

curious interpenetration between the facts of actual society and the mythic reality of America. Because of "more free play in the economic realm" (to use Mannheim's words quoted in the last chapter), realism in American fiction did not involve a concern with social questions similar to that of European realism. The myth of America could operate powerfully on the novelists' sensibility because individuals were still felt to be free agents, and society did not impose itself on the imagination as an inexorable complex of permanently stratified institutions. The meaning of the American experiment lay in the fact that individuals had been freed from the necessity of either conforming to or reforming the existing society. That compulsive alternative belonged to Europe. The American social situation, as the novelists saw it, offered a third and vital possibility: the possibility of withdrawal and the formation of a new community; the opportunity, in other words, of repeating the experiment along new lines.

Accordingly, preoccupation with social questions led the American novelists to ideas of total overhauling and intimations of ideal community life. Their imagination worked in terms of radical substitutes rather than localized improvements. Concerned with the basic fact of human relationship, which alone can provide a foundation for social organization, they were visionaries rather than reformers.

The lack of reformist intention in the American novel can go a long way in explaining some of its other distinctive characteristics. For instance, the terms "optimist" or "pessimist" can be applied with less relevance to Cooper, Hawthorne, Melville, and Twain than to their English contemporaries. Furthermore, whatever effects they achieve or fail to achieve, it is only rarely that they attempt the effect of pathos. And finally, though they have many faults of their own, they seldom fall into sentimentality.

These tendencies, prominent even in the best English fiction of the mid-nineteenth century, are directly connected with its particular kind of social purposiveness. The novelist whose motivation includes a desire for the amelioration of social evils sees his function as essentially mediative. He tends to regard his work as a plea entered on behalf of certain segments of society and addressed to those other segments which possess the power to alter the conditions in question. If he is hopeful of improvement, he will be an optimist, like Dickens; if, on the contrary, his idea of the ruling powers is less encouraging, he will be, like George Gissing, a pessimist. This fact will also color the general cast of his characterization, for, as Chesterton argues, if you want men saved, you must paint them as worth saving. Pessimistic reformers like Gissing, who show them reduced to worms, make them contemptible. But Dickens describes them as gods, and society rushes to elevate them to that position. In the same way, sentimentality and pathos are, for the reformer, ready means of arousing quick sympathies for the amelioration of easily remediable evils. "Dickens," as Chesterton says, "did help to pull down the debtors' prisons; and if he was too much of an optimist he was quite enough of a destroyer. . . . If Dickens was an optimist he was an uncommonly active and useful kind of optimist. If Dickens was a sentimentalist he was a very practical sentimentalist."[7]

The reformist motive lies also behind the use that Dickens made of children in his novels. In this field, as in many others, he was a literary innovator, for to put a child at the center of a novel for adults was virtually unknown when Dickens wrote *Oliver Twist* and the *Old Curiosity Shop*. One can see this pioneering effort in terms of Dickens' own life, especially the experiences he had undergone in childhood. But as Kathleen

7. G. K. Chesterton, *Charles Dickens* (New York, Dodd, Mead, 1929), p. 272.

Tillotson points out in *Novels of the Eighteen-Forties*, one must also remember how important a social problem child labor was at the time, and how it had been publicized by the Royal Commission, which issued five reports on it between 1831 and 1843. Thus the pathos in which Dickens enveloped the stories of children in his work was directly geared to his social purpose. Gissing defended it on these grounds when he said: "Such pathos is called 'cheap.' I can only repeat that in Dickens's day, the lives, the happiness of children were very cheap indeed, and that he had his purpose in insisting on their claims to attention."[8] Mrs. Tillotson, who quotes Gissing, goes on to add: "Dickens's pathos had its social purpose. Nell, Smike, Jo, even Paul are all in different ways social victims: as much as the Wilson twins in *Mary Barton*."[9]

Children figured extensively in nineteenth-century American fiction also, but no American novelist of Dickens' caliber regarded the theme of childhood as an occasion for pathos, except perhaps in rare cases like Hawthorne's "The Gentle Boy." From Annie in Hawthorne's early sketch "Little Annie's Ramble" to Henry James' Maisie, these little men and women have had many roles assigned to them: they have acted out the novelist's conception of innocence or of moral ambiguity; they have been corrupt or incorruptible; their purity has been used to reflect the evil of the surrounding adult world; they have served the novelist as tools for moral and social commentary; they have been passive spectators or active agents; they have provided their creators with the necessary means for satire and irony; but never have they been depicted as the helpless victims of a society whose inexorable machinery trammels up and destroys their lives.

8. Gissing, p. 230.
9. Kathleen Tillotson, *Novels of the Eighteen-Forties* (Oxford, Clarendon Press, 1954), p. 50.

Mark Twain uses children extensively for the purpose of social criticism, but not in the Dickensian manner. Though there are obvious resemblances between the two writers, and though Twain came to admire Dickens, Dickensian pathos was the one great shortcoming which he could forgive neither the English novelist nor his imitators. His own social purpose was very different from that of the English writer. Dickens would have seen in Huck Finn an opportunity for creating another Oliver Twist. But Twain could consider making his hero's homeless condition an occasion for appealing against the drunken fathers of Hannibal as little as Cooper could be expected to retire Natty finally to a judgeship in Cooperstown. Dickens' purpose was to awaken a heartless society to its professed civilized or Christian duties by opening its eyes to the plight of the Oliver Twists of England and by arousing it to the need of befriending them. On the contrary, the American novelist, true to the workings of the American myth in his imagination, has no truck with a corrupt society apart from the necessity of passing judgment on it. He does not seek to reform it, broadening its virtue from precedent to precedent. His hero refuses to compromise with evil by seeking a secure social position for himself. Unlike Oliver Twist, Huck and Natty do not lack virtuous friends and families who will adopt them. It is not society which has turned its back upon them but rather they who from the fullness of their moral judgment reject society—or civilization, as they call it.

The heroes of American fiction affirm at once the vitality of the American myth in the pre-Civil War period and the extent to which literary imagination still regarded the individual as essentially unfettered by social restrictions and pressures. The great novelists of this time seldom project the established social order as the ultimate arbiter of man's destiny. Equally rarely do they see this order as established beyond the possibility of further experiment along fundamentally different lines. In the last analysis, individuals retain the right to fashion for themselves a society which conforms to their highest ideals. The positive values which emerge from this novel are, accordingly, not bound so much to social institutions as they are addressed to the basic needs of ideal community life, or, what the elder Henry James would call perfect fellowship among men.

Society then does not exist in the mid-nineteenth century American novel either as a ubiquitous presence or as the all-important determinant of human life and attitudes. This is the fact which finally distinguishes American from European fiction. The reformist intention of the English novelists, the fact that they regarded their work as an appeal addressed to society itself, is only a humane corollary which follows from the attitude of regarding the existing social order as the most potent factor in the human situation. Not all European novels of this time are reformist by any means, but they are all society-bound in this sense. The dramas of Balzac, Dostoevsky, and Emily Brontë, as much as those of Dickens, are wholly worked out in terms of the social institutions and values of the nineteenth century. Established society provides not the background but the very tissue and fiber of the actions of their novels, none of which lead their characters, on a raft or along a trapper's path, away from the civilization of the time and put them in a position where they can enter into, or create, radically different social relations and thereby a different social world. The Australia where that chronic social failure, Micawber, makes good is not a new world but only a wishful projection of the old: it represents not new values but only different circumstances.

Dickens himself, however, did not always write with the expectation of reforming society. For instance, in a novel like *Dombey and Son*, as Kathleen Tillotson has pointed out, "a pervasive uneasiness about contemporary society takes the place of an intermittent concern with specific social wrongs."[10] In other words, Dickens' attitude here, as well as the un-optimistic strain in which the novel is cast, comes close to the kind of concern with society that is the hallmark of the great American fiction of this period. Nevertheless, though this novel does not attack superficial and easily remediable evils, Dickens, unlike his American contemporaries, focuses his criticism entirely on social institutions—business, church, and the family—even as his story remains confined within the limits of existing society.

This difference between the mid-nineteenth century fiction of the two countries can perhaps be illustrated better by re-ferring to Emily Brontë's *Wuthering Heights*, which appeared about the same time as *Dombey and Son* and has generally been recognized as the least typical of English novels. Indeed, in many of its characteristics it comes closer to the American tradition: in its setting on the wilderness of the Yorkshire moors, in the ungenteel quality of the passions with which it deals, and in the extension of its theme to include a pre-occupation with the more elemental aspects of the human situation. Its hero combines the Ishmael-like condition of the outcast with the will, the determination, and the passionate intensity of an Ahab. But—and this is where one begins to see the contrast—Heathcliff, unlike Ishmael and Ahab, does not act out his role in an institutional vacuum. To become the hero of an English novel—even an untypical hero—he has to be introduced not only into a family but, more significantly, into a firmly delineated social milieu which, with its estab-lished institutions and hierarchy of values, becomes, and remains to the last, the scene of his life and struggles. Though Cathy recognizes and affirms the elemental power of the pas-sion which binds her to Heathcliff, this bond is not strong enough to withstand the pressure of those more purely social

10. Ibid., p. 157.

attractions which work within her own self and which, by leading her to marry Edgar Linton, become the source of the subsequent tragic action. Her capitulation to the forces of genteel piety, property, and social prestige convinces Heathcliff that society cannot be disregarded even on the wild Yorkshire moors and that, in order to battle against it successfully, he must acquire and wield its own weapons.

Organized society plays no comparable role in the great American novels of the same period. Their heroes too engage in social conflict, but in their pursuit of ideal relationships or their passionate struggles the constituted social order is not an equally powerful antagonist. They can more easily turn their backs on it. On the level of plot and action, the only parallel American fiction offers to the story of the frustration of Heathcliff's passion is the story of Gatsby in the twentieth century, but by then society had acquired an equally compulsive character for the American imagination as well. As for the American novelists of Emily Brontë's own generation, in spite of the comparison which her imagination invites with theirs, on this point they offer only a contrasting picture. What possible role could Natty or Ishmael or Huck play in an English novel when, unlike even Heathcliff, they not only start by being unrelated to any recognized social order but deliberately stay in that condition to the end of their fictional careers? Whereas Emily Brontë found it necessary to launch her hero in a hierarchical social milieu, it is interesting to note that in *The Marble Faun* when Hawthorne decided to take one of his chief characters from the ranks of the Italian nobility, he had to see his hero without the encumbrance of social position, relation, custom, and manners before his imagination could set to work on him.

If we say that it is open to the novelist to explore human experience in three different spheres: the subjective world of the individual and of his private relations, the domain of relationships dictated by social institutions, and finally the larger and less easily realizable realm of man's relationship to the constitution and workings of certain cosmic forces essentially beyond human control, and if we call them the personal, the social, and the metaphysical dimensions of experience, we will be able to state the difference between English and American fiction in a simple form. It can scarcely be maintained that the fictional themes of any particular culture or time monopolize any one of these aspects of human life to the exclusion of the other two. The extent to which the various strains enter the theme of a novel depends on the individual genius of the writer concerned. Nevertheless, one can assert safely that whereas European fiction of the mid-nineteenth century works out its themes predominantly in social terms, the contemporary American imagination concerns itself directly with the world of man's personal and metaphysical relations. In English fiction the celebration of personal relations, unencumbered with, or in defiance of, socially sanctioned forms and customs, appears in its own right only with the novels of E. M. Forster in the twentieth century. In rare cases where the theme possesses a definite metaphysical dimension, the novel still turns heavily, as in the case of *Wuthering Heights*, on society and its institutions. By contrast, American fiction, with which I am concerned in this book, provides the exploration of essentially social themes, on personal and metaphysical levels.

Behind this characteristic of the American imagination we can see the workings of two related forces: the pressures exerted on the artist's sensibility by the archetypal American experience and those by the more visible forces of democratic individualism. I have already indicated the persistent relevance of the former. For a contemporary discussion of the problem in terms of the latter one can turn to two chapters of Tocqueville's *Democracy in America*. In the first, "Of Some

Sources of Poetry Among Democratic Nations," after defining poetry as the "search after, and the delineation of, the Ideal,"[11] Tocqueville observes how democracy robs literature of certain poetic effects connected with settled institutions, traditions of the past, and the picturesque refinement of some social classes as well as the equally picturesque rudeness and poverty of others—such effects, in short, as are readily available to aristocratic literature. But this does not leave democracies without poetic ideas. According to Tocqueville, democratic writers will draw their inspiration not from the observation of socially differentiated individuals but from the contemplation of the more universal attributes of humanity and from man's relation to the cosmos rather than to social hierarchy. Democracy "diverts the imagination from all that is external to man and fixes it on man alone. . . . Here," Tocqueville adds, "and here alone, the true sources of poetry among such nations are to be found." Unconcerned with the past, their thoughts are of future possibilities only, and "they are haunted by visions of what will be; in this direction their unbounded imagination grows and dilates beyond all measure."[12] Furthermore, democratic writers will appear "trivial and frigid" if, in imitation of older literatures, they seek to invest heavenly powers with corporeal forms and assign mundane roles to them, but "if they strive to connect the great events they commemorate with the general providential designs that govern the universe and, without showing the finger of the Supreme Governor, reveal the thoughts of the Supreme Mind, their works will be admired and understood, for the imagination of their contemporaries takes this direction of its own accord."[13] Tocqueville sums up his discussion by concluding (as though in anticipatory answer to Henry

11. Tocqueville, *Democracy in America*, 2, 71.
12. Ibid., 2, 73.
13. Ibid., 2, 75.

James' later strictures on the poverty of literary materials in America) that, though many resources fail the democratic writer, "Man remains, and the poet needs no more. The destinies of mankind, man himself taken aloof from his country and his age and standing in the presence of Nature and of God, with his passions, his doubts, his rare prosperities and inconceivable wretchedness, will become the chief, if not the sole, theme of poetry among these nations."[14]

Tocqueville is only one among the many commentators who have remarked on the absence of the "social" dimension in American literature. Like the others, he too connects this fact with the character of American society: "the principle of equality," he says, robs democratic poetry of that variety and picturesqueness which European society offers to its poets:

> Among aristocratic nations there is a certain number of privileged personages whose situation is, as it were, without and above the condition of man; to these, power, wealth, fame, wit, refinement, and distinction in all things appear peculiarly to belong. The crowd never sees them very closely or does not watch them in minute details, and little is needed to make the description of such men poetical. On the other hand, among the same people you will meet with classes so ignorant, low, and enslaved that they are no less fit objects for poetry, from the excess of their rudeness and wretchedness, than the former are from their greatness and refinement.[15]

More than a half century earlier, Crèvecoeur had similarly attempted to define American society by contrasting it with European institutions:

14. Ibid., *2*, 76.
15. Ibid., *2*, 72.

It is not composed, as in Europe, of great lords who possess everything, and of a herd of people who have nothing. Here are no aristocratical families, no courts, no kings, no bishops, no ecclesiastical dominion, no invisible power giving to a few a very visible one; no great manufacturers employing thousands, no great refinements of luxury. The rich and the poor are not so far removed from each other as they are in Europe.

If the newly arrived immigrant, Crèvecoeur goes on to add, "travels through our rural districts he views not the hostile castle, and the haughty mansion, contrasted with the clay-built hut and miserable cabin, where cattle and men help to keep each other warm, and dwell in meanness, smoke, and indigence."

In touching upon the literary consequences of such a situation, Tocqueville was preceded by Cooper in *Notions of the Americans* and followed by Hawthorne in the preface to *The Marble Faun* and, most notably, by James, who provided in his *Hawthorne* a fairly comprehensive list of the "items of high civilization" lacking in his native country. There would be no point in quoting these three celebrated and well-known passages, but it is worth while to make two observations about them. In the first place, the materials which Cooper, Hawthorne, and James desiderate in the American scene relate, as in Tocqueville's discussion, to institutional variety and social picturesqueness. Secondly, and more importantly, these remarks of the American novelists, as James noted in his own case, are wholly negative. Cooper and Hawthorne, like James after them, were too powerfully aware of Europe and European literature to present their own different situation and work in any manner other than an apologetic one. It was thus left to a foreign observer like Tocqueville to attempt a more positive analysis of the correlation between the democratic social situation and the possibilities of democratic literature. Since, however, this lack of institutions in American society did not prevent Cooper and Hawthorne from writing but led them only to write differently, we should take even their remarks less as rueful apologies for their inability to recreate the European novel in America and more as rudimentary attempts to define the distinctive character of the American novel. Interpreted in this way, they provide a sort of definition by exclusion of the relation between society and literature in America.

The comparative absence of institutionalized relations in the American novel leads one to place in perspective not only its predominant themes and patterns but also certain of its other characteristics: its often-noted lack of concern with social reality at the level of manners, for instance, or the fact that its greatest characters tend to be archetypes rather than social types. To these one can add a few other points with the help of Tocqueville's illuminating insights. I have already pointed out how this astute student of democracy realized that American literature would emphasize the personal and metaphysical sides of human experience. In the following chapter, "Why American Writers and Orators Use an Inflated Style," he proceeds to relate this observation with the stylistic tendency of democratic writing, providing in the process hints for a theory of the sort of rhetoric most conspicuously exemplified by Melville. Rephrasing the conclusion he had arrived at in the previous chapter, Tocqueville says that the American writer's "ideas are all either extremely minute and clear or extremely general and vague; what lies between is a void." One can recall here the void which separates (almost literally) Melville's detailed description of the whaling industry from the vaster reaches of his theme in *Moby-Dick*, or the distance that lies between the "A" on Hester's and Dimmesdale's bosom and its heavenly projection on the nocturnal sky. It is in an effort to bridge this gulf, to reach from the personal to the metaphysical aspect of the universe, that the American writer uses (and at times abuses) those many distinctive literary and stylistic devices among which can be included the "immense and incoherent imagery," the "exaggerated descriptions and strange creations," the "monsters," and "the fantastic beings of their brain" of which Tocqueville speaks. One can also see in Tocqueville's observation that "among democratic nations the sources of poetry are grand, but not abundant"[16] a clue to the fact that the greatest achievement of the American novelists, more than that of any others, tends to be concentrated in single masterpieces. If, like continental writers, they had undertaken to write the "social" novel or the novel of manners, they could have derived endless inspiration from the wide panorama of society. That the means for such attempts were not entirely lacking to them can be noted from the Albany scenes in Cooper's *Satanstoe*, which achieve an almost Tolstoyan breadth and verve; the Dickensian urban description in Melville's *Pierre;* or Hawthorne's fine evocation of the Boston setting in *The Blithedale Romance*. But such opportunities stimulated their imagination only sporadically. It was fully engaged by the single and by no means inexhaustible theme of exploring the moral and social meaning of the American experience. The writer made repeated assaults on it, even stated it variously at various times, but once he had articulated it fully, the achievement tended to dwarf his other performances.

Henry James regarded social relationships as the primary source of even the most inward and personal of human experiences. "Experience, as I see it," he observed, "is our apprehension and our measure of what happens to us as social creatures—any intelligent report of which has to be

16. Ibid., *2*, 77–78.

based on that apprehension."[17] It is with this side of the American experience, its social meaning as reflected in the themes of nineteenth-century fiction, that I am chiefly concerned in this study. Obviously, no concise statement of it will either fit or cover all the individual novelists, much less all their works. Nevertheless, I attempt a general definition in the hope that it will provide a rough framework for the separate discussions to follow and, at the same time, indicate the nature of the theme pursued in them. This theme can be described as separation from established society and search for ideal community. While the separation may be voluntary or forced, physical or moral, complete or partial, brought about by the individual's alienation from society or society's rejection of him, by and large it is presented sympathetically. The criticism is of the established social order rather than the seceding individual. While the absence of compulsive institutions makes withdrawal possible, the situation is so fashioned in the context that for the individual not to withdraw would be to compromise his integrity. It is often argued that such acts on the part of American heroes represent immaturity, irresponsibility, or escapism. This would indeed be an accurate reading if the hero stopped short with the assertion of his individual and absolute freedom. In reality he only withdraws from one particular complex of institutions, from an order which has falsified the very basic premises of personal and social relationships. That he is not a romantic escapist is evident from the fact that his first action is followed invariably by seeking, or entering into, other and more satisfactory relationships in which he displays a remarkable ethical sensibility and a cheerful willingness to bear the burden of mutual responsibility. This search for a truer community life is as much a part of what he represents as his earlier

17. Preface to *The Princess Casamassima, The Novels and Tales of Henry James*, New York Edition, *5* (New York, Scribner's, 1908), x.

repudiation of society. The one fact complements the other in the total picture.

These novelists are thus concerned with the theme of society rather than with any particular social theme. Separation from Europe was the great fact of the American experience even as the creation of a regenerate society was its highest ideal. Through the generations, in varying ways and with changing terms of reference, the American sensibility has never ceased to respond to both the fact and the ideal, constantly interpreting the meaning of the one and exploring the possibilities of the other. Seen in this light, the American hero's assertion of the right to separate himself from a society which he judges to be corrupt becomes a testament to the vitality of his American heritage. In the early nineteenth century the literary imagination was still comparatively unfettered by the restrictions of an imposing and ubiquitous social machinery, and it could still deal with the problem of society in simple and ideal terms. I do not think, however, that because these novelists retained the ability to look beyond particular social arrangements to fundamental questions of social ethics, they were for that reason fanciful utopians. On the contrary, their vision was circumscribed by a recognition of those more permanent limitations which are inherent in the moral nature of man and the universe he lives in. This fact extended the scope of their drama and at the same time disciplined both their social criticism and their ideals.

In this particular also we can see the operation of the American heritage on the nineteenth-century imagination. The novelists shared the glib idealism and hopefulness of the contemporary utopian thinkers as little as the elder Henry James did. In its austerity and rigor their view of man and the universe was closer to that of the Calvinists, though their human values differed radically from those of their forebears.

Even in Cooper, the most romantically hopeful of the four, man's natural environment is not always benevolent. If at times Nature wears the peaceful aspect of the Lord's temple, its stillness is more often broken by scenes of violence and savagery whose enactment is not altogether confined to human actors. Like Crèvecoeur before him, Cooper suggests a correspondence between the conflicts of men and the struggle that is latent everywhere in the natural world. Marius Bewley has pointed out an example of this in a scene in *The Water-Witch* where a seaman's philosophy of "eat or be eaten" is immediately vindicated by the sharks when a fellow-seaman loses his foothold on the stranded raft and falls into the sea.[18] The same effect of the precariousness of existence, of the ambiguous character of the surrounding reality, is created in the land novels by the ever-present imminence of danger and death that lurk in all corners of the immense wilderness. This involvement of the human situation with a suprahuman reality is more readily evident in the works of Hawthorne, Melville, and Twain. In Hawthorne's case the present is very often a hostage of the past, and the past itself is dominated by the rigorous Calvinist view of sin and damnation. In Melville's sea novels, the sea becomes the chief objective correlative for the imponderable nature of the cosmos which environs human existence and with whose forces man has to battle or reconcile himself. And finally, in Twain's deterministic view of the universe, most starkly set forth in *The Mysterious Stranger*, we can see a latter-day restatement of the Puritan belief in an existence that is essentially preordained.

At times the metaphysical extension of the human situation gives to these novelists' critical evaluation of human behavior a depth and an earnestness which we commonly associate

18. Marius Bewley, *The Eccentric Design* (New York, Columbia University Press, 1959), pp. 74–76.

with great satire. More often it is the source of the urgency that lies behind their exploration of the ideal of human fellowship. Man, they may have said with Shakespeare,

> proud man
> Drest in a little brief authority,
> Most ignorant of what he's most assured,
> His glassy essence, like an angry ape,
> Plays such fantastic tricks before high heaven
> As make the angels weep . . .

A wiser attitude toward the reality of his own self as well as of the universe he lives in would inculcate in man a spirit of humility and understanding: self-righteousness would give place to the tolerance of cosmic piety, self-assertion to human sympathy, and fanatical zeal to mutual compassion. These values are enforced by the necessities of the human situation as these novelists conceive it. If life were a pleasant excursion, the best way to live it would be for each participant in the enterprise to assert his independence and go his own way, as Hazlitt says men should do on such occasions. But human existence resembles more closely a precarious journey through a cosmos which incorporates elements of savagery, hostility, inscrutability, or simple indifference to man's fate— a universe, in short, not calculated to promote automatically the happiness of human beings. In the face of such somber surroundings men should draw together in mutual fellowship rather than aggravate the menace by turning away from, or against, each other.

Subjected to a rough paraphrase, the themes of many great works of American fiction would reveal some such meaning as their common denominator. Hawthorne, to take the most difficult case, could utilize the Calvinist belief in the universal sinfulness of humanity as a premise for the exploration of the problems and possibilities of man's life, but his conclusions were radically opposed to those drawn from this world view by his forefathers. The Hawthornes, Endicotts, and Bellinghams of the early Puritan settlements responded to man's inveterate corruption by inflicting on him ceaseless punishment and persecution—an attitude that would seem strangely contradictory, if not altogether illogical, to the humane novelists of the nineteenth century. If sin is the universal destiny of mankind, its manifestation should occasion sympathy, understanding, and compassion rather than pietistic arrogance and moral blindness. Accordingly, in a remarkable combination of metaphysics with social values, Hawthorne often conceived pride, hypocrisy, coldness of heart— all that obstructs the flow of human sympathy—as the true bosom serpent, whereas the metaphysical notion of sin could only suggest, as it does in "Young Goodman Brown," a basis for the communion of the whole race.

More obviously, the urge toward community, the individual's desire to belong to a larger social unit, was a response to the contemporary social situation in America. European society, in which the forces of democratic freedom had to establish themselves in the face of a surviving feudal order, offered its novelists ready-made possibilities for dramatic exploitation. There was a new exhilaration in according to nameless, ordinary men the dignity of full-length literary treatment. The first English novelists often took for their theme the celebration, the championship, or simply the portrayal of the democratic man. Defoe celebrated the omnipotence of the individual in *Robinson Crusoe* and, in *Moll Flanders*, took a low character for his protagonist; Fielding's heroes numbered among them a footman, a foundling, and a notorious criminal; while in *Clarissa Harlowe* Richardson fashioned a tragic action out of the conflict between personal freedom and feudal familial and economic institutions. In contrast to this, American society presented to the creative imagination an altogether different theme. Here the freedom and supremacy of the individual constituted not a battle to be fought and won but rather a generally accepted principle, the starting point rather than the end of further search and struggle. In a society where equality was becoming increasingly a compulsion toward conformity and where individualism was rapidly draining social relationships of their human content, democratic values needed to be critically appraised as well as celebrated. Individual freedom could be used as a moral shield against the obligations of a corrupt social order, but by itself it was not enough. The principle of individualism could become self-stultifying unless it was related to the responsibilities of a larger social life. The problem of the novelist was thus not only to vindicate individual freedom in all its moral and psychological complexity but also to show how it could acquire positive meaning only when it was defined within the needs of the family or the civil community.

The ideal of a community life explains, in part at least, the constant, though seldom uncritical, pre-occupation of these novelists with the forest, the wilderness, an uninhabited scene for an altogether fresh start generally, as well as, in some cases, with the life and customs of simpler civilizations. The key to the thematic pattern of many of their works is to be found in the fact that the concepts of society and community figure in them with something of the dialectical opposition which the terms "civilization" and "society" had for the elder Henry James. It is true that Hawthorne seldom employs, except in *The Blithedale Romance*, a geographically discrete locus for the enactment of the positive aspect of this theme, such a locus as is provided by the raft in *Huckleberry Finn* or by the ships and distant lands in Melville. Nevertheless, in Cooper, Melville, and Twain as much as in Hawthorne, the essential search is not for a means of escape but for values. It has often been observed that American fiction assumes typically the pattern of a journey. Whether the journey is only inward or whether it is accompanied by outward physical movement, the important fact is that, unlike other literary journeys, such as the one in Chaucer's *Canterbury Tales*, it is not a mere functional device. It does not merely provide a means for the serious or satirical portraiture of contemporary society, nor is its purpose entirely that of holding together an episodic narrative of adventure, anecdote, or escape. The journey is more nearly the essential form of these novels because it represents in physical terms an approximation to their theme: the individual's alienation from the established social order and his reaching out toward community relationships and values.

Here we have the distinctive character of the American novelist's handling of the social theme. The criticism of existing society is balanced in his treatment by the imaginative constructs of community life, these microcosmic units providing the means for exploring the values on which new social relationships must be based. The over-all sense conveyed is that society can be remade without the necessity of compromising one's ethical principles by countenancing its corruption even temporarily. The protagonist thus figures as "Man the Reformer" in the Emersonian sense of the term, for, as Emerson asks in the essay of that name: "What is a man born for but to be a Reformer, a Re-maker of what man has made; a renouncer of lies?" The Americans, he goes on to add, have little faith in such a possibility, "and no class more faithless than the scholars or intellectual men. . . . But the believer not only beholds his heaven to be possible, but already to begin to exist,—not by the men or materials the statesman uses, but by men transfigured and raised above themselves by the power of principles. To principles something else is possible that transcends all the power of expedients."

The exigencies of such a theme involve a radically original view of human relationships, and I should like to comment on some of the more significant fictional forms assumed by these relationships. For instance, there is the "men without women" theme which appears so widely in American fiction and which is generally interpreted in psychological, sexual, or auto-biographical terms. Without implying that these interpretations are not valid in individual cases, I should like to point out an aspect of this recurring motif that relates it more closely to the novelists' common social preoccupation. My suggestion is that the American hero's drive toward celibacy can be seen profitably as a negative response to the contemporary social situation, as a part, in other words, of the novelist's criticism of a society in which even the most intimate personal relationships were not free from the influence of the dominant commercial values. One can take Hawthorne's short story "Mrs. Bullfrog" as an illustration, because viewing marriage as a commercial transaction provides the serious point of this otherwise light-hearted sketch. The narrator of the story, Mr. Bullfrog, is a dry goods merchant who requires such varied excellence in the woman who can win his love that he is faced with the risk of either not getting married at all or "of being driven to perpetrate matrimony with my own image in the looking-glass."[19] He is saved from this cruel fate by a stroke of good fortune which takes him into another state where at last he meets the right woman and marries her. Driving back immediately after the wedding, however, Mr. Bullfrog begins to discover that his

19. Unless otherwise stated, the edition used for quotations from Hawthorne is *The Complete Works of Nathaniel Hawthorne*, ed. George Parsons Lathrop, 12 vols. Boston, Houghton, Mifflin, Riverside Edition, ca. 1882–99.

bride is in reality a Gorgon-like parody of the innocent and beautiful Eve which he had imagined her to be. Her silken curls turn out to be a deceptive wig, her gums are toothless, she has the temper and strength of a virago, and her bottle of face lotion contains cherry brandy. The final blow comes when the unhappy man chances upon an old newspaper report of a lawsuit for damages arising from breach of promise of marriage, and finds out that the plaintiff in the case was none other than his present bride. Mr. Bullfrog is prostrate with despair. What hopes of connubial happiness can one entertain when one's wife is not only without personal beauty but also totally devoid of innocence, dignity, and modesty? Why, indeed, had Mrs. Bullfrog suffered the shame of such a trial and not treated the villain who had wronged her "with the silent contempt he merited?"

"That is all very well, Mr. Bullfrog," said my wife, slyly; "but, in that case, where would have been the five thousand dollars which are to stock your dry goods store?"

"Mrs. Bullfrog, upon your honor," demanded I, as if my life hung upon her words, "is there no mistake about those five thousand dollars?"

"Upon my word and honor there is none," replied she. "The jury gave me every cent the rascal had; and I have kept it all for my dear Bullfrog."

"Then, thou dear woman," cried I, with an overwhelming gush of tenderness, "let me fold thee to my heart. The basis of matrimonial bliss is secure, and all thy little defects and frailties are forgiven. Nay, since the result has been so fortunate, I rejoice at the wrongs which drove thee to this blessed lawsuit. Happy Bullfrog that I am!"

The ironic point of this ending is essentially the same that Emerson makes more seriously in "Man the Reformer,"an essay which attacks nineteenth-century commercialism in terms that make it almost a new version of the Original Sin. Commenting on the far-reaching evils of "Trade," Emerson says:

> I do not charge the merchant or the manufacturer. The sins of our trade belong to no class, to no individual. One plucks, one distributes, one eats. . . . The trail of the serpent reaches into all the lucrative professions and practices of man. . . . Inextricable seem to be the twinings and tendrils of this evil, and we all involve ourselves in it the deeper by forming connections, by wives and children, by benefits and debts.

Such statements suggest the social background to the American hero's "purity" or "chastity." Seen in this light, it becomes a desire for noninvolvement in relations which can only be founded on false values. The protagonist conceives of wives and children as hostages given over to a corrupt society. He even renounces the less intimate forms of social intercourse, as Natty does when he bids goodbye to the manorial Hall of Templeton, because he hates, as he may have said with Emerson again, "the prostitution of the name of friendship to signify modish and worldly alliances. I much prefer the company of ploughboys and tin-peddlers to the silken and perfumed amity which celebrates its days of encounter by a frivolous display, by rides in a curricle and dinners at the best taverns."

If the protagonist's rejection of these institutions is intended as a part of the novelist's criticism of contemporary society, the less institutionalized and less worldly friendships, which are so constant a feature of American fiction, constitute the main repository of its positive values. To define the exact nature of these relationships is difficult. However, to say that they are based on "love," with all the misleading associations of the term, seems to me to misconstrue their meaning, for such relationships are not confined to Melville's sailors but figure with equal persistence in Cooper and Twain, not to mention their numerous successors in American fiction. Even in Melville the writing in which the friendships are portrayed hardly ever acquires that tumescent covertness which always accompanies literary hintings at abnormal sexual relations. On the whole, it seems to me that nothing is gained by approaching these situations with our newly acquired knowledge of unconscious psychoses. We would do better, if we must use the word "love," to define it, in terms of Emerson's contemporary essay on the subject, as essentially a matter of man's personal relations, as a force which "unites him to his race, pledges him to the domestic and civic relations, carries him with new sympathy into nature" and beams "upon the universal heart of all."

In this way we can see the connection between these friendships and the American mystique of democracy. By and large they are represented as ideal relations rather than intense emotional unions. In his essay on "Friendship" Emerson declared: "Maugre all the selfishness that chills like east winds the world, the whole human family is bathed with an element of love like a fine ether." Friendship itself he described as "that select and sacred relation which is a kind of absolute, and which even leaves the language of love suspicious and common." The elder Henry James, as we have seen, thought in similar terms when he considered that the proper function of democracy was to lead humanity to universal brotherhood and perfect fellowship. Such formulations come very close to describing the relations between Natty and the Indian chief Chingachgook, Ishmael and the outlandish heathen Queequeg, and Huck Finn and the Negro slave Jim. If we want a more modern and perhaps also more exact definition, we can call them cases of "civic friendship." The term is Jacques

Maritain's, and in *The Rights of Man and Natural Law* he considers the relationship which it describes as the necessary condition for the political task of establishing a "brotherly city." "In the bourgeois-individualist type of society," Maritain says, "there is no common work to do, nor is there any form of communion."[20] But human beings crave community life. "The person is a whole, but it is not a closed whole, it is an *open* whole. It is not a little god without doors and windows, like Leibnitz's monad, or an idol which sees not, hears not, speaks not. It tends by its very nature to social life and to communion." This is so not only because of the individual's own need "but also because of the radical generosity inscribed within the very being of the person."[21] In a section entitled "The Conquest of Freedom," Maritain seeks to clear what would seem to be a paradox: the relation between the freedom of the individual and the demands of social life. The ideal goal of a perfect human society can be achieved, he says, through the feeling, "in some sense sacred," for justice and "the development of civic friendship."

> For justice and law, by ruling man as a moral agent and appealing to reason and free will . . . transform into a relation between two wholes—the individual and the social—what would otherwise have been a mere subordination of the part to the whole. And love, by assuming voluntarily that which would have been compulsion, transfigures it into freedom and into free gift. While the structure of society depends primarily on justice, the vital dynamism and the internal creative force of society depend on civic friendship.[22]

20. Jacques Maritain, *The Rights of Man and Natural Law*, tr. Doris C. Anson (New York, Scribner's, 1943), p. 39.
21. Ibid., p. 5.
22. Ibid., p. 35.

The nineteenth-century novelists' problem was also the reconciliation of individual freedom with the necessity of a larger social life, and they too responded to it often with imaginative portrayals of civic friendship. It is significant that one of their common values should be the idea of loyalty, a bond which involves a personal as well as a social commitment, and without whose active presence no community life is possible. The American Kantian philosopher Josiah Royce made loyalty the cornerstone of his philosophy of community, and fashioned out of it the categorical imperative of his own system of ethics: "Be loyal to loyalty." We need not concern ourselves here with the metaphysical aspects of Roycean thought, but, in the field of social morality, Royce's dictum, as John Smith has pointed out, is far from being a vague and meaningless formulation:

> Although this appears at first sight to be the most hazy of commands and perhaps worthy only of an idealist, Royce was careful to point out that in so far as every individual, wherever he be, stands in some social relationship, his duty is to manifest loyalty by concrete deeds *in his particular situation*, and that in this way he indirectly contributes to the extension of loyalty to the whole of mankind.[23]

Since, however, loyalty is a voluntary response and, unlike obedience, can never be coerced, it does not operate in socially enforced relationships. It requires by implication the creation of a community life to which the individuals concerned can owe free and spontaneous allegiance.

By the time Royce came to write his philosophy, the social situation in America had changed. To the imagination it

23. John E. Smith, *Royce's Social Infinite* (New York, Liberal Arts Press, 1950), p. 9.

presented a radically different picture. The elder Henry James had warned that the auroral beauty of the democratic morning might only lead to a clouded noon.[24] Many people thought that this had happened, and that the great differential between the European and American societies had all but vanished. Toward the end of his life Hawthorne is reported to have told W. D. Howells that he wished he could find some part of America "where the cursed shadow of Europe had not fallen."[25] The individual was no longer felt to be a free agent. A gigantic social machinery had grown up everywhere around him, and he could no longer assert his independence and break through it. Joseph Dorfman, who has evoked and documented the social atmosphere of the last decades of the nineteenth century in America, quotes Ignatius Donnelly, the Populist leader, posing the great question which agitated the whole country: "Could the ordinary man retain his economic independence, or must he become the wage slave of the possessor of great wealth?"[26] The same question was being asked by Henry George in *Progress and Poverty*, for George felt that America had lost its earlier consciousness of freedom and that social and economic conditions now approximated the European situation where the child of ordinary people, as he grows to manhood, "finds all the best seats at the banquet of life marked 'taken,' and must struggle with his fellows for the crumbs that fall, without one chance in a thousand of forcing or sneaking his way to a seat."[27] Henry George's own early career bore testimony to the general feeling that the world had closed in and left Americans without that sense of

24. See above, p. 43.

25. Moncure D. Conway, "My Hawthorne Experience," *The Critic*, 45 (July 1904), 23.

26. Joseph Dorfman, *Thorstein Veblen and His America* (New York, Viking Press, 1934), p. 16.

27. Henry George, *Progress and Poverty* (New York, Modern Library, 1929), p. 390.

boundless opportunity which had earlier made individualism a meaningful principle.

The pragmatic philosophers responded to the situation by postulating an open universe, attempting thereby to rehabilitate the American tradition of endless experimentation. In William James' thought the individual still held the central place on the stage of omnipotence. But the creative imagination could no longer ignore the new forces, and, as society and its institutions became increasingly the chief determinants of the individual's life and fortune, American fiction began to approximate the European novel in theme and intention. To illustrate the point, one can cite a true-life story told by Judge Ben Lindsey—one which could have come from a page of Charles Dickens. In the nineties in Denver a child was brought to court for stealing coal from railway tracks and Lindsey sent him to the state reform school. Hardly was the verdict out when the mother of the boy rushed down the aisle screaming "the most soul-piercing scream of agony that I ever heard from a human throat." Lindsey decided to investigate and found that the boy's father, a smelting worker, was dying of lead poisoning in a slum tenement. In the jail itself he found the youthful delinquents lodged in vermin-ridden cells and debauched by older criminals. The experience turned the judge into a lifelong crusader for the reform of the penal code and the treatment of criminals.[28] Lindsey thus adopted the career which Hollingsworth had set out for himself in *The Blithedale Romance*, and the point of relating the story here is to wonder if Hawthorne would have treated the Judge as he did his own protagonist forty years earlier. The important difference between Hawthorne and the new novelists of the succeeding generation lies in the fact that, whereas Hawthorne could ignore social institutions in his concentration upon the

28. Eric F. Goldman, *Rendezvous with Destiny* (New York, Knopf, 1952), p. 122.

moral personality of free individuals, to his successors the two were inseparably bound up with each other.

Accordingly, in the last decades of the century American novelists turned to writing the "social" novel in the European manner. In 1892 Edward Bellamy declared that "the novel with a sociological motive now sets the literary fashion."[29] Almost a decade earlier Henry James had come to a similar conclusion as the idea of *The Bostonians* first occurred to him. When he confided to his notebook that he "wished to write a very *American* tale, a tale very characteristic of our social conditions" and asked himself "what was the most salient and peculiar point in our social life": "The answer was: the situation of women, the decline of the sentiment of sex, the agitation on their behalf."[30] This novel, as well as *The Princess Casamassima* which was also published in 1886, represented, as the editors of his notebooks observe, "James' attempt to handle the Dickensian type of social novel."[31]

Other novelists considered other sociological motives more urgent, and by treating sympathetically such themes as poverty, prostitution, urban slums, sweatshops, agricultural distress, etc., they created the novel of social protest on a large scale in America. Together with this went the realism associated with Stephen Crane, Theodore Dreiser, and Frank Norris. William Dean Howells had prepared the way by extending the social frontiers of fiction. As Charles Kingsley and Disraeli had done forty years earlier in England, he explored the life of a poor New England community in *Annie Kilburn*, and in *A Hazard of New Fortunes* reached down to the lower and impoverished strata of urban society. Henry Adams wrote in *Democracy* a roman à clef which

29. Quoted by Aaron, *Men of Good Hope*, p. 104.
30. *The Notebooks of Henry James*, ed. F. O. Matthiessen and Kenneth B. Murdock (New York, Oxford University Press, 1947), p. 47.
31. Ibid., p. 69.

remains the most distinguished American political novel.

Insofar as this body of fiction approximates thematically the English social novel, it suggests once again by contrast the general quality of the works with which I am concerned. It also defines the historical period of the earlier fiction. Perhaps we can take the Civil War as a convenient though far from precise line of demarcation between the two phases of American sensibility even as it is generally considered to be the watershed of American social experience. The war dramatized for the imagination the end of an era and climaxed a growing sense of disillusionment. Among other things, it spelled disaster for the ideal of democratic brotherhood. The very antithesis of the concept of community, it demonstrated with conclusive finality that America was not moving toward the social harmony envisioned by hopeful prophets. On the contrary, like the nations of the Old World, it had become divided into mutually antagonistic classes. The events of the sixties and the seventies seemed to prove that the worst fears of imaginative men had at last come true. The American poets and novelists of the time may indeed have said of the Civil War what Henry James was to say later of the first World War: "The plunge of civilization into this abyss of blood and darkness . . . so gives away the whole long age during which we have supposed the world to be, with whatever abatement, gradually bettering, that to have to take it all now for what the treacherous years were all the while really making for and *meaning* is too tragic for any words."[32]

Out of a similar shock of betrayal, a sense of shattered dreams, arose the bitterness of Whitman's *Democratic Vistas* (1871), the satire of Twain's and Warner's *The Gilded Age* (1873), and the anguish of Melville's *Clarel* (1876). These writers, born to admire and hope, had stayed to be

32. Letter of August 4, 1914, to Howard Sturgis, *The Letters of Henry James*, ed. Percy Lubbock (2 vols. New York, Scribner's, 1920), *2*, 384.

THEMES AND PATTERNS

disillusioned. Melville, for one, definitely conceived of the Civil War as marking the point of no return when he called it in *Clarel:*

> True Bridge of Sighs—so yet 'twill be
> Esteemed in riper history—
> Sad arch between contrasted eras . . .[33]

Mark Twain, the author of *Huckleberry Finn* as well as *The Gilded Age*, appears on both sides of the arch. If, as has been said, all modern American fiction derives from him, he is also the last representative figure of the older tradition. He takes his place with the realists, reformers, and radicals as well as with the social visionaries of an earlier America.

33. Herman Melville, *Clarel: A Poem and Pilgrimage in the Holy Land*, ed. Walter E. Bezanson (New York, Hendricks House, 1960), p. 422 (IV. v. 78–80).

3. James Fenimore Cooper:

THE HISTORY AND THE MYTH
OF AMERICAN CIVILIZATION

The political work in which human persons may
truly find communion, and to whose realization, all
through the centuries to come, the earthly hope of
our race and the energy of human history must
normally be applied, is the establishment of a
brotherly city . . . If we understand it as brotherly
conduct by all men, each to the other, and as the
victory of the "New Man" thereby implied, it
relates to something beyond history, and represents
for human history a "myth"—the "myth" which
temporal history needs.

—Jacques Maritain,
The Rights of Man and Natural Law

The Littlepage Trilogy and the Leatherstocking Tales may be
considered as representing, respectively, Cooper's response to
the history and the myth of American civilization. Cooper, as
a recent critic puts it, was "both the analyst and the visionary
of American conditions,"[1] and the terms suggest something

1. Richard Chase, *The American Novel and Its Tradition* (New York,
Doubleday, 1957), p. 46.

of the divergence between the thematic assumptions of the two works. Yet they are similar in their concern with the moral foundations of American society, and taken together they provide the best artistic embodiment of Cooper's most vital interests. To be sure, the Littlepage novels were written with a definite thesis in mind, and since they were intended to draw attention to the evils of the contemporary Anti-Rent Movement, they are akin to a work like *Ways of the Hour*, Cooper's last novel, whose purpose, as he said in his preface, was "to draw the attention of the reader to some of the social evils that beset us; more particularly in connection with the administration of criminal justice."[2] After his unfortunate embroilment in a series of unpopular libel suits and the loss of his earlier hopefulness, Cooper tended increasingly to focus his novels on particular social evils—attacking with equal intensity the licentiousness of the press, the Anti-Rent agitation, political demagoguery, and the jury system; and championing alike the right of the landlords to receive rent from their tenants and of sea captains to flog their sailors. In short, one might say that Cooper turned to writing "social" fiction somewhat in the manner of his English contemporaries, though from a conservative rather than a radical point of view. Nevertheless, his novels—the most significant ones at least—hardly ever confined themselves to the evils of the hour. Almost inevitably the social themes reached fundamental moral principles, and plots stemming primarily from contemporary problems were defined against both past history and possible future development.

Such at any rate is the case with the Littlepage Trilogy. As a sociological novel it examines its main thesis in the context of historical development, while as a historical novel it belongs

2. Unless otherwise stated, the edition used for quotations from Cooper is *The Complete Works of J. Fenimore Cooper*, 32 vols. New York, Putnam's, Leather-Stocking Edition, 1893(?).

to that small class of works that deal not with isolated episodes and personages of history but with the dynamics of a whole society. Cooper, as Howard Mumford Jones has observed, "recorded better than any of his contemporaries the first stage in the transition from the world of George Washington to the Great Barbecue of the Robber Barons."[3] Written in the middle period of American history, the Trilogy takes its stand on the values of the first Republican phase of the country and points critically toward the ominous shadows of coming events. Over and above this main preoccupation it takes stock of what might be called the prehistory of American civilization and investigates the moral basis upon which the society had initially laid its foundations. It is the latter fact which provides a sort of link between this series of novels and the Leatherstocking Tales. In the 1840s American society was still in the making; it was fluid enough to induce the novelist critically evaluating the first evidence of its emerging structure to re-examine the whole question of the mold into which it should finally settle itself. Thus the Littlepage Trilogy, which is a work of social protest of a topical nature, becomes also a work which cannot solve in its own terms the problem it has generated—the dilemma of applying moral principles to practical social questions.

The three novels which constitute the series—*Satanstoe* (1845), *The Chainbearer* (1845), and *The Redskins* (1846)—are all concerned with land: the ownership of land, and possible forms of social organization based upon land. Though land provides the focus and the chief integrating principle of the series, the work also concerns itself with the nature, values, and changes of civilization generally. More specifically, its action turns upon the Anti-Rent agitation which was aimed at ending land tenancy in the state of New York and which

3. Howard Mumford Jones, *The Pursuit of Happiness* (Cambridge, Harvard University Press, 1953), p. 105.

represented an important episode in the transition from Jeffersonian Republicanism to the populist democracy associated with the rise of Jackson. The land, which had passed from the possession of Indian tribes into the hands of landlords and patroons holding royal patents, was now claimed by tenants settled upon it. Cooper, whose "sympathies and pocketbook lay on the side of the old squirearchy and the even older patroons" (to use Charles A. Brady's words[4]), undertook to write the novels professedly for the purpose of justifying the ways of God and the rights of the landlords—two principles which in this series he tends to equate, somewhat arbitrarily and against his own subtler recognitions. In order to do this effectively, he invents the Littlepage family of landlords, and, by making three generations of Littlepages tell their own stories, attempts to reconstruct the history of the land from its acquisition and the slow and difficult process of surveying and settling it—a process involving considerable patience, foresight, and outlays of expenditure on the part of the owners—down to Cooper's time, when its ownership was challenged by the agitation of tenants.

Cooper not only sought to prove the justice of the landlords' ownership of their estates and the corresponding iniquity of the tenants' claims; he also set out to demonstrate the superiority of the Littlepage concept of civilization over the new principles that were challenging it. In order to analyze the thematic meaning of this trilogy, therefore, it is necessary to inquire what value, apart from his pocketbook, Cooper saw in the civilization he championed, and how far, within the framework of the novels, he was successful in animating his sympathies in a communicable manner. In other words, to what extent do we respond sympathetically to the novelist's

4. Charles A. Brady, "James Fenimore Cooper: Myth-Maker and Christian Romancer," in *American Classics Reconsidered*, ed. Harold C. Gardiner, S. J. (New York, Scribner's, 1958), p. 61.

claim of the moral and social superiority of the Littlepages and to what extent do we feel that he is merely and unconvincingly loading the dice in their favor?

One way to answer this question would be to say simply that Cooper watched with distrust the replacement of the older Republican virtues by the new spirit of commerce, speculation, and avariciousness, and that he conceived of his landed gentry as a bulwark against the rising tide of a moneyed oligarchy. The point has been made often, and indeed it is too obviously broadcast throughout Cooper's writings to be missed. The impending change was made more dangerous by the growing alignment between the forces of popular press and political demagoguery on the one hand and the power of money and trade on the other. To Cooper it seemed to spell the abandonment of all principles, moral, social, and political, in favor of self-interest, and the eventual vulgarization of the whole culture when money values would remain its only guiding standards. "As the man who lives only to accumulate," he observed in *The Crater*, "is certain to have all his nobler and better feelings blunted by the grasping of cupidity . . . so do whole communities degenerate into masses of corruption, venality, and cupidity, when they set up the idol of commerce to worship in lieu of the ever-living God. So far from denoting a healthful prosperity, as is too apt to be supposed, no worse signs of the condition of a people can be given, than when all other interests are made to yield to those of the mere money-getting sort." He saw increasingly a connection between this tendency and the character of New Englanders, their false piety as well as their spirit of speculative expansionism. Whereas in *The Last of the Mohicans* he only made mild fun of the maladroit David Gamut, the Puritan psalmodist whose piety is misplaced but "honest," the New England characters of his later books are usually petty villains and their motives are likely to be mean and selfish. In *Satanstoe* Yankees are described as "the locusts of the West"—a memorable image which, in its implied charge of parasitism, goes beyond Henry Adams' later description of Western frontiersmen as busy beavers totally unburdened with any moral purpose.[5] In *The Chainbearer* Cooper observes that the New England "spirit of improvement" only conceals under a respectable mask the indulgence of "malice, envy, covetousness, rapacity, and all the lowest passions of our nature." Like Emerson and Dickens, he saw in this spirit a danger to moral and social values. In the Littlepage Trilogy the drama is chiefly embodied in the opposition between the successive generations of the Newcome and Littlepage families.

As between the values represented by these two families, there is no question of Cooper's success in establishing the superiority of the Littlepages. By comparison with the Newcomes' selfishness and sharp-dealing, the landlords embody an almost selfless exertion to achieve an ordered development of their estates. It is true that their scruples about trade and quick money-making break down occasionally, as happens in *Satanstoe* when Corny is commissioned by his father to sell pork and horses in Albany on his way to Mooseridge. Though his grandfather had earlier admonished him somewhat loftily not to have anything to do with army contractors ("Money, and not honor, is their game; and you will be treated like a barrel of beef, or a bag of potatoes, if you fall into their hands."), Corny, with Guert Ten Eyck's expert help, strikes a stiff bargain with the same contractors, and exacts from them, in a maneuver of literal horse-trading, better terms than even his father had stipulated. By the time we come to *The Redskins* and Uncle Ro's financial dealings regarding the development of Satanstoe into the town of Dibbletonborough, the Littlepages are themselves in the business of speculation.

5. See above, p. 29.

By and large, however, in the first volume Cooper successfully presents an attractive picture of the landed gentry. The
reader responds sympathetically to the class, not on account
of any bias external to the presentation itself but because it
establishes its superiority unaided and unhindered by one's
particular preferences and prejudices. The reason for this is
that the Littlepages become associated with such values as
kindliness in personal relationships, warm family affections, a
genuinely enjoyable mode of social intercourse, as well as
with the ripeness which derives from the consciousness of
belonging to a continuing tradition. The best proof of
Cooper's success in this respect is the brilliant evocation of
the *modus vivendi* of the tightly knit squirearchy in the Albany
scenes of *Satanstoe*. It is a novel in which, unchallenged as
yet by the rights and wrongs of the Anti-Rent controversy,
the novelist can concentrate on the portrayal of a graceful
civilization, all the more poignantly because of his awareness
that the world in which he himself was living had more or less
settled its fate.

Working successfully on the basis of a correlation between
manners and moral values, Cooper suggests at the same time
the evil which underlies the vulgarity of Jason Newcome: the
evil of a civilization based entirely on the philosophy of
money and the doctrine of getting on, and the consequent
substitution of the cash nexus for all relationships. This is
brought out early in the novel in the amusing characterization
of Jason, who insists that Corny's father must maintain a
ledger in which are charged against Corny all the various
sums spent on the boy's education, and advises Corny accordingly that he "ought to begin to think of bringing suthin' in,
to pay for all the outgoin's." In the same line, though much
more pointed in intention, is the comic episode at the
Pinkster festival in New York in which Jason tries unsuccess-
fully to give a "treat" to Anneke Mordaunt by paying for her

admission to the lion show, while at the same time feeling thankful that the attempt was foiled because "it saved me three ninepences." "How often do you think," he admonishes Corny, "young ladies will accompany you to shows, and balls, and other sights, if you make them pay?" Of his subsequent dealings with Herman Mordaunt and Mordaunt Littlepage, his maneuvers for obtaining possession of the mill seat at Ravensnest, and his later machinations, one can say perhaps that they make him an early representative of the type recently projected and developed by William Faulkner in the more sinister person of Flem Snopes: the unprincipled and ambitious climber who schemes tirelessly against the very family which has harbored and befriended him. "This man was one of those moneyed gluttons, on a small scale," Cooper says of Jason in *The Chainbearer*, "who live solely to accumulate; in my view, the most odious character on earth." The class to which he belongs—"Newcomites; and that means that each is for himself"—stands for a cold and calculating individualism that perverts even the most intimate relationships, as can be seen by the contrast between the warm family ties among the Littlepages on the one hand, and "Seneky" Newcome's attitude toward his sister, Opportunity, on the other; the name "Opportunity" itself suggesting the moral character of the Newcomes.

By comparison, the values of the Littlepages are relatively independent of pecuniary considerations. To them, as Uncle Ro says, "money is no compensation for the affections." Their attitude toward the all-important question of land— their love for it and the care and patience with which they seek to survey and settle it—is not exclusively determined by love of personal gain. As Herman Mordaunt explains to Corny, he expects no profits to accrue for several generations from "all this outlay of money and trouble" at Ravensnest. If his descendants benefit eventually from his exertions, so

will the numerous tenants and the whole country, for the enterprise he has launched is not just a commercial scheme but
a part of the great communal task of putting to the plow
the vast and virgin lands of the continent.

This view of the landowner's function, constructive rather
than parasitic, informs the first two volumes of the trilogy and
contributes greatly to the pattern of sympathies which Cooper
weaves. In its light we can see, for instance, the point of
Cooper's naming the central and perhaps the most significant
volume after the land surveyor. The surveyor himself,
Andries Coejemans, brings to his task a dedication which has
nothing to do with any expectation of personal rewards and
benefits and which lies at the back of the force that his otherwise uncertain character possesses for us. Though poor and
old, he is altogether above money considerations. As Corny
says to his son, Mordaunt, at one point: "I have known him
actually suffering for money when he was too proud to accept
it from his friends, and too benevolent to part with family
slaves, in order to raise it. 'They were born Coejemans,' he
always said, 'as much as I was born one myself, and they
shall die Coejemans.'" Cooper felt, and perhaps rightly, that
from the point of view of the human relationships involved,
the Littlepage mode of developing the land was preferable to
its being seized by "thousands of heartless speculators," as he
puts it elsewhere, who "regard everything, even to the graves
of our fathers, as only so much improvable property." In
describing his first visit to Ravensnest, Mordaunt observes
that the tenants "crowded around me in a frank, hearty manner, in which good feeling was blended with respect. They
desired to take my hand. I shook hands with all who came, and
can truly say that I took no man's palm into my own that day,
without a sentiment that the relation of landlord and tenant
was one that should induce kind and confidential feelings."
If this relationship is destroyed, Cooper asks in the preface to

The Chainbearer, what elements would take the place of the landlords? "We know of none half so likely to succeed," he warns, "as the country extortioner and the country usurer!"[6]

It is easy enough to sympathize with this part of the case for the landlords. But it constitutes only a fraction of Cooper's total argument. These virtues—the constructive function of American landlordism and the "kindly and confidential" relations which it fostered within the community—were connected in Cooper's mind, as we shall see, with the spirit of early settlements. They do not belong to the fully developed aristocracy that he envisioned in theory and presented in the subsequent volumes of the trilogy. As for the warning that the landed gentry would be replaced by a moneyed oligarchy, it should be observed at the very outset that, though history has amply justified Cooper, the issue is irrelevant to both *The Chainbearer* and *The Redskins*. These novels do not develop the theme along the lines of the conflict between agrarian and commercial values. The dramatic opposition to the country gentlemen in these volumes comes not from "the country usurer" but from squatters and tenants. And this, needless to say, marks a radical shift in the theme.

Cooper's championship of the landlords was more positive in the sense that it rested on the merit he saw in the existence of the class itself. As several commentators have pointed out, he conceived of it as a social and cultural elite: a class enjoying enough leisure and wealth to be able to develop taste and refinement; an aristocracy in the midst of a democratic society which would justify its necessary aloofness from the rest of the community by serving as a guide and model for it. Cooper realized, of course, that on a virgin continent the constituent classes of such a social organization could hardly be

6. *The Chainbearer* (2 vols. New York, Burgess, Springer, 1845), *1*, vi; or (3 vols. London, Richard Bentley, 1845), *1*, xii.

expected to spring up in a day, full grown and armed like warriors from dragon's teeth. The task of settling the land necessitated a certain amount of egalitarianism and cooperation, but it was to be only a transitional phase in the advance toward the emergence of a class-bound society headed by a landed aristocracy.

The novelist has left a succinct little essay on the process of social evolution in a "new country," to which Robert Spiller has drawn attention and which prefaces the description of Templeton in chapter 12 of *Home as Found*. Here he divides "the progress of society" into three stages:

> At the commencement of a settlement, [he observes] there is much of that sort of kind feeling and mutual interest which men are apt to manifest towards each other when they are embarked in an enterprise of common hazards. The distance that is unavoidably inseparable from education, habits, and manners is lessened by mutual wants and mutual efforts; and the gentleman, even while he may maintain his character and station, maintains them with that species of good-fellowship and familiarity, that marks the intercourse between the officer and the soldier in an arduous campaign. . . . To this period of fun, toil, neighborly feeling, and adventure, succeeds another, in which society begins to marshall itself, and the ordinary passions have sway. Now it is that we see the struggles for place, the heart-burnings and jealousies of contending families, and the influence of mere money. . . . This is perhaps the least inviting condition of society that belongs to any country that can claim to be free, and removed from barbarism. . . . The third and last condition of society in a 'new country,' is that in which . . . men and things come within the control of more general and regular laws.

In short, Cooper held that social progress demanded, as a first and all-important step, the transition from a state of communal struggle for a common aim to one of struggle and contention within the community. This analysis is realistic enough, perhaps even quite penetrating in its own way. Nor does one quarrel with Cooper because he maintained that this was a necessary, almost an inevitable, process. History would bear out the case for him with a dozen instances, not excluding the early history of the first Puritan settlement in America itself. The difficulty of accepting the view lies rather in the fact that Cooper believed it to be a desirable development and built the main thesis of the Littlepage Trilogy on that basis. We quarrel with it, not because it is undemocratic and militates against our own preference but because Cooper himself entertained a deep-seated resistance to this idea of progress. At many crucial points his rational belief warred with his sympathies, and, if the public aspect of the debate over landlordism resulted in the rhetoric which ruins the later part of the work, it is equally true that the most dramatic conflicts in the trilogy owe their power and significance to Cooper's quarrel with himself. The best proof that his deepest sympathies did not coincide with his chart of social progress—or at least that he was unable to communicate them in consonance with his theory—is that his successive heroes are progressively less sympathetic, and that Hugh, the last of the Littlepages, who should have been the finest flower of the civilization represented by them, strikes us actually as quite unpleasant. Of the three novels which record this progress with regard to the Ravensnest-Mooseridge estate, and by synecdoche with regard to the whole land, the first presents the most attractive picture of Cooper's aristocracy and the last the least.

In reality, whatever continuing power the later generations of Littlepages possess derives from the storehouse of sympathy with which Cooper initially invests them in *Satanstoe*.

Notwithstanding his concern for progress and civilization, there is no doubt that Cooper himself responded with lasting fervor to the social conditions of the first settlements—to the world he had half known and half imagined during his childhood in Cooperstown. Commenting on the first of his three stages in the passage from which I have already quoted, he says:

> This period may be termed, perhaps, the happiest of the first century of a settlement. . . . Good-will abounds; neighbor comes cheerfully to the aid of neighbor; and life has much of the reckless gayety, careless association, and buoyant merriment of childhood. It is found that they who have passed through this probation, usually look back to it with regret, and are fond of dwelling on the rude scenes and ridiculous events that distinguish the history of a new settlement, as the hunter is known to pine for the forest.

Here we have the social implications of what Brady calls "Cooper's *nostalgie du temps perdu*"—a nostalgia which extends, with similar effect, to the history of the supplanted Indian tribes—and which is, to use Brady's words once again, "always one of his most compulsive themes."[7] Here too, in Cooper's linking his instinctive preference for a vanished, or simply imagined, past with the hunter's pining for the forest, we get a clue to the meaning of that Robin-Hood-like principle of good-fellowship whose great embodiment is his creation of the Leatherstocking. It is this feeling which lies behind the power of those pastoral scenes in *The Pioneers* (which moved D. H. Lawrence so deeply) and elsewhere: the scenes of communal labors, shared and enjoyed in simple cooperation, of house-raising, hunting, and fishing; the richly communicated picture of a rude and elemental existence

7. *American Classics Reconsidered*, p. 79.

which at the same time maintains the essential graces and pieties of life; the evocation of a world in which landlords and tenants, surveyors and laborers, hunters and forest messengers, Indians, Negroes, and white settlers all meet on an equal footing and work together, and where, notwithstanding the superior social claims of the high-born or the well-mannered, the leadership belongs to those who deserve it on the basis of personal ability and skill.

On the other hand, however, Cooper was committed to his ideal of the gentleman and with it to the desirability of creating social and economic distinctions. His pocketbook apart, there was that side of him, so hilariously and bitterly satirized by D. H. Lawrence, which took great satisfaction when he could count his knees among the knees of counts, cardinals, and milords under one common dining-table in a Parisian saloon.[8] The artistic consequence of this dual, if not discordant, pressure is the breakdown of the manners-morals correlation. Though never maintained with extensive firmness, it was Cooper's main formula for the work; a formula, moreover, upon whose successful application alone he could justify artistically his theoretical claims for the superiority of the Littlepage civilization. But such a correlation demands, if it is to be meaningful, in literature as in life, a well-integrated cultural response that sanctions outward forms only because, and only insofar as, they represent values of human and demonstrable worth. Cooper's response to American conditions was divided, and the test of manners, successful in the case of Jason Newcome, loses all effectiveness in the face of other and later challenges introduced by Cooper himself. For instance, its application seems curiously inept, if not positively irrelevant, in the case of Aaron Thousandacres, and Cooper's insistence on the Littlepage manners, when the

8. D. H. Lawrence, *Studies in Classic American Literature* (New York, Thomas Seltzer, 1923), p. 69.

moral issues are far from settled, becomes tiresome. The novelist indeed requires us increasingly to accept manners, not in a representational capacity but for their own sake, almost as a final good in themselves.

In his essay on Cooper, Yvor Winters has pointed out how the distinction between Genteel and Vulgar, when it is maintained with the intensity which properly belongs to the conflict of Good and Evil, leads to an effect of priggishness.[9] While this is true, I think the basic failure arises, not from misapplied intensity but from Cooper's easy assumption that the genteel is the good per se and that the vulgar can approach goodness only to the extent to which it sides with the genteel. It is an assumption which dominates the tone of the trilogy but which, as I shall attempt to show, is defeated by certain important, though not proportionately represented, elements within the work itself. The same can be said of Winters' observation that at the present time "an act of sympathetic historical imagination is necessary to understand Cooper."[10] Although such an attitude is perhaps desirable and is indeed only too often accorded to the novelist, the argument should not be used as a charitable cover for what is ultimately a weakness of organization: a confusion between theme and technique as well as a discord between the pattern of dramatized sympathies and that of rhetorical assertion. The recognition of this fact is not a disservice to Cooper because if it points to his technical imperfection it also leads to an understanding of the fullness of his theme.

A literary work that organizes its sympathies to the pattern of its "rational" theme can usually afford to dispense with the reader's prior convictions. For instance, in responding to Jane Austen's moral dramas as she intends us to do, we do not

9. Yvor Winters, *Maule's Curse* (Norfolk, Conn., New Directions, 1938), p. 30.
10. Ibid., p. 31.

need to sympathize with the historical existence of the English squirearchy upon which those dramas are based. She sustains artistically the issues which she defines. Questions like the sources of her heroes' wealth or their relationship with the tenants on their land form no part of her theme. To inquire into them would be as irrelevant as to tax Cooper with not discussing the rights and wrongs of Negro slavery just because an important character like Jaap is a Negro slave. However, although the morality of slavery is not an issue in the Littlepage Trilogy, the morality of landownership and land tenures is, and Cooper attempts, but fails, to resolve it on the basis of gentility versus vulgarity.

This failure, symptomatic of the novelist's sensibility, is reflected in the gradual deterioration of tone in the successive volumes of the trilogy. After *Satanstoe* his easy assurance of the landed gentry's moral superiority is all but lost. As the family progresses toward the higher phases of life promised by the civilization for which it stands, Cooper finds it necessary to bolster its claims with a rhetoric and an abusive petulance which reach their final declamatory climax in *The Redskins*. In this final novel the case for the Littlepages rests heavily on authorial asides and on verbal arguments conducted, mainly and somewhat unfairly, between Uncle Ro and Hugh Littlepage—two persons belonging to the same side of the question. Here Cooper is at his worst, and, in order to make his viewpoint persuasive, he employs many small devices which are as irritating as they are comic in their desperation. For instance, he repeatedly uses a circular argument based on such characters as Mr. Warren and Tom Miller—"good" people whose "goodness" is first postulated on the ground that they support the rights of landlords and subsequently used to show how just these rights are because good people support them. More objectionable still is the use he makes of the Indians at the end of the trilogy—more

99

objectionable because, in making the dispossessed Indians the
allies of the landlords who had dispossessed them, Cooper
was flagrantly violating his truer and more humane intuitions.
By permitting the Littlepages to press the native chiefs into
armed service in a white man's quarrel from which they stand
to gain nothing, he was re-enacting with approval a fact of
history which he himself had often deplored with penitential
poignance. The lapse can be excused perhaps by saying with
Charles Brady: "It is nearly the end of Cooper's career before
he lets his braves degenerate into protectors of the great
landed proprietors."[11] Nevertheless, it is worth noting that in
Satanstoe and *The Chainbearer*, only a year earlier, Cooper
could afford to leave the Indian sullenly unconvinced of the
landlord's convenient theory of landownership, allowing the
drama of opposed convictions to speak for itself. It is only
when that theory has worked out to its last phase that he uses
these somewhat ridiculous devices in order to support a
conviction which his unaided sensibility is far from according
to his rational belief.

That there was something deep in this novelist of the
American scene which militated against the conception of a
hierarchic society crowned by a wealthy and leisured elite is
evident at the outset from the ambivalent attitude toward the
British aristocracy in *Satanstoe*. It is true that Cooper, or
Corny, is suitably impressed by the elegance of soups and
toasts at Herman Mordaunt's table, and that, as Bulstrode,
Harris, and others make endless conversation about my lord
this and bishop that, no one cries "Faugh!" as Goldsmith's
hero does to the pretentious talk of the sham nobility in *The
Vicar of Wakefield*. Nevertheless, by means of a persistent
though irregularly maintained irony, Cooper does suggest the
comparative frivolity of an existence whose only claim to
worthiness rests on noble birth and aristocratic breeding. The

11. *American Classics Reconsidered*, p. 80.

distance between the British gentlemen and Cooper's more serious-minded protagonists is widened into total separation toward the end of the novel when the party of Americans façes one way and the wounded Bulstrode and his friends the other: the Americans preparing to encounter their destiny in the uncharted wilderness while the English make ready to return to a settled and orderly England. The entry of the tale into the forest signalizes the final irrelevance of manners to its action, and also perhaps the impossibility of sustaining it any further on that basis.

There is a passage in chapter 22 of *Satanstoe* which brings home dramatically the radical difference between the situations of the English and the American characters in the novel, and the consequent unreliability of the rules and usages sanctioned by the past. In the chapter previous to this, Susquesus, the Indian guide, has led the American party (consisting of a surveyor and his laborers as well as Corny, Guert, Dirck, and their Negro servants) to the tree which marks the corner of Mooseridge, the map which they carry having proved useless in locating or identifying the spot. Now, after a brief disappearance, the guide returns to inform the party of the impending operations between the French and the English and to lead them to Ticonderoga. They do not follow the highway with the rest of the army. Their route lies through the trackless forest. It is during this march that Susquesus, piqued by the remark that a compass can provide better direction than the sun or the bark of trees, defies them to try the experiment for themselves. The high-spirited Guert takes up the challenge, and speedily admits defeat: "There was no resisting the truth; we had got turned completely round, without knowing it . . . . any one who has tried the experiment, will soon ascertain how easy it is for him to lose his direction beneath the obscurity and amid the inequalities of a virgin forest." The incident suggests a comparison with a later moment in American fiction which, though rendered with much greater poetic skill and concentration of significance than Cooper's more leisurely paced narrative can achieve, is nevertheless similar in its basic intuition: the moment in Faulkner's *The Bear*, where, guided by Sam Fathers' careful if somewhat obscure intimations, Ike McCaslin takes off his watch and compass and hangs them on a bush before entering the primeval forest to encounter its daemon in the elusive and mythic Old Ben.

While discovering the futility of their reliance on maps and compasses, Corny and Guert, too, learn the lesson of humility in the face of the forest and its laws. It is true that in the Littlepage Trilogy the lesson enters the narrative as an almost casual effect and that its implications are not followed up in the career of the protagonists. The forest itself, however, in all its mystery, stays with them almost to the end of *Satanstoe*. Later in the novel, when the party is surprised by marauding savages at Mooseridge and Corny is led by Susquesus into the darkness in order to hear and identify the man whom the Hurons have scalped and left hanging by the arms on a tree, its terrifying inscrutability makes a memorable impression on him:

> It was impossible [he says] to see for any distance, and the objects that were visible were only those that were nearest at hand. Notwithstanding, one might imagine the canopied space beneath the tops of the trees, and fancy it, in the majesty of its gloomy vastness. Of sounds there were literally none, when the Indian first bade me listen. The stillness was so profound, that I thought I heard the sighing of the night air among the upper branches of the loftier trees. This might have been mere imagination; nevertheless, all above the summits of the giant oaks, maples, and pines, formed a sort of upper world as

regarded us; a world with which we had little communication, during our sojourn in the woods below. The raven, and the eagle, and the hawk, sailed in that region, above the clouds of leaves beneath them, and occasionally stooped, perhaps, to strike their quarry; but to all else it was inaccessible, and to a degree invisible.

But my present concern is with the world I was in; and what a world it was! Solemn, silent, dark, vast, and mysterious.

When Corny returns to tell his companions of the scalping and the presence of the Indians, Guert says that he should have taken his friends with him: "We must stick together, in future, let what may happen."

The image of America which Cooper draws here is essentially an intensified version of his own picture of the first settlement in a new country: a common campaign against a resisting environment in the conduct of which it is necessary that considerations of rank and custom should yield to the spirit of good-fellowship. It is not surprising therefore, that, with the introduction of this theme, the drama of manners should be severely dislocated. "Every chronicle of manners has a certain value," Cooper had observed in the preface to *Satanstoe*. "When customs are connected with principles, in their origin, development, or end, such records have a double importance." In reality, however, the connection between customs and principles is hardly evident in the subsequent two volumes, and whatever historical importance Cooper's continued portrayal of manners may possess, the dramatic significance of the trilogy after the Albany scenes in *Satanstoe* centers on unadorned moral issues.

The great moral principle involved in the theme is of course the rightful ownership of land. Its definition begins properly with the entry of Susquesus, the tragic representative of the people whom Cooper never failed to designate as the "original owners of the land." It is important to realize this, because Cooper, concerned as he was with fundamental moral questions, with the very origin of issues, does not focus the theme entirely on the contemporary quarrel between the landlords and the tenants but extends it backward to include the dispossessed Indians. The reaching beyond the expediency to the basic morality of historical development is one of the chief distinctions of Cooper's genius, even though in the Littlepage Trilogy such a concern goes against his own case and demonstrates in an unacknowledged way that his Littlepages are after all only better educated and not necessarily better men.

The very first words spoken by Susquesus, or Trackless as he is called in *Satanstoe*, suggest the Indian's tenacious refusal to accept the Littlepages' title to the land, or at least his puzzlement that Corny should own a piece of it which he has not even seen before. When the surveyor shows him the map of Mooseridge and, in appealing to him to lead them to the tree which marks the corner of its boundary, asks him if the map is drawn to suit his fancy, the guide answers that the map is good enough, adding, with unconcealed irony: "Now show Susquesus *your* oak tree."[12] When the surveyor points out the tree on the map, he replies in the same strain of irony: "Good. *Very* good. The palefaces know everything! Now, let my brother find the tree." The question involved here is taken up more explicitly in chapter 24. Trackless, who has led the party to the battle of Ticonderoga with a sort of cynical detachment, startles Corny when, on their return to Mooseridge, he says suddenly and with no apparent connection with the subject they are discussing: "All Injin land, once!" "This last remark was made in a way I did not like," Corny goes on

12. The italics in this and the following quotation are Cooper's, although they do not appear in the Leather-Stocking Edition. See *Satanstoe* (2 vols. New York, Burgess, Springer, 1845), *2*, 82.

to say; "for the idea seemed to cross the Onondago's brain so suddenly, as to draw from him this brief assertion in pure bitterness of spirit." In reality, however, the Indian's observation is not unrelated to what has gone before, for what he has witnessed at Ticonderoga is only a later phase of the continuing struggle for the mastery of the continent which had earlier resulted in the dispossession of his own people. Indeed, in the ensuing dialogue between Corny and Susquesus, the rights of conquest arising from the victory of the King's army over the Indian warriors, are cited by Corny as one of the two reasons in justification of his title to the land, the other being the fact that his father and Colonel Follock had paid the Mohawks for it.

The question is taken up again in chapter 8 of *The Chain-bearer*, this time between Susquesus, or Sureflint, and Corny's son, Mordaunt Littlepage, when the latter falls in with the Indian on his way to Ravensnest. The debate is opened here, as earlier, with the Indian's half-naive and half-astute puzzlement: "How you own land, when nebber see him?" But the Littlepage defense is now extended to include several other arguments, all of them connected in one way or another with what Cooper believed to be the inevitable requirements of progress. Mordaunt's answer to the Indian's puzzled query is that he owns the land by inheritance, and that it is the laws of inheritance, the rights of property, paper deeds, and scientific knowledge which constitute the superiority of the white man's civilization and the secret of his success. This being so, he implies, the red man should acquiesce in the sad but necessary and just course of history. Why after all, he asks the Indian, have the white people been able to defeat the natives? To which the Indian replies:

> "Be sure, differ; one strong, t'oder weak; one rich, t'oder poor; one great, t'oder little; one drive 'way,

105

t'oder haf to go; one gets all, t'oder keep nuttin'; one march large army, t'oder go Indian file, fifty warrior, p'raps—dat reason t'ing so."

"And why can the pale-faces march in large armies, with cannon, and horses, and bayonets, and the redman not do the same?"

"Cause he no got 'em; no got warrior—no got gun— no got baggonet—no got nuttin'."

"You have given the effect for the cause, Sureflint, or the consequences of the reason for the reason itself. I hope I make you understand me. . . . The white man is stronger than the redman, and has taken away his country, because he knows most."

"Even that fire-water," Mordaunt adds a little later, "which doubtless has proved a cruel gift to the Indians, is one of the fruits of the white man's knowledge." The cornerstone of this civilization, he concludes, is to be located in man's self-interest: "It is by encouraging man's love of himself, in this manner, that he is got to do so much."

The Littlepage defense against the challenge of the past (a moral rather than a physical challenge) thus consists of three arguments: rights of purchase and conquest, superiority of force and numbers, and the demands of a progressive civilization. Of course, they fail to win from Susquesus the moral conviction which the Littlepages expect. His attitude of resignation does not exclude that defiance, physically as ineffectual as it is morally potent, which is associated with the tragedy of a just but lost cause. "Why come so late?" he says of the new tribe of "Injins" (the Calico Indians of the Anti-Rent war) in *The Redskins*—"why no come when 'e foot of Susquesus light as feather of bird?— why stay away till pale-faces plentier dan leaf on tree, or snow in air? Hundred year ago, when dat oak little,

106

sich Injin might be good; now, he good for nuttin'."

If Susquesus is not completely convinced, we are less so; for the novelist has made the issue of ownership a three-cornered moral question, and the arguments he uses against the claims of the past are either ignored or glossed over when the Littlepages face the challenge of the future. Here again we notice Cooper's dilemma, the tension between his moral sensibility and his personal and social commitments. This tension is the secret of his power as a novelist. Without it he would not have been able to provide his rather colorless landlords with such memorable adversaries as Susquesus and Aaron Thousandacres, and the Littlepage Trilogy would have hardly amounted to anything more significant than fictionalized polemics. The unfortunate thing is that he did not leave his dramatized sympathies to speak for themselves but often ruined the effect by intruding upon the narrative his non-artistic bias. It is to this fact that we must attribute the persistent disquisitions on accent and personal hygiene in the later volumes when, on the novelist's own showing, the Littlepages can claim no other grounds of superiority over their opponents. For with regard to the great question of landownership, it is not at all evident how the threat of dispossession which the landlords face differs materially from their own dispossession of the previous owners. Cooper forgets his recognition of "man's love of himself" as an agency of democratic civilization when the argument shifts to one between the landlords and the tenants, and he berates the latter ceaselessly for their being motivated by self-interest. Corny's rights-of-conquest claim is travestied only a little later in *Satanstoe* when Jason argues that the driving away of the Indian party which had temporarily taken possession of Ravensnest constitutes a reconquest, and hence he is free to consider himself a freeholder and no longer a tenant of the mill seat on the estate. The travesty is no doubt intended as a reflection on Jason

Newcome, but it points equally to the moral unworthiness of the original claim which it parallels. The superiority of force and numbers belongs as much to the side of the tenants as it had gone against the Indians in the earlier struggle. As for the purchase of the land from the Mohawks, one remembers that the tribe had received a total value of ninety-six dollars in rum and blankets and that the tenants do not want to seize the land without purchasing it either. Each one of them is prepared to pay to the landlords a sum which, in many cases, exceeds the original cost of the whole estate at Mooseridge. Cooper, of course, leans heavily on the fact that the Littlepages had secured a contract from the Indians, but, legalistic sophistry apart, what moral validity does a bargain possess when it is made with a demoralized and ignorant people and when it is so ridiculously unequal? Nor must we forget that, as presented by Cooper himself, the tenants' agitation is only a pressure tactic employed to win eventually a legal approval of their demands in the state legislature.

Cooper's double standards are most evident in his failure to accept the fact that the Anti-Rent struggle is only another phase in the evolution of that same civilization in whose name the Indians had been dispossessed earlier. Had he accepted this further manifestation of historical necessity in the spirit of acquiescence with which he had invested the character of Susquesus, he would have written a much greater work. Lack of acceptance, however, does not mean lack of recognition. If Cooper's annoying rhetoric is the result of the former, we owe to the latter the strength and dignity of Thousandacres' character in *The Chainbearer* as well as the serious part of the Anti-Rent case which Cooper, almost in spite of himself, leaves intact in *The Redskins*. What Thousandacres represents is not lack of all principle, as the narrator's commentary would have us believe, but only a principle different from, and opposed to, the one upon which the Littlepages take their stand. "Thief back ag'in, old measurer!" he cries at the Chainbearer when the latter accuses him of being a thief for squatting on other people's land. "Do not the sweat of the brow, long and hard days of toil, achin' bones, and hungry bellies, give a man a claim to the fruit of his labors?" "There's two rights to all the land on 'arth, and the whull world over," he says later to the same adversary. "One of these rights is what I call a king's right, or that which depends on writin's, and laws, and sich like contrivances; and the other depends on possession." In short, Thousandacres argues on the one hand against absentee landlordism, not unlike Susquesus and the later Anti-Rent tenants; on the other, he pleads for a labor theory of value as against exploitative property rights. The progress of democracy in America, a land of abundant resources but limited manpower, has been based precisely on the increasing acceptance of these principles.

It is the same with the concept of democratic equality. The Littlepage narrators misinterpret it constantly and unfairly by taking it to signify equalization of personal effects. They distort it in argument to suggest that, on its basis, people will start taking away each other's guns and gowns and livestock. This provides yet another example of Cooper's loading the dice at all costs in favor of the Littlepages. Surely he realized that land does not fall into this category of articles inasmuch as it is of no value in itself, that its fruits are entirely those of human labor, and that it is a far cry from the Littlepages' idea of equality to the tenants' demand for a more democratic land distribution based on reasonable compensation to the landlords. I say he realized these facts because, notwithstanding the ridicule which he pours on the Anti-Renters' bad grammar and worse pronunciation, their case comes through strongly. For one thing, it is not as lawless as that of Thousandacres. As the demagogue says in *The Redskins*, what the tenants want is "an equality that is substantial, and which must be restored, when the working of the law has deranged it." This is an argument for political change and not for lawlessness, a fact that becomes clear when in the same speech Cooper goes on to define, without approval of course, the concept of the "political leap-year": periodic social and economic adjustments to save democratic equality from becoming an empty phrase.

> Thus will it be with democracy. Human natur' can't devise laws yet, that will keep all things on an exactly equal footing, and political leap-years must be introduced into the political calendar, to restore the equilibrium. In astronomy, we must divide up anew the hours and minutes; in humanity, we must, from time to time, divide up the land.

In the time when this was written, Jacksonian democracy was effecting such a readjustment. America has gone through other leap-years since, and it would be needless to insist that it presents a better civilization to the world for having done so.

Thus Cooper, who set out to justify the moral claims of the Littlepages, leaves these claims finally as a wide open question. On the assumptions underlying his theme in the trilogy he was unable to prove the justice of their cause with regard to both the Indians, whom they had dispossessed, and the tenants, who were threatening to dispossess them in their turn. That he presented the case in this way is a tribute to his honesty. In *The Redskins*, as though to underline the fact, he employs the historical episode of the Calico Indian war to bring together the two challenges to the Littlepages' ownership of land. It is one of the few artistic triumphs of this otherwise uninspired novel. By combining the two sides of the moral drama it gives final shape to the theme of the trilogy, the tenants masked as Indians representing the appropriate nemesis of the landlords; for, as Susquesus says toward the end of the novel,

"But the wicked spirit that drove out the redman is now about to drive off the pale-face chiefs. It is the same devil, and it is no other. He wanted land then, and he wants land now."

Was moral perfection, then, not possible to any civilization, however graceful? The answer in the Littlepage Trilogy is no. The history of American civilization, like any other history, points rather to the impossibility of reconciling moral principles with social expediency. In *The Chainbearer* Cooper states this dilemma explicitly by drawing a distinction between "the gentleman" and "the Christian": "one of which is a mere human embellishment of the ways of a wicked world, while the other draws near to the great end of human existence. The last is a character I revere; while I am willing to confess that I never met with the first without feeling how vacant and repulsive society would become without it; unless, indeed, the vacuum could be filled by the great substance of which, after all, the gentleman is but the shadow."

This is only a restatement of the old American dilemma, a dilemma as old as the founding of the Plymouth colony. It is born of that visionary tradition which clung tenaciously to the belief that the new continent was not to be the prospective scene for a repetition of the wicked ways of the old world. Its settlement was to manifest rather the final advance toward "the great end of human existence" itself. It is hardly surprising that Cooper, who shared the moral idealism of this tradition as much as he did the hard-headed materialism of his day, should have presented his favorite civilization as finally wanting in the highest requirements of moral principle. To him the development of America could be justified only if it was done with righteousness—a righteousness that included what Natty calls "doing what's right between man and man." Accordingly, the fact that the Littlepages had developed the land was not enough for him. Since his land-lords could not fall back upon a Doomsday Book whose verdicts could be cited with the finality of Doomsday itself, they, unlike Jane Austen's squires, had to validate their original claims, and this, in its turn, involved the morality of Indian dispossession. Thus in Cooper, as in Faulkner in our own time, there is a constant feeling that the history of the land was tainted at the very outset and that, as he makes his "up-right" Indian say at the end of the trilogy, the unprincipled acquisitiveness of his time was only a further manifestation of the evil spirit that had crossed the ocean in the first boats of the palefaces.

If Cooper was unable to justify the foundation of American civilization, he watched the signs of its future development with greater uneasiness. He felt that American democracy was becoming increasingly, to use Richard Hofstadter's words, "a democracy in cupidity rather than a democracy of frater-nity."[13] Comparing America with Europe, he warned his country, in words like those of the elder James, that "the brightest dawns often usher in the darkest days; that the most brilliant youths frequently precede manhoods of disappoint-ment and baffled wishes; that even the professed man of God can fall away from his vows and his faith, and finish a career that was commenced in virtue and hope, in profligacy and sin. Nations are no more safe from the influence of tempta-tion than individuals."[14] Before he died, he had lost all hope in the distinctive destiny of the new civilization. "What is true in the Old World will, in the end, be found to be true here," he wrote in his posthumously published and fragmen-tary history of New York.[15] He ended *The Crater*, a novel in

13. See above, p. 2.
14. Cf. Henry James, Sr., above, p. 43.
15. James Fenimore Cooper, *New York*, ed. Dixon Ryan Fox (New York, William Farquhar Payson, 1930), p. 61.

which he allegorized the history of the discovery and development of the New World, by making a volcanic eruption destroy the colony which had been started in great hope but which had become inevitably corrupted by the growth of "civilization" and the consequent conflict between material interest and moral principle. Less savagely and more realistically, he observed in the history of New York: "Nevertheless, the community will live on, suffer, and be deluded: it may even fancy itself almost within reach of perfection, but it will live on to be disappointed. There is no such thing on earth—and the only real question for the American statesman is, to measure the results of different defective systems for the government of the human race."[16]

Measurement of imperfect achievement, however, presupposes a standard of perfection, a conceived if unrealized or even unrealizable goal. This, for Cooper, as for many another American of the nineteenth century, was provided by the myth of American civilization: an unanalyzed but persistent belief in new ideals, of man, of human relationships, and of human society. As Jacques Maritain says of his "brotherly city," such ideals may constitute a limit attainable only at infinity; nevertheless they are indispensable to temporal history if this history is to develop in consonance with "the earthly hope of our race." Cooper's moral idealism, which was applied to, and frustrated by, the development of American history, had earlier found freer play in creating the myth which lies embodied in the Leatherstocking Tales.

It would hardly be a revelation to say that this work is unsatisfactory in many ways, most of all perhaps in the fragmentary, almost casual, manner in which Cooper pursues the serious concerns of his theme and the determined effort he makes to stifle it under a heavy clutter of adventure, plottiness, and the ridiculous decorum of sentimentality. Nor

16. Ibid., p. 58.

113

would it profit much at this date to debate whether the responsibility for these lapses should be laid at Sir Walter Scott's door or his own—at the feet of Mrs. Cooper. Long ago Mark Twain made it unnecessary for all future readers to labor the case against Cooper. Twain, however, made the mistake of losing Cooper's significance because he chose "to study him in detail—word by word, sentence by sentence"[17]—a mistake repeated many times since then by other close readers of the text. Fenimore Cooper's literary offenses certainly damage his literary achievement, but they do not quite reduce it to zero. To miss the largeness and vitality of Cooper's theme would be as absurd as to see nothing in Bradford's epic narrative of Plymouth colony except the now meaningless details about the quantity and quality of beaver skins and livestock. The comparison is not entirely fortuitous. The Leatherstocking Tales derive their significance, as much as Bradford's history does, from the constant interpenetration of history and myth, of the actual and the ideal, of mundane concerns and visionary hope.

Before turning to these tales, however, it would be worth while to enlarge upon the difference between the assumptions underlying the themes of these and the Littlepage novels. In chapter 14 of *Home as Found*, whose scene is laid on Lake Otsego, the scene also of the first and the last of the Leatherstocking Tales, the following bit of dialogue occurs in the course of a general and lively conversation:

> "I have heard the old settlers affirm that the Leather-Stocking used to talk for hours at a time with the animals of the forest."
> "You knew the Leather-Stocking, commodore?"
> "No, young lady, I am sorry to say I never had the

17. Mark Twain, "Fenimore Cooper's Further Literary Offenses," *New England Quarterly, 19* (1946), 293.

pleasure of looking on him even. He was a great man! They may talk of their Jeffersons and Jacksons, but I set down Washington and Natty Bumppo as the two only really great men of my time."

Washington and Natty Bumppo! The collocation seems odd even after one has made allowance for the fact that at Templeton local legend would have done for the Leatherstocking what history had done for George Washington in the country at large. It is a little hard to believe that the man who wrote such an astute political treatise as *The American Democrat* should have found reason to elevate a "lawless squatter" to the dignity of a place beside Washington, suggesting even a comparison with St. Francis of Assisi. Yet the reason can be seen in the very comparison which is barely hinted at. To Cooper here, Washington and the Leatherstocking are the representatives of the two extremes between which the American sensibility has attempted through the centuries to locate and identify its destiny: the principle of material advancement and that of ascetic detachment from all material interests. John Cotton, the seventeenth-century Puritan divine, thought that there was a "combination of virtues strangely mixed in every lively, holy Christian: and that is, diligence in worldly business, and yet deadness to the world."[18] In the twentieth century there is Jay Gatsby, the tycoon of Fitzgerald's novel and one of the more significant heroes of modern American fiction, who is neither a Christian nor very holy but to whom nevertheless the world is "material without being real."

Washington and Natty would seem to represent the two divergent possibilities which Cooper saw in American civilization. One of them was being realized in the history of the country while the other could only form the subject of an imaginative myth. If Natty carries with him the thematic

18. *The American Puritans*, ed. Miller, p. 171.

meaning of the Leatherstocking Tales, Washington can serve as a motto for the Littlepage novels, which, as I have attempted to show, deal realistically with the social, economic, and political problems of the new Republic. The Littlepages, and the novelist in this series, take their ultimate moral stand on the sanctions of the Constitution, strict legality, the sacredness of contracts, and the inviolable rights of property. All the main characters are firmly delineated as recognizable social types, and people generally are described as "order-loving, law-loving, property-loving Americans" even though temptation leads them only too often away from absolute adherence to these principles. Society itself is visualized as a hierarchic organization with the first families of landed gentry at the top, and the dynamo of its past and future progress is located in the self-interest of the individual. The *beau ideal* of such a society is the gentleman of leisure, his chief ornaments, cultivation and refinement. Persons lacking wealth can be admitted to the title of "gentry" if their genealogies reveal a close connection with good families on both sides, as happens to be true in the case of Dus Malbone; or, if, like Mr. Warren, they serve God in a church, for even the English squires did not quite banish their parsons to the servants' hall. Over the gate leading into this closely guarded sanctuary are inscribed the words: "Manners maketh man."

Natty would surely not qualify on a single ground to enter this elite circle. He is ignorant, rude-mannered, and speaks bad English. He is not only unrelated to a genteel family but actually has no family that one knows of. As for the Constitution and the laws of the land, he has not even heard of them and refuses stubbornly to obey any commandments except those of God as he understands them. Rather than accept the principle of a hierarchic society, he would subscribe to the rank idealism of the Declaration of Independence: "all men are created equal." He stands for a woolly-headed concept of universal brotherhood, an aristocracy of personal merit and skill, natural piety, and a civilization whose frontiers are open. If Judge Temple is equated with the neighbor in Robert Frost's short poem "Mending Wall," who believes that "good fences make good neighbors," Natty would be the protagonist who is not convinced by the argument and who keeps repeating: "Something there is that doesn't love a wall / That wants it down."

Natty and his uncouth companions are visualized indeed on an altogether different plane. They are born of what Charles Brady has called Cooper's "fundamental revulsion from the dialectics of property."[19] Although there are gentlemen enough of the Littlepage variety in the Leatherstocking Tales, it is Natty, Chingachgook, Uncas, and others, rather than they, who are assigned the first place in the novelist's, and the reader's, sympathies. In *The Chainbearer* Cooper's spokesman, Mordaunt Littlepage, says of his first visit to Ravensnest: "I examined the view with the interest which ownership is apt to create in us all. The earth is very beautiful in itself; but it is most beautiful in the eyes of those who have the largest stake in it, I fear." This is the voice of reason, of nineteenth-century reason at least, but it leaves unexplained the emotion which the American land arouses in Natty Bumppo, for, although he has less "stake" in it than the smallest of Littlepage tenants, his utterances about it form a moving paean of praise to the beauty of God's earthly creation.

The difference between the assumptions on which the two works are organized can be seen succinctly in the contrast between Natty's constant imprecations against that symbol of advancing civilization, the axe, with Cooper's panegyric on it in *The Chainbearer:*

The American axe! It has made more real and lasting

19. *American Classics Reconsidered*, p. 61.

conquests than the sword of any warlike people that ever lived; but they have been conquests that have left civilization in their train instead of havoc and desolation. More than a million of square miles of territory have been opened up from the shades of the virgin forest, to admit the warmth of the sun; and culture and abundance have been spread where the beast of the forest so lately roamed, hunted by the savage. . . . A brief quarter of a century has seen these wonderful changes wrought; and at the bottom of them all lies this beautiful, well-prized, ready, and efficient implement, the American axe!

It would be useless to deny that Natty's attitude is unpractical, for civilization cannot remain perpetually in the happy hunting stage of its growth. One can argue of course that his diatribes against the axe are really meant for the particular kind of civilization which it was heralding on the virgin continent, but this does not solve the whole difficulty, since positively he is definitely committed to an obsolete culture. This means that, speaking in realistic terms, he is headed for defeat at the hands of the civilization which he opposes, and that his attitude, if taken literally and translated into a blue-print for action, would prove worthless for all practical purposes. But this still leaves the values for which he stands, and, however idealistic, these perform the same function with regard to questions of practical social conduct as his mythic career does with regard to the actual history of the country: a moral function which is constructive because it is critical.

The Pioneers (1823) can be regarded as the common matrix of Cooper's two important series of novels. Although it is the first of the Leatherstocking Tales, it comes closer to the Littlepage Trilogy in theme and fictional technique and, in its general atmosphere, resembles *Satanstoe* rather than *The Last of the Mohicans* or *The Deerslayer*. Being "A Descriptive Tale," as its title page declares it to be, Cooper was faced with the "constant temptation to delineate that which he had known [in his childhood in Cooperstown], rather than that which he might have imagined." Realistic in its portrayal of a frontier settlement, its main focus falls on the description of a well-mannered gentry—the pioneers of a civilization struggling to establish itself on the edge of the American wilderness. The moral problem of landownership makes a marginal appearance in the persons of Natty Bumppo and Oliver Effingham. The former, who is described as a "lawless squatter" by Sheriff Richard Jones and who comes close to the description in his transgression against the new laws introduced by Judge Temple, maintains a sullen resistance to the landlord's authority throughout the novel, declaring in the very opening scene: "There's them living who say that Nathaniel Bumppo's right to shoot on these hills is of older date than Marmaduke Temple's right to forbid him." Young Effingham combines in himself the more substantial claims of the Effinghams and the Indians, since his grandfather had been adopted by the Delawares and he is looked upon by both Chingachgook and Natty as the legitimate heir of that tribe. These two themes, as I have attempted to show, constitute the moral drama of the Littlepage Trilogy.

However, notwithstanding these similarities, the Leatherstocking Tales go on to develop the theme of American civilization along the lines of an altogether different tension. Starting from a more or less common social milieu, while the heroes of the Littlepage novels move forward in history from the days of the colonial settlements to Cooper's own time of democratic stress and strain, Natty and Chingachgook are carried backward, in spirit much more than in time, to the very beginnings of American society and the promise which its foundations had proclaimed. "When the colony's laws, or even the King's laws," Natty declares in *The Deerslayer*, "run ag'in the laws of God, they get to be onlawful, and ought not to be obeyed." This is not merely a restatement of the visionary concept of the American experiment; it is a statement of the basic tension which unifies the Leatherstocking series as a whole and gives thematic meaning to each of its constituent novels. If actual social development defines one side of this tension, the other is provided, not by an alternative historical possibility but by an archetype of what a new society should be. That American civilization had postulated such an archetype for itself even before it came formally into existence makes significant the inverted chronology of the events recorded in the series. The development here is not from history into a future utopia. On the contrary, the Leatherstocking Tales attempt to recreate the myth which history was supposed to validate but which in reality it had violated from the outset.

The fictional career of Natty Bumppo is perhaps the clearest statement in literature of the archetypal American experience. It is so clear indeed that it seems almost as simple-minded in its moral idealism as Bradford's history of America. Yet perhaps it is the simplicity that helps to give it the distinctive outline of a memorable and meaningful myth. The narrative begins quite appropriately in *The Pioneers*, a novel which projects a society speedily molding itself in the image of the Old World: a hierarchic order, built on landed property and centering around the Manorhouse, the Church, and the Lawcourt. The squire, Judge Temple, who has been a wealthy trader, now combines in himself also the power of the landlord and the magistrate. Under his direction the social world at Templeton has already achieved the firm contours of a civilized state: it is becoming increasingly industrious, orderly, and impersonal; everyone knows his place and is beginning to respect authority; tenants buy and sell their holdings;

there are lawyers, sheriffs, and justices of peace; disputes between neighbors are pleaded in the lawcourt; search warrants are issued and executed; game laws are enacted and enforced; and everywhere, irrespective of personal considerations, the demands of justice are fulfilled to the letter. It is against this emergent civilization that the hero of the Leatherstocking Tales takes his sullen and implacable stand. On the level of the plot, Natty's opposition arises of course from his loyalty to the Effinghams, the family of his erstwhile master whose property Marmaduke seems to have usurped. Though softened, he is far from reconciled to it even at the end, when the great wrong has been righted and his master's scion is duly installed as the lord of Templeton Hall. He simply declines the invitation to receive his share of poetic justice. "I know you mean all for the best, but our ways doesn't agree," he says in answer to the Effinghams' entreaties that he stay at Templeton and live happily ever after.

Whether Natty's repudiation of civilization has any moral justification or is merely the expression of the lawless instincts of a frontierman is a question that can be answered fully only in the context of all the novels in which he figures. Here it is important to realize that, whatever hints for an answer this first novel provides, they are not to be found in the intricacies of its story. As R. W. B. Lewis has observed, Cooper's "most illuminating clashes and insights occur on the margins of his plots."[20] In creating the character of Natty Bumppo especially, Cooper had touched a chord of imaginative energy far more compelling than the surface force of his plot machinery. Its vibrations echoed over a period of almost twenty years from *The Pioneers* to *The Deerslayer*, and if we would understand the meaning that lies behind its power we should turn to those marginal illuminations of which Lewis

20. R. W. B. Lewis, *The American Adam* (University of Chicago Press, 1955), p. 101.

speaks. These occur usually at the beginning of individual tales, before the avalanche of adventures has been unleashed; at the end, when the complications have been successfully resolved; and only in one or two cases, during a fortunate breathing space, somewhere in the middle of the book. Perhaps a similar law of arithmetical distribution of meaning governs the series as a whole, for its two most significant components are the first and last volumes.

In *The Pioneers* Cooper's hero rejects a world he believes to be corrupt and corrupting, a world which represents, in his view, not a new civilization but only a cruder version of the old: "might often makes right here," he says to Judge Temple in the opening scene of the novel, "as well as in the old country, for what I can see." He himself is as old as the civilization he repudiates but he possesses a moral conscience which, for all its unreasonable promptings, is radically new. The figure of Natty, then, as he stands at the end of the novel ready to march into the wilderness, is, if one may make a bold statement, the very incarnation of the spirit of American separation from Europe. At least, much of its otherwise inexplicable power derives from such correspondence in our own minds.

The theme that is launched here is taken up in all the subsequent novels as Natty repudiates, one after another, various gradations and manifestations of civilization. In the middle book of the series he dies, facing west (not east as Lawrence says incorrectly) when he can no longer move physically in that direction. In the last novel, *The Deerslayer*, however, he is reborn as an untried youth, and his final literary avatar links with the first to round out the mythic movement of the whole action. Here the geographical location is the same as that of *The Pioneers*, and yet what a different world! As several commentators have pointed out, the atmosphere in which the novel opens suggests the world before the Creation.

The lake on whose banks the action is laid—Lake Otsego of the first novel—is still unnamed officially. It is called Glimmerglass, and like the virgin forest around it seems ready, for better or worse, to take the impression of whatever world is created on the scene. It is Nature's unblemished mirror and functions physically as Natty's conscience does in a moral sense: it reflects back to man his true image of himself even if it is powerless to alter him or his eventual course. The anticipatory mood of the novel, its suggestion that the world is ready for a fresh start, is further heightened by the biblical name of Tom Hutter's floating sanctuary. This particular Ark, it is true, carries anything but the possibilities of a new moral order. That, however, is a part of Cooper's ironic scheme, his constant juxtaposition of the ideal archetype and historical reality. The character who bears the burden of re-enacting the myth is Natty Bumppo, and, if his departure from the world of *The Pioneers* represents the break with the corrupt old order, his reappearance in *The Deerslayer* approximates the first encounter with the new continent. Here there is no established civilization which demands conformity, but only possibilities of good and evil, and no lawgiver except the human conscience. The struggle is not between this and that form of defective civilization; it is rather the old conflict between God and Satan, acting through their surrogates, for the establishment of a morally perfect society in the chosen land.

Thus, starting from the reality he knew, Cooper worked—fragmentarily to be sure but nonetheless effectively—toward the hope which lay at the back of it all and which seemed now lost. Read according to the chronology of the hero's life, the Leatherstocking Tales record the loss of the ideal in the actual; read more or less as written, they reaffirm the great American myth. History and myth function in a mutual critique, since we realize that the world of *The Pioneers* is not Europe but

123

America, not European past but American future. *The Deerslayer*, which provides the clearest celebration of the mythic possibilities of American civilization, is also weighted with the fullest consciousness of its actual historical development. It is a fresh but not a sunny book. Certainly its mood is far less hopeful than that of *The Pioneers*. What makes it poignant in a strange and somber way is our knowledge, derived from the novels preceding it in the series, that, although Natty here enjoys our unequivocal dramatic sympathies, he and his values are marked out for defeat.

What are the moral and social values that he represents? Some of them have already been indicated in a general way, but it is necessary to attempt a more specific analysis. It is easy enough to say, as Cooper does in *The Pathfinder*, that he is a living picture of "simplicity, integrity, and sincerity," or to repeat with Middleton in *The Prairie* Duncan Heyward's judgment: "He was a man endowed with the choicest and perhaps rarest gift of nature, that of distinguishing good from evil." These and the many other similar statements reinforce Natty's position as the center of moral reference in the work. But they are too abstract and their dramatic meaning can be discovered only in the concrete clashes as they develop from novel to novel. It would be helpful to observe at the outset that in the series as written, while the complex of social behavior and institutions, or what might be called the image of actual civilization toward which Natty stands in a critical relation, becomes progressively less attractive, Natty's own character and values become proportionately more idealized and sympathetic. The result is to make his successive escapes from civilization more and more readily endorsable. Before taking this up in greater detail, however, one can mention briefly two of the many constants of his personality: his inveterate gravitation toward Nature with a capital N, and his friendship for the Indian chief Chingachgook. It is pointless to deny that both these involve a great deal of the contemporary Romantic attitudes. But it is equally true that neither can be dismissed as mere attitudinizing. They have worn too well to make such summary judgment valid. Since the positive aspects of the relationship between Natty and Chingachgook will be considered later in the essay, it is enough to say here that one of its functions is to stand in critical contrast with the relationships observable in "civilized" society. There is, however, more Romanticism of an objectionable variety in Natty's craving, to use his own favorite term, for unspoiled Nature. But even this serves as a commentary on the dubious morality of what goes on in the settlements. Such at least is Natty's own view, as can be seen from his sorrowful statement in *The Prairie:* "I passed the spring, summer, and autumn of life among the trees. The winter of my days had come, and found me where I loved to be, in the quiet—ay, and in the honesty of the woods!"

In *The Pioneers* the balance of sympathies is held perhaps even between Natty and the civilization he hates. To Judge Temple's vision—to commemorate which he has assigned the name "Vision" to the hill from which he obtained the first view of his newly bought estate—of a thriving and orderly settlement at Templeton, he opposes a misty vision of his own. In chapter 26 he recounts to Oliver Effingham the deeply moving experience he had years earlier when he beheld, as it were, the whole earth from a peak in the Catskills. When young Effingham asks what exactly he had seen up there, he answers: "Creation, all creation, lad." Although one registers its force, Natty's vague mysticism belongs altogether to a different order of existence to invalidate Marmaduke Temple's more practical plans. It is likewise difficult to see in this novel what superior claims Natty's personal predilection for hunting has over those of a more settled and agrarian way of life.

His hostility, or at least sullen indifference, to organized religion, however, has more point, since it rests on the belief that outward Christian forms have not been incompatible with an inner abandonment of moral principle, or even with downright dishonesty and hypocrisy, as in the case of the treatment meted out to the Indians. In the opening scene of the novel Natty observes that his "dog is more to be trusted than many a Christian man" and later declares to Mr. Grant, the local parson, that he has never known "preaching come into a settlement but it made game scarce, and raised the price of gunpowder." These reflections cannot be dismissed as crotchety notions of a garrulous old man chafing at unaccustomed restraints, for the simple reason that Natty is not a man without a moral conscience and his outbursts tie in with his indignation against the deprivation and Christianized degradation of the Indians: a fact to which his friend Chingachgook bears a living and mournful testimony. For instance, when Oliver Effingham taxes the Indian, now called John Mohegan, with being a drunken old beast, he replies:

> Is John old? When was a Mohican a squaw, with seventy winters! No! the white man brings old age with him— rum is his tomahawk! . . . John is a beast. The smokes were once few in these hills. . . . But warriors and traders with light eyes followed them. One brought the long knife, and one brought rum. They were more than the pines on the mountains; and they broke up the councils, and took the lands. The evil spirit was in their jugs, and they let him loose. Yes, yes—you say no lie, Young Eagle; John is a Christian beast.

It is against this background that one sees the justice of the claim that Natty makes before Judge Temple: "as for honesty," he says, "or doing what's right between man and

126

man, I'll not turn my back to the longest-winded deacon on your Patent."

While this is true, the society at Templeton is not presented unsympathetically either. On the contrary, taken as a whole it makes an attractive picture of rural bliss. It is friendly and genial, and, barring a few characters, the people who compose it are decent and wholesome. Life has not yet become so completely institutionalized as to rule out all forms of personal and kindly relationships. Judge Temple himself does not lag far behind Natty in deprecating the wasteful and disorderly spoliation of Nature and its resources. What finally gives the edge to Natty in the drama, however, is that Marmaduke Temple has built his kingdom on the basis of a questionable past. Of course the plot makes it clear eventually that the Judge's conscience is clearer than his record and that he has really had no reason to feel the guilt which makes him say to Oliver Effingham early in the novel: "Yet your face is one that I have seen; though it would not be strange, such has been my affright, should I see thee in thy winding-sheet walking by my bedside to-night." But if the enormity of the feeling expressed here cannot be explained away in terms of the minor wound the young man has received accidentally at the Judge's hands, the denouement of the story cannot quite cancel its effect either. Moreover, notwithstanding the trick by which young Effingham is made out to be a Delaware chief, his rehabilitation still leaves the Indian John to function as Banquo's ghost at the feast.

The next novel, *The Last of the Mohicans*, presents again a a fairly decorous image of organized society, but compared with that in *The Pioneers* it is heavily burdened with sentimental chivalry and is considerably less vigorous. The truly effective characters here are Natty, Chingachgook, and Uncas, who, in their undemonstrative but strong feeling for each other, represent something new and vital in the field of social relationships. Natty and Chingachgook, the one no longer disgruntled and the other no longer drunken, play their parts as exemplary warriors. The war itself is conducted with heroism, grace, and a strong sense of honor on the part of both the English and the French. It is important to note this fact, since most of these qualities are gone when Cooper projects the image of society at war again in *The Pathfinder*. If Major Duncan, the English commander of that novel, does not possess quite the loftiness of Colonel Munro, Lieutenant Muir turns out to be a traitor secretly in league with the French. In place of the sentimental love of Major Heyward for Alice we have a matrimonial intrigue whereby Lieutenant Muir, with Major Duncan's complaisant assistance, seeks to annex Mabel Dunham, the Sergeant's daughter, for his fifth wife, and the luster, or what passes for luster in Cooper's mind, has quite departed from the topmost surface of civilized society. By the time we come to *The Deerslayer*, this class of society is only marginally represented by the British garrison —a heartless company of elegant seducers.

In *The Prairie* civilization is in its true pioneer stage, heralded by the appearance of the large and uncouth, though far from unattractive, patriarch Ishmael Bush. It is a somber book with, as D. H. Lawrence puts it, "a shadow of violence and dark cruelty flickering in the air."[21] This time there is treachery and murder within the family—something unknown even to savagery—which makes Natty say of the murderer: "a shame and a disgrace is it to our race, that he is of the blood and family of the dead." The treachery, cruelty, and violence depicted here are combined with the hypocrisy, the acquisitiveness, and the unscrupulousness of civilization hinted at earlier, to form one powerful and repulsive image of actuality in *The Deerslayer*. "Plunder," a term which not-withstanding its usual meaning signifies baggage in *The*

21. Lawrence, p. 83.

Prairie, becomes the real product of plunder in this novel. Natty's criticism of organized religion is likewise more cogent: "Forts and churches almost always go together, and yet they are downright contradictions: churches being for peace, and forts for war." Warfare itself has degenerated entirely into taking scalps for bounty, a cruelty encouraged and paid for by both the English and the French. Natty alone maintains his concept of "open and generous" warfare, a concept which no rational description can explain as effectively as Cooper's art does in that justly celebrated scene in which Natty kills his first enemy and is rewarded by the dying man with affectionate admiration and the gift of a new name. As this episode demonstrates, Natty's attitudes—his desire for peace and harmony, his deep piety, and his reverence for life—are not necessarily unfit for the practical tasks of life. What he stands against are unnecessary cruelty, killing out of cupidity, intolerance, racism, wasteful exploitation, and unprincipled acquisitiveness. These are the very things that Tom Hutter and Harry March, especially the latter, stand for. The contrast is so markedly drawn and has been so extensively and illuminatingly commented on by more than one critic[22] that it is needless to labor it.

The Deerslayer thus dramatizes the social theme of the Leatherstocking Tales with all the intensity of which it is capable: the clash between Natty's ideal of the brotherhood of man based on true principles of Christianity and Hurry Harry's insidious avariciousness. The irony, if we consider the novel in its place within the series, is that the ideal possibilities of the new civilization should have been poisoned at the very roots by its more materialistic drives. As a matter of fact, as I have said earlier, the fresh and virgin world of *The Deerslayer* is also a world laboring under the heaviest burden of Cooper's historical awareness. The evil which presides over

22. See especially Marius Bewley, *The Eccentric Design*, pp. 87–100.

129

it is not unlike the evil whose manifestations dominate Twain's *Huckleberry Finn*. Although the scene of the novel is laid in an epoch earlier than that of *The Pioneers*, Tom Hutter and Hurry Harry represent the spirit of a later historical period. As Marius Bewley has pointed out, in "Hurry Harry and his moral vision of life we have an early representative of a type that was to become a dominant element in American civilization as it moved along toward the Gilded Age—a type that could supplant moral motives by motives of commercial expediency, and pretend, even to itself, that the substitution had never been made."[23] Another critic had earlier said much the same thing about Tom Hutter by observing that he "reminds us of later captains of railroads and industry, who were equally unprincipled and exploitative."[24]

It seems indeed that Cooper, his dream of a squirearchic order rudely jolted, not only looked prophetically into the future but also recognized with acute insight that the seeds of such development had been laid in America simultaneously with the proclamations of its ideal moral and social mission. If history was violating the myth, it was also perhaps fulfilling its destiny. The result was an ironic vision that puts one in mind of Yeats' "The Second Coming":

> The darkness drops again; but now I know
> That twenty centuries of stony sleep
> Were vexed to nightmare by a rocking cradle,
> And what rough beast, its hour come round at last,
> Slouches towards Bethlehem to be born?

The irony can be illustrated by one final example: the play upon the word "Ark." That the boat in which God saved

23. Ibid., p. 95.
24. David Brion Davis, "The Deerslayer: A Democratic Knight of the Wilderness," *Twelve Original Essays*, ed. Charles Shapiro (Detroit, Wayne State University Press, 1958), p. 9.

Noah so that he could be the patriarch of a new humanity should here be the habitat of Tom Hutter is of course the obvious ironic meaning of the name. But "Ark"—or "Ark of the Covenant"—is also the biblical word for the wooden coffer containing tables of divine law and guarded in the sanctum sanctorum of the temple. The wooden chest which Tom Hutter guards with equal vigilance, however, so far from being the repository of God's commandments contains instead a part of Captain Kidd's booty: a naval flag, old pistols, rich garments, ivory chess-pieces which Natty takes for idolatrous icons—the plunder, in short, which, as Hurry Harry says, Hutter has come into the wilderness to enjoy "peacably in the woods." It also contains the old letters which reveal to Judith the story of her mother's life: a tale of broken promises, a coarse and brutal lover, approaching insanity, and death. However, if in *The Deerslayer*, as in the world of Yeats' "The Second Coming," "the worst are full of passionate intensity," the best certainly do not "lack all conviction." That was to come after Cooper's time. Here, Natty and his moral vision, more idealized than in the other novels, also carry the deepest conviction.

Natty's function is, as we have seen, mainly critical. Nevertheless his attitude toward "civilization" implies, as all worth-while critical attitudes do, certain positive social values of its own. Before taking this up, however, it would be well to consider briefly the thorny question of his attitude toward marriage. Although many critics have made heavy weather of it, perhaps the sanest way to look at the whole matter of Natty and love is to view it, with Henry Nash Smith, as a sign of "Cooper's reluctance to break with the conventions of the sentimental novel."[25] It certainly is in no way an important

25. Henry Nash Smith, *Virgin Land* (Cambridge, Harvard University Press, 1950), p. 65.

part of the theme of the Leatherstocking Tales. Whatever little significance it possesses is again negative. Natty's rejection of marriage is a part of his general rejection of the institutions of an unworthy social order. He has, as Master Cap says in arguing against the proposed marriage of Mabel to him, "no more idea of the main chance than you have of spherical trigonometry." The surprising thing indeed in *The Pathfinder* is that, is spite of his being in "love," Natty should so often express his reservations about marriage. Most of them are self-deprecatory, it is true, but there are some which point the other way with telling effect: "I once hunted for two summers during the last peace," he says at one place, "and I collected so much peltry that I found my right feelings giving way to a craving after property; and if I have consarn in marrying Mabel, it is that I may get to love such things too well, in order to make her comfortable." This is precisely what happens to Jasper, who marries her and goes on to become "a successful and respected merchant." In *The Deerslayer*, where Natty is the pursued rather than the pursuing party, he owns with as much delicacy as truthfulness will allow that he cannot entertain the idea of marrying Judith because of Hurry Harry's revelations about her past. It would be a compromise with precisely that sinfulness of the past which the American hero has renounced. Perhaps such a harsh attitude is unbecoming in a true lover, but, as Natty makes clear repeatedly, he does not love Judith at all. Such being the case, marriage would mean nothing more than a surrender of principles in exchange for the security and comfort of Tom Hutter's "Castle."

Natty's critical attitude extends to social rebels of the frontier type. Although he himself is described as something of a lawless squatter in *The Pioneers*, the remarkable thing in that novel is Cooper's firm suggestion of the distance which separates Natty from such characters. In the subsequent novels this distance increases until he becomes not a class type at all but a moral type. The true squatter in the Leather-stocking Tales, the counterpart of Aaron Thousandacres in the Littlepage Trilogy, is, of course, Ishmael Bush. These people are rebels, not because they reject "civilization" but because they want unlimited opportunity to compete for its benefits. Products of an unrestrained individualism, they reject institutions only when they go against them. Fugitives from the law of the land, both of them hold lawcourts and trials of their own. They are traders and accumulators as much as Judge Temple, and indeed their rebellion only marks the first crude and dusty stage of the road that leads eventually to the Temples or the Hurry Harrys of the future, as the case may turn out to be in history. Natty, on the contrary, would think as little of striving toward Templeton Hall as he would of trafficking in slaves, like Ishmael Bush's brother-in-law, or of trading in lumber, like Thousandacres.

Thus one is pushed inevitably to the question: If Bush's frontier democracy is rejected together with Temple's squire-archy and Harry's robber-baronry, what on earth is left? Perhaps nothing is left on earth. To put it another way, Natty's answer to this historical problem is about as useful and as satisfying as is to be expected from a beautiful myth when it gives a visionary answer to a practical question. To the question where do we go from here?—as it is usually phrased—Natty's reply would be simple if we follow him literally: Go into the wilderness (an answer, incidentally, for which he had an estimable precedent in the decision of the Pilgrim Fathers). But should this not satisfy us, as it did not quite satisfy himself, he would say that the best thing to do would be to find a nice tribe, preferably of the Delaware or even Pawnee Indians, and get ourselves adopted and duly initiated into its life.

It is perhaps reasonable for us to laugh at the whole business of Cooper's Indians. At least it is easy—as easy as it was for the romantically inclined of Cooper's nineteenth-century readers to admire them, and more or less for the same reasons. But do we not miss something if we see in this theme only the romanticization of the noble savage, something of the effect if not the conscious intention? After all, Cooper does not admire the Indians because they are primitive, in the sense that they wear paint and feathers and delight in taking scalps. Nor does he represent them as innocent and uncorrupted. On the contrary, he divides his red men as mercilessly into the good and evil categories as any other novelist who deals in the drama of heroes and villains. Indeed it is a tribute to Cooper's tolerant humanity that he does not make moral distinctions along race lines but examines persons of all colors alike in the light of such values as courage, honor, and fortitude on the one hand, or cruelty, greed, and treachery on the other. The difference between those who judge a person by the color of his skin and those who judge his intrinsic worth provides perhaps the single most dependable moral test of characters in Cooper. Natty, who faithfully reflects what may be called his creator's humane if somewhat imaginative interest in comparative civilization draws attention to the importance of this test by firmly and repeatedly distinguishing between what he calls "gifts," or traditions, customs, and codes of various cultural groups, and "nature," or the common humanity of all men. Cooper's ultimate interest was not in traditional picturesqueness but in moral and social values, and if he idealizes his Indians it is for the same reason he idealized Natty or other writers have idealized their own heroes: because they represent in some way ideal values.

It is somewhat unfortunate that Cooper's quite open idealization has not been accepted on its own terms as an artistic device. From the very outset his portrayal of Indians was challenged as a violation of reality, and critical discussion has since continued to focus itself on the social and anthropological verisimilitude of the picture. This is unfortunate because it obscures the thematic function which the close-knit community life of the tribes performs in the Leatherstocking Tales. Like Crèvecoeur's "new man," Cooper's hero is powerfully attracted to it and to the "social bond" which holds it together.[26] As a matter of fact, of the five Leatherstocking novels, the only two (*The Last of the Mohicans* and *The Prairie*) which do not end with Natty's "escape" are the ones whose stories terminate in a tribe. The concluding note of all the others, whose action is confined within the settlements, is struck by Natty's resolute departure for the wilderness. Natty is undoubtedly a pronounced, even a dogmatic, individualist, but his individualism is not incompatible with a willing acceptance of certain forms of social organization, and for all his insistence on the difference between white and red men he can live only in a tribal community. He feels warm affection for all sorts of people, but, when it comes to adopting a son in *The Prairie* he rejects Middleton in favor of the young Pawnee chief Hard Heart, and though he can indulge his passion for hunting no longer he stays for the rest of his days in the Pawnee tribe, to which he is a stranger, in preference to returning to the settlements with the Middletons or Paul Hover and Ellen Wade.

Thus Cooper's fascination with tribal life was not confined to its picturesqueness or to the personal moral attributes of the individual members of particular tribes. It also included a preoccupation with its social organization, with such community values as absolute but unenforced loyalty, the absence of internecine conflict, freedom from "the dialectics of property," voluntarily assumed restraints and disciplines and the many traditions and rituals which unify the tribe and

26. See above, p. 27.

135

connect the present with the past in a satisfying social con-
tinuum. Even the Indian custom of giving names fascinated
him endlessly, since such names reflected an appreciation of
skill or merit and were the gifts of fellow members of the
tribe. Cooper's great Indian heroes are great precisely because they embody the spirit of a whole community. That they
speak out of a deep sense of wrong and woe is only part of the
secret of their moving eloquence. It is effective because the
feeling to which they are giving utterance is not one of personal loss but rather the tragedy of a whole nation. One can
see this if one contrasts Colonel Effingham's ludicrous and
anticlimactic entry upon the scene at the end of *The Pioneers*
with the magnificent appearance of Tamenund at the end of
The Last of the Mohicans. The two scenes are obviously
arranged for similar effect. What is more, Effingham is an
Indian chief too, though an adopted one. Both men are intended as ancient and patriarchal figures who almost rise
from the dead to proclaim verdicts of wisdom and justice
upon a troubled world. The only difference is that while
Effingham represents only himself and his wronged family,
through Tamenund speaks the voice of his whole tribe:

> Go, children of the Lenape, the anger of the Manitou is
> not done. Why should Tamenund stay? The pale-faces
> are masters of the earth, and the time of the redmen has
> not yet come again. My day has been too long. In the
> morning I saw the sons of Unamis happy and strong;
> and yet, before the night has come, have I lived to see
> the last warrior of the wise race of the Mohicans.

All this, however, can be dismissed, perhaps justifiably, as
nostalgic hankering after the primitive mores of a vanished
past, an impossible infatuation comparable only to Melville's
temporary enthusiasm for the Polynesian tribes in *Typee*. But
the myth that Cooper created in the Leatherstocking Tales

has another positive facet of social meaning that is embodied in the relationship between Natty and Chingachgook. It is a relationship which lies as much outside the Indian tribal past as it does outside the contemporary white civilization, yet which bridges them both and perhaps also points toward the future. Certain recent interpretations of the theme by professedly Lawrentian critics notwithstanding, the best thing on it was said by D. H. Lawrence himself when he observed with his usual apocalyptic insight:

> What did Cooper dream beyond democracy? Why, in his immortal friendship of Chingachgook and Natty Bumppo he dreamed the nucleus of a new society. That is, he dreamed a new human relationship. . . . This is the new nucleus of a new society, the clue to a new world-epoch. It asks for a great and cruel sloughing first of all. Then it finds a great release into a new world, a new moral, a new landscape.[27]

This is, of course, as Lawrence suggests, a dream—a concept not unlike the elder James' vision of postdemocratic "Society." It is therefore absurd to see it in terms of ordinary fictional realism and read in it a psychologically or socially faithful transcript of actuality. A better way for twentieth-century readers would be to approach it in the light of a work like Hart Crane's *The Bridge*, which represents a more modern attempt at recapturing the positive myth of American civilization. Such ideal affirmations can become sources for cultural renewal and endless inspiration precisely on account of the moral distance which separates them from existing reality. Cooper certainly did not believe that the ideal had been realized in America. On the contrary, as I have pointed out in a previous section, toward the end of his life he regarded it as essentially unrealizable. There is, however, a

27. Lawrence, p. 78.

137

passage written a few years earlier in *The Crater* which states precisely the relation he saw between myth and history. It also indicates that he realized what endless travail human history would have to go through before human society could achieve the perfection of which it had dreamed:

> Everything human follows its law, until checked by abuses that create resistance. This is true of the monarch, who misuses power until it becomes tryanny; of the nobles, who combine to restrain the monarch, until the throes of an aristocracy-ridden country proclaim that it has merely changed places with the prince; of the people, who wax fat and kick! Everything human is abused; and it would seem that the only period of tolerable condition is the transition state, when the new force is gathering to a head, and before the storm has time to break. In the meantime, the earth revolves, men are born, live their time, and die; communities are formed and are dissolved, dynasties appear and disappear; good contends with evil, and evil still has its day; the whole, however, advancing slowly but unerringly towards that great consummation, which was designed from the beginning, and which is as certain to arrive in the end, as that the sun sets at night and rises in the morning. The supreme folly of the hour is to imagine that perfection will come before its stated time.

4. Nathaniel Hawthorne:

HEIR AND CRITIC OF THE PURITAN TRADITION

> Man is a political animal, which means that the
> human personality craves political life, communal
> life, not only with regard to the family community,
> but with regard to the civil community.
>
> —Jacques Maritain,
> *The Rights of Man and Natural Law*

The pertinence of Hawthorne's themes to the problems of
modern life is widely recognized today. It is equally necessary
to emphasize their relevance to the author's own time. In the
course of this chapter I shall have occasion to point out how
some of the issues he explored were basically the same ones
that were confronted, in their own way, by Cooper, Emerson,
and the elder Henry James. As in the case of Cooper, however,
Hawthorne's themes were only superficially of a topical
nature. To a greater degree than his predecessor, he was preoccupied with the very origin of things, and repeatedly saw
the present in terms of the past. He holds a central place in
the history of the American imagination precisely because he
responded with adequate complexity to certain central problems of American civilization. This is particularly true of such

themes as the alienation of the individual and the possibility of social regeneration—themes with which Hawthorne dealt extensively but which were implicit in the American situation from the outset and which have continued to find expression in the nation's literature right down to the contemporary works of William Faulkner. It is a measure of Hawthorne's diagnostic insight that, whether he dramatized the society of the nineteenth or the seventeenth century, the issues upon which he seized are equally applicable to the experience of the twentieth.

There is a sense, of course, in which Hawthorne, like the best of his American contemporaries, was not a social novelist at all. He was not interested in portraying realistically the everyday life of his time. There is undoubtedly a good deal of social description in both *The House of the Seven Gables* and *The Blithedale Romance*, but when compared with the European fiction of the mid-century or the American novel of a generation later, Hawthorne's work exhibits, as Henry James noted in 1879, "the absence . . . of that quality of realism which is now so much in fashion." Henry James' discussion of the problem is worth stopping over a moment because, although Hawthorne's practice differed so radically from that of the school with which James was aligning himself at the time he wrote the study, it is remarkably balanced. He does not dismiss Hawthorne as a fanciful fictionist. On the contrary, he recognizes that the current conception of realism is only a different convention and not a permanent standard for testing the social significance of fiction. He observes that Hawthorne has "not proposed to himself to give an account of the social idiosyncracies of his fellow citizens," that his "portraiture never suggests a rigid standard of accuracy," that his characters are not "portraits of actual types," that he has not attempted to present "the usual Yankee of comedy, and that he has been almost culpably indifferent to his opportunities for commemorating the variations of colloquial English that may be observed in the New World." At the same time, however, "he testifies to the sentiments of the society in which he flourished almost as pertinently" as Balzac, Flaubert, and Zola "testify to the manners and morals of the French people." He "offers the most vivid reflection of New England life that has found its way into literature," and his work "is redolent of the social system in which he had his being."[1]

The one thing that James makes clear here is the difference between the realism of European fiction and Hawthorne's concern with American society. With regard to this concern itself, however, he is not equally helpful. He mentions but leaves unanalyzed the relation between Hawthorne's work on the one hand, and his age, his region, and his country on the other. We can perhaps meet the problem better by noting what might at first sight appear a contradiction in James' account. In the passage from which I quoted above, James says that Hawthorne "has none of the apparatus of an historian"[2] while in a later chapter he maintains that "Hawthorne had, as regards the two earlier centuries of New England life, that faculty which is called now-a-days the historic consciousness."[3] Of course the contradiction is only apparent, and James is not only clear but correct. Hawthorne was not a historian in the sense that Jane Austen was—that is, he was not a historian of manners. But his approach to American civilization was profoundly historical because it was essentially genetic. As a novelist he sought not to describe the society in which he lived but to understand it; and for him, as for many other imaginative Americans of the time, the logical

1. Henry James, *Hawthorne*, English Men of Letters (London, Macmillan, 1879), pp. 4–5.
2. Ibid., p. 4.
3. Ibid., p. 67.

starting point for the inquiry was the society of the seventeenth century. Of his "three American novels"—to use the term under which James groups *The Scarlet Letter*, *The House of the Seven Gables*, and *The Blithedale Romance*—the first is concerned with an early Puritan settlement; the story of the second makes a bridge, as it were, between the seventeenth century and the author's own time; while the third is placed entirely within the nineteenth century.

As my putting the facts in this manner perhaps suggests, Hawthorne was more interested in the continuities of tradition, of underlying principles, of hopes and frustrations than he was in the contrast of ages or even social development in the ordinary sense. His interest in the past was of the utmost importance in his work, but it was not an antiquarian interest. In his artistic vision the seventeenth century was decisive in fostering the essential American attitudes, character types, and ideals; and his fiction focused on the recurring type in historically altered situations rather than on any basic alteration in society itself. To him the past was the moral fountainhead from which issued the stream, pure or addled, whose deepest current his sensibility recorded at various points along its course down to his own time. If the nineteenth-century subject which he chose to dramatize in *The Blithedale Romance* admitted a kinship with the American experience of the seventeenth century, the seventeenth century itself was explored for clues helpful to the understanding of the future. Whatever their historical or sociological accuracy, these explorations provide thus an imaginative response to American civilization which is, in spite of the severe limitation of Hawthorne's subject matter, remarkably inclusive on the one hand and admirably unified on the other.

If it were not so fascinating and so representative of the American imagination, Hawthorne's preoccupation with the past would seem incredibly obsessive. In the biographical sketch which he appended to *The Scarlet Letter* he laments the irresistible compulsion he feels to fling himself "back into another age" while the solid materiality of his daily life at the Custom House is "pressing so intrusively" upon him:

> The wiser effort would have been to diffuse thought and imagination through the opaque substance of to-day, and thus to make it a bright transparency; to spiritualize the burden that began to weigh so heavily; to seek, resolutely, the true and indestructible value that lay hidden in the petty and wearisome incidents, and ordinary characters, with which I was now conversant. The fault was mine. The page of life that was spread out before me seemed dull and commonplace, only because I had not fathomed its deeper import. A better book than I shall ever write was there . . . only because my brain wanted the insight and my hand the cunning to transcribe it.

Thus, while he left the life of the Custom House "like a dream behind me" and while the living personages seemed "but shadows in my view," he set out upon his career as a serious novelist by conjuring up a tale of the seventeenth century and "imagining the motives and modes of passion that influenced the characters who figure in it." There is no novel of his whose action does not turn momentously upon some event consummated in the past, and some at least of whose principal characters do not find themselves struggling against the bondage of their past history. Hawthorne's own attitude toward the past is complex if not paradoxical, inasmuch as he conceives of it at times as a source of wisdom and balance in human affairs and attitudes, while more often he visualizes it as a dead and ghostly weight upon the present which living men must exorcize, at some inevitable sacrifice, if life is to advance untrammeled into a fresh and better future. Likewise, the limits of what constitutes the past for Hawthorne

143

are far from fixed. Under this one artistic conception he includes the Adamic past of all humanity, the European past of America, and the New England past of his own society. In the works with which I am dealing, I shall be concerned mostly with the last—and, in the case of this particular author, I think it is perhaps more important than the others. The European past, so essential to the workings of Henry James' imagination, occupies no similar place in the themes of Hawthorne's best novels, although Mrs. Q. D. Leavis has argued strongly for considering them in that light, for seeing Qld England, that is, as the other side in Hawthorne's social equation.[4] Paradoxical as it may sound, Hawthorne's preoccupation with the American past went hand in hand with a forward-looking inquiry. He, like the elder James, Emerson, and even Cooper, regarded the break with Europe as a salutary, though incomplete or even negative, development, and the positive side in his theme, as in theirs, was supplied by a visionary conception of what democracy means and what a truly democratic future should be.

If we wish, we can explain Hawthorne's absorption in his country's past in biographical terms, in terms of the influence of Sir Walter Scott, or only as an attempt to choose a picturesque subject. To do so, however, is not so important as to see its literary effect and to give an account of its thematic value in the body of his work. Once we remember that the American experiment was supposed to be a new beginning for humanity, we realize that Hawthorne's combining a critical exploration of Puritan society with an idealistic concern for human and

4. Q. D. Leavis, "Hawthorne as Poet," *Sewanee Review*, 59 (1951), 179–205, 426–58. Since I have expressed this difference with Mrs. Leavis' point of view, and since I have made below one other reservation with regard to her account, it is necessary for me to add that I consider her essay one of the most illuminating pieces of criticism on Hawthorne. My own debt to its insights is too obvious to need formal acknowledgment.

social regeneration so far from being a paradox presents actually a case of imaginative logic and coherence. Was the Puritan establishment in reality a new beginning for humanity? Is it possible to separate from a corrupt world and form a regenerate community? If so, how can regeneration be achieved and what are its manifestations? Or, to put Hawthorne's basic criticism in different words, one can say that, while he was deeply preoccupied with both the beginnings of civilization in the New World and the possibilities of a new civilization, unlike his ancestors in New England he did not regard the two as identical.

A similar critical attitude distinguishes the author's treatment of the communitarian experiment which forms the subject of *The Blithedale Romance*. It is a remarkable fact, and one highly indicative of Hawthorne's imaginative response to the meaning of the American experience, that of all possible themes offered by contemporary life he should choose to dramatize this particular one. It is the more remarkable since this man of resolute good sense had as little faith in quixotic demonstrations of this sort as Emerson himself. We can no doubt view the whole matter biographically again, but Hawthorne's brief association with the Brook Farm experiment, like his association with men and matters at the Custom House in Salem, testifies only to the availability of certain diverse kinds of raw material which the artist may or may not use, the choice depending essentially upon the nature of the theme which appeals most deeply to his imagination. Hawthorne had a mind which, descended as he was from the most true-blue Puritans, worked irresistibly in types and correspondences; and if Brook Farm became to him the most significant offering of his times, it was because he could see in it an interesting parallel to the venture of the American Puritans themselves. Here again was the American theme of exodus: a determined band of people separating from a corrupt society to form a regenerate community, and expecting thereby to light the beacon flame of new hope for the rest of the world.

Hawthorne laughed at the idea of course, but not entirely. He was also critical of it, which means that he posed certain serious questions. Is the fact of physical separation enough to ensure regeneration? Do ideals suffice? And in any event, what are the true ideals which should inspire a community, whether of saints or citizens? In what manner these questions enter Hawthorne's theme I shall attempt to show when I discuss the novels individually. Here I should like to note how, in dismissing in the Custom House sketch the life of his own times as a possible subject for fiction, he was only ruling out certain modes of dealing with its realities. "Henceforth," he declared in conclusion, speaking not only of the Custom House but also of the whole town and its everyday life, "it ceases to be a reality of my life. I am a citizen of somewhere else." This suspenseful leave-taking was intended for a journey not into the land of fantasy but only into that region of the imagination where, free from the distractions of commonplace events, the artist could, among other things, come to terms with the essential meaning of the American experience; a region where, like a good democratic citizen, he would be free to evaluate his national inheritance and free to become its critic. Thus in writing a masterpiece about the society of the seventeenth century, Hawthorne was also understanding that of the nineteenth. He was acquiring the "insight" and the "cunning" whose lack he deplored in the passage I quoted above. He was fathoming the "deeper import" of the otherwise dull page of contemporary life.

Puritan or Blithedalean, Hawthorne tested the claims of each community to regeneracy in the light of the effect its mode of life and its beliefs had on the concerns of this world: on human relationships and on such necessary values as love

146

and loyalty and compassion. His was entirely a social theme. His imagination, unlike Melville's, was not challenged by the metaphysical problem of man's relation to the unknown mysteries of life. Even *The Scarlet Letter*, which of all Hawthorne's novels is most heavily weighted with an awareness of Puritan dogmas, is not so much a book about Hester's breaking one of God's commandments as it is about the social effect of such an action. It deals not with the sin of adultery but with the diverse repercussions on human relationships resulting from the consciousness of this sin. As Hawthorne says at one place, making explicit the social nature of the novel's essential concerns: "The effect of the symbol [of adultery]—or, rather, of the position in respect to society that was indicated by it—on the mind of Hester Prynne herself, was powerful and peculiar." The parenthetical clause of this statement is its most revelatory part, and what is said here of the effect of the scarlet A on Hester applies also to its effect on the other characters of the story. For this novelist, who characteristically hid his meanings behind a fascinating veil of ambiguities, that is perhaps a bold declaration. It is nonetheless representative of his basic strategy, his method of working the theme out by inviting rather than bypassing the complexities of life.

One should therefore be wary of dismissing lightly the ubiquitous machinery of Puritan metaphysics in *The Scarlet Letter*, or of passing it over in silence as Mrs. Q. D. Leavis does. Whether Hawthorne personally believed in it or not is perhaps an irrelevant question, but not so the artistic use to which he put it. It seems to me that, in writing this story of the Puritans, Hawthorne was engaging them on their home field, as it were, and while accepting their version of metaphysical reality as the starting point and the framework for his story he was questioning not their religious beliefs but rather the validity of human conclusions drawn from the accepted

premises. This to my mind makes his criticism more searching, and his humanist sympathies warmer and less superficial
than would otherwise appear to be the case. For instance,
Hawthorne never dismisses the concept of universal sin as the
imaginary bogey of Puritanism. On the contrary, whatever his
personal belief in the matter, he enforces its implications with
a simple seriousness that would have denied to the old worthies their smug satisfaction in being the worst of sinners. It is
not by disregarding sin, but rather by insisting on its universality that Hawthorne finally rules it out as a standard of
ethical judgment in human affairs. In other words, though he
used the terms interchangeably, he draws a broad distinction
between sin and evil—or sin and the unpardonable sin, as he
would perhaps prefer to put it himself. From a theological
point of view one may only be a manifestation of the other;
but Hawthorne's themes center less on the former, with its
metaphysical reference, and more on the latter, whose reference is social and which governs the relationship between man
and man rather than between man and God.

It was thus by quietly accepting the Christian account of
man's fallen nature and his future destiny that Hawthorne
could devote his critical exploration to the problems of his
earthly predicament and the values which should govern his
life here below. If men recognize their common sinfulness and
their common weakness before God, they should also
acknowledge their essential brotherhood and fellowship, and
not do violence to the many ties which bind them to other
human beings in the family and the civil community. He
would have agreed with the elder Henry James that the great
mistake of Protestant Christianity was to regard human life
as personally rather than socially constituted, and that egotism or intellectual and spiritual pride, all that alienates
man from man, was the result of what the latter called "the
church spirit." Time and again Hawthorne demonstrated the

difference between ethical rightness and self-righteousness. He analyzed repeatedly the calamitous effects on life of such things as fanatical zeal, bigotry, greed, and acquisitiveness, what he called the coldness of the heart, and of that species of ruthless ambition which, however one may judge the value of its original motivation, leads inevitably in the end to a warping of the aspirant's moral personality. If there is any single "message" in his work, it is the one which pleads for the wisdom of recognizing the limitation of man's reach and capability, and for a relaxed attitude of brotherly tolerance, love, and compassion.

To put Hawthorne's values, sympathetic or otherwise, in this manner might make them sound as trite as the Virtues and Vices of the Moralities; and indeed one cannot deny that some of his inferior sketches approach the simple personifications of that genre. But in his mature fiction he invests the opposition of these values with a human richness and a depth of understanding which give to his themes, however one may simplify them in paraphrase, an abiding relevance to the problems of modern life. For whether we place its origin in the seventeenth or the nineteenth century, and whether we ascribe it to "the church spirit" or to democratic individualism, man's sense of alienation is an increasing fact of modern society. And so is his quest for community.[5]

5. I have taken the phrase from Robert A. Nisbet, to whose book *The Quest for Community* (New York, Oxford University Press, 1953) the interested reader should refer for an illuminating discussion of this problem. Mr. Nisbet maintains that of all the symptoms of the impact of modern conditions on the human personality in the Western world, the most revealing is "the preoccupation, in so many spheres of thought and action, with community—community lost and community to be gained." However, although he recognizes that "behind this preoccupation there lie many historical changes and dislocations—economic, religious, and moral," his book deals chiefly with "the *political* causes of the manifold alienations that lie behind the contemporary quest for community." (For the quotations used here see p. vii.)

Of Hawthorne's four major novels, the three I propose to discuss are *The Scarlet Letter* (1850), *The House of the Seven Gables* (1851), and *The Blithedale Romance* (1852). Published within a short period of just over two years, they possess an underlying thematic unity that is not often recognized. *The Marble Faun*, which appeared several years later, clearly falls outside the scope of this study. Set in Europe, it introduces a dialectic different from the one that lies at the heart of the earlier work. Even among the three American novels, however, I shall not be concerned extensively with *Seven Gables*. Since its social theme has been fully commented on by F. O. Matthiessen, I shall restrict my remarks on it to an area that connects it with the two other works in the group.

But before turning to the novels, it would be useful to consider some of Hawthorne's shorter tales. Many of these are not perhaps masterpieces in their own right, but nonetheless they possess great interest for the reader because of the insight they afford into the nature of this writer's themes. At times a Hawthorne tale is a sort of intermediate sketch, an uninvolved variation on a theme, less cryptic than a notebook entry and not quite so complexly developed as a longer work. The stories with which I shall deal in this section can be loosely grouped into three categories: the tales which center on the predicament, more or less tragic as the case may be, of individuals alienated from society; those which have for their theme the essential, one might say the inescapable, fellowship of all men; and, finally, a few in which Hawthorne explores the possibility of achieving a regenerated society in this world.

To the first of these groups—numerically larger than any other in Hawthorne—belong such diverse stories as "Wakefield," "The Minister's Black Veil," "The Man of Adamant," "Egotism; or, The Bosom Serpent," "Rappaccini's Daughter," and "Ethan Brand," as well as all the tales which deal with the figure of the artist. The theme of isolation which is common to these stories can be viewed, of course, as Hawthorne's statement of some innate perversity in human nature which drives it to repudiate, sever, or violate the ordinary ties that bind human beings one to another. Alternatively or simultaneously, at any rate more specifically, it can be interpreted as a comment on the American social situation, as the artistic diagnosis of a possible perversion inherent in the attitudes and values fostered by a democratic society. Insofar as it has this social implication, it is necessary at the outset to make a few general comments on the nature of the theme. It is necessary, I may add, in view of certain prevalent confusions on the subject. For instance, in his recent book *The Dungeon of the Heart*, Edwin T. Bowden has interpreted the theme of isolation in the American novel in terms of what he calls "the frontier isolation."[6] I should like to point out that the isolation which Hawthorne writes about is not a matter of physical solitude but of moral alienation, of "solitude in the midst of men," as Oberon says in the early sketch "The Devil in Manuscript." Oberon, the struggling young writer, it will be remembered, bears Hawthorne's own nickname of college days and is in other thinly disguised ways a dramatization of Hawthorne himself. For a more specific comment on the erroneousness of blaming it all on the lonely woods, one can turn to the following statement about the heroine of "Roger Malvin's Burial," who has traveled deep into the frontier with her husband and son: "The heart of Dorcas was not sad; for she felt that it was better to journey in the wilderness with two whom she loved than to be a lonely woman in a crowd that cared not for her."

As is obvious here, Hawthorne's theme was the warping of human relations in society and not isolation in any physical

6. I have already remarked in general terms on the limitations of this view. See above, pp. 13–14.

sense. Marius Bewley seems to me right when he sees the tension between society and solitude as lying "near the centre of all of Hawthorne's art." But it is characteristic of the general incoherence of his account that he should go on to equate "solitude" with "aristocratic withdrawal" which "seemed to side with Europe rather than with America."[7] This is the physical isolation theory again, in an unnecessarily sophisticated garb. It is somewhat difficult for amateur sociologists to decide offhand on the comparative values of aristocratic and democratic civilizations, but I would much rather rely on the authority of an older critic, who was a penetrating observer and who had the advantage, moreover, of being contemporary with the times on which he was commenting. Tocqueville, as is well known, made the following statement in contrasting the social conditions of Europe and America: "Aristocracy had made a chain of all the members of the community, from the peasant to the king; democracy breaks that chain and severs every link of it."[8] In the light of this observation one can see that the alienation of the individual which Hawthorne studied—whether in artist, priest, or medicine man—was a product of democratic society itself. "Aristocratic institutions," as Tocqueville says just before the statement quoted above, "have the effect of closely binding every man to several of his fellow citizens." It is true that this sense of immediate community extends primarily to one's family or class, but since men living in "aristocratic communities" occupy "fixed positions, one above another," they are conscious of belonging to a unified social structure. They count on the patronage of the person above and the cooperation of the one below them. They are "therefore almost always closely attached to something placed out of their own sphere, and they are often disposed to forget themselves." In democratic

7. Marius Bewley, *The Eccentric Design*, p. 115. See also p. 123.
8. See above, p. 28.

societies, on the other hand, there is no comparable sense of secure relation to the community at large, no kinship of class, and no warm and close ties within smaller social units such as the family: "the bond of human affection is extended, but it is relaxed."[9] Democracies are based on individualism, and "individualism, at first, only saps the virtues of public life; but in the long run it attacks and destroys all others and is at length absorbed in downright selfishness."[10]

The loss of a sense of community, obsession with self, exploitative individualism—Hawthorne's major themes—are thus the dangers latent in democratic society and not the products of geographical solitude or "aristocratic withdrawal." Furthermore, the positive side in the tension which lies close to the center of Hawthorne's work is not provided by aristocratic as opposed to democratic values at all. If the solitude he wrote about was the result of the democratic atomization of humanity, the society he envisaged could only result from a further development of democracy. Tocqueville's chain of aristocracy was a chain of hierarchic institutions which enforced such links as class, privilege, and patronage. Hawthorne was a good democrat in the fact that he, like many of his contemporaries, accepted its dissolution without trepidation. To the coldness and fragmentation involved in a superficial attitude of individualism, however, he, like the elder Henry James, opposed the findings of a deeper exploration into the moral nature of the individual. He had himself experienced a powerful sense of isolation, but as Malcolm Cowley has observed, "It is characteristic of Hawthorne that he should have drawn a social lesson from a solitary experience."[11] The lesson was, of course, that the

9. Tocqueville, *Democracy in America*, 2, 98–99.
10. Ibid., 2, 98.
11. Malcolm Cowley, "Hawthorne in the Looking-Glass," *Sewanee Review*, 56 (1948), 550.

existence of the individual has no meaning apart from the ties which bind him to other human beings—a lesson, incidentally, which Conrad teaches us in every one of his great novels. The social bond that Hawthorne visualized, however, was not the old chain of aristocracy but simply "the magnetic chain of humanity." Insofar as it can be paraphrased, his attitude represented a hope that democratic men would achieve a better community than the one they had left behind—the European community of class and privilege—if they acknowledged the inescapable fellowship of all human beings and translated the theoretical claim of universal brotherhood into the values and conduct of living relationships. Thus the essential tension in Hawthorne's theme is not between aristocratic pride on the one hand and democratic sociality on the other; it is rather between the actual products and the ideal possibilities of democracy. Europe and Europe's old institutions do not have the importance for him which they had for Henry James, and to this extent it is a mistake to read into his work a preparatory footnote to the younger writer's fiction. Hawthorne was not only a critic of America, not merely a "restless analyst," he was also its visionary, albeit a refreshingly skeptical one. He shared something of the land-of-promise hope together with a great deal of doubt whether any lands of promise are to be ever discovered anywhere—unless it be in the altered hearts of men.

Among Hawthorne's tales of isolation, as we may call them, there is finally an important distinction to be made between those which deal with protagonists who have willfully alienated themselves from "the magnetic chain of humanity" and others where the hero has not deliberately withdrawn himself but where, on the other hand, he has been forced into isolation by society. If "Ethan Brand" is the classic example of the former type, all but one of the artist-stories belong to the latter category. It would be a slight exaggeration to say that in the drama of solitude and society, or of the individual and the community, which is common to them both, the two kinds of characters are treated respectively as villains and victims. Perhaps a more accurate observation would be that in comparison with the former the latter are more sinned against than sinning. It is partly a question of the motivating discord and partly of the final consequences for the individual concerned. The important thing in Hawthorne is the human personality, and, in the cases where its original attitudes are wholesome, isolation frustrates but does not warp the sympathies. The consequences are truly catastrophic only where the original motivation is inhuman. To bear this distinction in mind is necessary if one is to do justice to the subtlety of Hawthorne's moral evaluations. To overlook it is to invite confusion, as I shall attempt to show a little later.

With regard to these tales, therefore, my purpose is to note only the initial drives which lead the protagonists on to the road of alienation and the eventual destination reserved for them in the scheme of Hawthorne's world. Take, for example, a simple sketch like "Wakefield." It tells a fanciful story about a man who, somewhat whimsically and quite deliberately, absents himself from his household for a period of twenty years. Leaving his wife and children to believe him dead, he takes lodgings in a neighboring street and starts keeping a stealthy watch over their reactions. It can perhaps be considered as only an eccentric thought, a plan not unlike the celebrated one executed by Tom Sawyer; for Wakefield, observing how his wife will take the event, is resolved not to return "until she be frightened half to death." But in Hawthorne's world the matter is not so simple. By giving in to his "morbid vanity," Wakefield has committed the unpardonable sin, and he ends by becoming "the outcast of the Universe." He has, in other words, willfully stepped outside the family community in order to subject to a perverse experiment the reciprocal affections and sympathies which inform it. Thus what seems originally an eccentric fancy, undeserving of the heavy punishment meted out to it, is in reality an inhuman action stemming from a defective moral personality; for, as Hawthorne carefully indicates at the outset, Wakefield's heart, though neither depraved nor wandering, is cold, and there is in his character "a quiet selfishness, that had rusted into his inactive mind." What we have in Wakefield's strange career, then, is a story of warped family relations, a theme whose wider applicability can be recognized by adjusting the parable to reality. By eschewing the fanciful element of Wakefield's actual absence of twenty years from his family, we can see in him a representative figure: a man who is "we may figuratively say, always beside his wife and at his hearth, yet must never feel the warmth of the one nor the affection of the other."

If Wakefield's retribution is to become the outcast of the universe, Richard Digby in "The Man of Adamant" is turned into stone. His fate is the reward of a false piety, an unrighteous religiosity, which is indistinguishable from a bigoted obsession with his own self. "His plan of salvation was so narrow, that, like a plank in a tempestuous sea, it could avail no sinner but himself," especially since he took "special care" to keep it outside the reach of other sinners. Convinced that he is the one man God has decided to redeem from eternal death, he shuns all contact with sinful humanity, looks with sour disfavor upon the ordinary joys and sorrows of life, and finally seals himself into total seclusion in a cavern which Nature could have meant for no purpose except as a burial place for "the victims of a pestilence." Although Richard Digby considers it a divine sanctuary, the cave is his most appropriate sepulcher, because his bigotry is in effect a pestilence, a malady which is gradually changing "his fleshly heart to stone." His last chance of redemption is to return into the fold of humanity through the love that is offered to him by the girl (or rather her apparition) who has followed him from England, "a great Physician" having given her the skill to cure his diseased soul. "Come back with me!" she says, "come back to thy fellow-men; for they need thee, Richard, and thou hast tenfold need of them." But he rejects the appeal and, as he does so, falls down dead, only to be discovered a century later turned into a figure of adamant which "seemed to have been carved in the same gray stone that formed the walls and portal of the cave": the cave of a loveless, compassionless, impious, and therefore lifeless, heart.

As variations on the theme of these two stories, one can consider two others: "The Minister's Black Veil" and "Egotism; or, The Bosom Serpent." Mr. Hooper, the clergyman of the former, also decides, like Richard Digby, to seclude himself, although only in a symbolic way by draping his face in a black veil. There is something adamantine, and to that extent inhuman, in his resolution not to let his face be seen even by the woman whom he loves and proposes to marry. But it is a more complex story than "The Man of Adamant." For one thing, unlike Richard Digby, Mr. Hooper does not believe himself to be the only regenerate man, set above and beyond the rest of mankind. On the contrary, the veil is his acknowledgment of universal sinfulness, including his own, and though withdrawn forever behind this dreadful screen, he loses neither his love nor his sympathy. His gesture of piety is nevertheless equally deluded because his recognition of the sinfulness before God of all men does not lead him to a deeper and more compassionate sense of communion. He sees sin rather as a barrier, a black veil hanging on every human face and separating man from man, husband from wife, as well as the clergyman from his congregation. Therefore, like Young Goodman Brown after his vision of universal

157

sin, Mr. Hooper lives and dies a gloomy and alienated man: "All through life that piece of crape had hung between him and the world: it had separated him from cheerful brotherhood and woman's love, and kept him in that saddest of all prisons, his own heart; and still it lay upon his face, as if to deepen the gloom of his darksome chamber, and shade him from the sunshine of eternity."

Compared with Mr. Hooper's story, the reference of "Egotism," like that of "Wakefield," is primarily secular. The snake in Roderick Elliston's heart—"the symbol of a monstrous egotism"—is at once the cause and the consequence of "his shattered schemes of domestic bliss,—wilfully shattered by himself." His alienation from the family community leads eventually to an estrangement "from all companionship. Not merely the eye of man was a horror to him; not merely the light of a friend's countenance; but even the blessed sunshine, likewise, which in its universal beneficence typifies the radiance of the Creator's face, expressing his love for all the creatures of his hand." Thus Roderick's alienation is also a turning away from God, while his diseased self-contemplation, as he calls it, is in effect devil worship, since the serpent of egotism has become to him "a divinity,—not celestial, it is true, but darkly infernal." The yearning for fellowship, which he cannot quite stifle, makes him realize how widespread the malady is in reality, the crowd of people who nourish reptiles including even a distinguished clergyman who has "swallowed a snake in a cup of sacramental wine." Roderick's redemption comes only when he takes his wife to his bosom again, and, forgetting his own self, recovers his place in the family community—and thereby a place in the human community at large.

These are thus the stories of a peculiar destiny: of an alienation which arises from cold selfishness, from deluded piety, and from egotistical individualism, and which leads in all cases to a corruption of the human personality and the break-down of normal social relations within the community. They are the parables of a culture in which the Puritan absorption with the self has shaded off into the democratic ideal of the individual's self-sufficiency. To the transcendental argument of the infinitude of the private man they seem to answer that man by himself is nothing: he is nonexistent, a hollow and meaningless shell, a figure of stone, a shade draped in black, a tortured being haunted by infernal furies; and that individual existence can acquire meaning only within the larger life of the community. The meaningful community life, it must be pointed out, was not for Hawthorne a matter of external slogans and schemes. It could arise only from the individual's deep realization of his own insufficiency, and it could be based only upon genuine emotion, upon such feelings as love and compassion. This was the conclusion to which Hawthorne's brooding over his own sense of isolation had led him. Commenting upon the long period of his solitary existence in Salem, he wrote in his Notebook for 1840: "Indeed, we are but shadows; we are not endowed with real life, and all that seems most real about us is but the thinnest substance of a dream,—till the heart be touched. That touch creates us,—then we begin to be,—thereby we are beings of reality and inheritors of eternity."

In other stories which I shall consider a little later Hawthorne explored this same theme of the inescapable fellowship of man from a different angle. We must first, however, take note of two tales in which alienation is the result of science: "Rappaccini's Daughter" and "Ethan Brand." Insofar as science enters these stories, one need scarcely point out, it is not condemned as the search for knowledge or as knowledge which results in human good. It is not a matter of the historic bias against science. Hawthorne is free of the vulgar attitude which regards science as the intrusion of an unnatural or ungodly view upon an otherwise beautiful and poetical world. If Rappaccini is a physician, so is the kindly Professor Baglioni "a teacher of the divine art of medicine." If one doctor poisons his own daughter, it is a doctor again who, in the legend within the story, saves Alexander from the poisonous woman sent to destroy him. "Science" is here indeed a name for the pursuit of power, the ruthless power which gives a man absolute control over other men and in whose acquisition he coldly speculates with human destinies. As Baglioni says of Rappaccini, "he cares infinitely more for science than for mankind. His patients are interesting to him only as subjects for some new experiment." The "scientific" world which Rappaccini has fashioned on this premise is a garden of deadly atmosphere and poisonous shrubs and flowers. "Was this garden, then, the Eden of the present world?" It is certainly the Eden of a world where the lust for power has supplanted the affections and sympathies of the natural world. Love cannot flourish in it. Beatrice Rappaccini, who, as well as her lover, has become an object of her father's experiment, lives in it as in a desert island. Herself a sympathetic character, her tragedy lies in the fact that though she is human, has "all gentle and feminine qualities," and is capable of "the height and heroism of love," the dreadful power with which Rappaccini has endowed her must forever seclude her from the rest of mankind. When she falls in love, it is only to poison her lover and die herself; for the very father who blesses their union with "conscious power" and who has contrived that it should take place on the basis of this same power has by so doing also "thrown poison into the stream of their lives."

If "Rappaccini's Daughter" is mainly the story of the victims of a scientific experiment, "Ethan Brand" goes on to tell what happens to the experimenter himself. Brand—the man whose search is for the unpardonable sin and who, after eighteen years, finds the object of his search in himself—turns into a Rappaccini-like scientist precisely at the moment when his pursuit of knowledge becomes a violation of the sanctity of human life. His sin is not intellectual inquiry but, as he himself says, the "sin of an intellect that triumphed over the sense of brotherhood with man and reverence for God, and sacrificed everything to its own mighty claims! The only sin that deserves a recompense of immortal agony!" In other words, he becomes sinful when, in the pride of his intellectual power, he willfully alienates himself from humanity, and, like Rappaccini, with "cold and remorseless purpose," makes Esther "the subject of a psychological experiment" that wastes and annihilates her soul. It is only then that he puts himself on that long road which ends with his suicide. Alienated from earth, mankind, and heaven alike, as he acknowledges before he jumps into the lime kiln, his only reward is the "deadly element of Fire,—henceforth my familiar friend!"

It is commonly assumed that Ethan Brand's unpardonable sin consists in the very nature of his pursuit, namely, the examination of the moral nature of man and the psychological study of human weakness. But this is not so. That constitutes, on the contrary, the heroic part of Brand's character, which is fully endorsed by Hawthorne:

> The Idea that possessed his life had operated as a means of education; it had gone on cultivating his powers to the highest point of which they were susceptible; it had raised him from the level of an unlettered laborer to stand on a star-lit eminence, whither the philosophers of the earth, laden with the lore of universities, might vainly strive to clamber after him.

But this was at a time when Brand's intellectual pursuit had not destroyed his sympathies, at a time when, as he himself remembers, he was "a simple and loving man" pursuing his inquiry without losing his human tenderness:

> He remembered with what tenderness, with what love and sympathy for mankind, and what pity for human guilt and woe, he had first begun to contemplate those ideas which afterwards became the inspiration of his life; with what reverence he had then looked into the heart of man, viewing it as a temple originally divine, and, however desecrated, still to be held sacred by a brother.

In this careful recapitulation of his protagonist's career, Hawthorne not only makes plain the worthy beginning of the pursuit which finally ends in the lime kiln, he also states clearly the nature of the unpardonable sin and the precise development which made Ethan Brand guilty of it:

> He had lost his hold of the magnetic chain of humanity. He was no longer a brother-man, opening the chambers or the dungeons of our common nature by the key of holy sympathy, which gave him a right to share in all its secrets; he was now a cold observer, looking on mankind as the subject of his experiment, and, at length, converting man and woman to be his puppets, and pulling the wires that moved them to such degrees of crime as were demanded for his study.
>
> Thus Ethan Brand became a fiend. He began to be so from the moment that his moral nature had ceased to keep the pace of improvement with his intellect.

I have made these lengthy citations in order to point out the erroneousness of the widespread assumption that Hawthorne's democratic bias, or his Puritan inheritance, made him antipathetic to the individual's pursuit of knowledge or art—or any other activity, for that matter, beyond the attainment of the mass of mankind. The inclusion of art here might seem uncalled for, but the correlation of Ethan Brand and the artist is not of my making. The responsibility for it belongs to Marius Bewley. He reads this story as being "fundamentally . . . concerned with the problem of the creative artist, and particularly the writer." Having made that assumption, it is understandable that Bewley should go on to conclude that Hawthorne here presents art "as a field of conflict upon which the artist conducts his nefarious trade of human exploitation."[12] Now it is true that the artist's and particularly the writer's trade, like that of Ethan Brand, involves the moral and psychological examination of human beings. But that is neither exploitative nor sinful. On the contrary, Hawthorne would agree with Alexander Pope that the proper study of mankind is man.[13] At least it is precisely this study which raises his unlettered laborer "to stand on a star-lit eminence" beyond the reach of university professors. Ethan Brand becomes sinful only when he loses "the key of holy sympathy" which alone gives the inquirer the right to explore "the chambers or the dungeons of our common nature" and the right to "share in all its secrets"; when, in other words and if we accept Bewley's correlation for the time being, he ceases to be an artist and becomes a Rappaccini-like scientist. The unpardonable sin consists of egotism and inhuman obsession, while the hallmark of the artist, as of the early Brand, is his "holy sympathy," or what we would call artistic sympathy. Hawthorne himself possessed this sympathy—what great artist is without it?—and, more often than not, so do his artists. In the preface to *The Snow-Image* he replied to the

12. Bewley, *The Eccentric Design*, pp. 116, 121–22.

13. Cf. the passage in Hawthorne's Notebook for 1838 in which he recounts the judgment of his character by a poverty-stricken and seemingly degraded man who was nevertheless an impressive "man of intellect": "'My study is man,' said he. And, looking at me, 'I do not know your name,' he said, 'but there is something of the hawk-eye about you, too.'"

charge of egotistical self-absorption, brought against him seemingly because of his providing some biographical data in earlier prefaces, with the following words: "And, as for egotism, a person, who has been burrowing, to his utmost ability, into the depths of our common nature, for the purposes of psychological romance—and who pursues his researches in that dusky region, as he needs must, as well by the tact of sympathy as by the light of observation—will smile at incurring such an imputation."

Hawthorne realized of course that the pursuit of art, like many other pursuits in the sort of society which he was writing about and which, in this as in other respects, mildly foreshadowed the problems of our own day, could become an obsession, a means of isolation from the world rather than a mode of communication with it. When this happens, when art is unrelated to human sympathy, its "diabolism," always alleged in Hawthorne's stories, becomes a fact in Hawthorne's moral vision. This is true of "The Prophetic Pictures," the story in whose light alone we can accept Matthiessen's remark about Hawthorne's not being "wholly sympathetic with his artists."[14] The painter in this tale, a European portraitist, is presented as a man who evades his moral responsibility as a human being. There is, indeed, even a suggestion that he is not only a prophet of evil but almost its diabolical agent. But we must not forget that this particular artist is also, as we learn in the very opening paragraph, a "scientist" and an almost Chillingworthian scholar and willful recluse. Furthermore, if his art has become an obsessive pursuit it is because like "all other men around whom an engrossing purpose wreathes itself, he was insulated from the mass of human kind."

14. F. O. Matthiessen, *American Renaissance* (London, New York, Oxford University Press, 1941), p. 223. Matthiessen, it must be noted, goes on to say that in "The Artist of the Beautiful" "Hawthorne made a more sympathetic sketch of the creative temperament."

What is condemned here, then, is not art but the insular tendency in man which even his being a gifted artist cannot wholly justify. However, before turning to Hawthorne's other artists and their role in the drama of solitude and society, it might be helpful to see how art enters, if it enters at all, into some of the stories I have already discussed. Bewley, in his eagerness to make Ethan Brand an artist, sees in the dioramist of that story an extension of Brand, as guilty as Brand himself of the unpardonable sin. Now, insofar as the dioramist has anything to do with the unpardonable sin, it is to carry a representation of it in his box and not its reality in his own heart. And, insofar as he is an artist, his function, like that of Shakespeare, is merely to hold the mirror up to nature, and thereby to reveal to Ethan Brand the true image of the latter's sin: the image perhaps of that barren emptiness which is the share of those who have lost their sense of community with mankind. But art itself is not malignant because it pictures malignity. On the contrary, in "Rappaccini's Daughter" it is actually the proffered antidote to science, because, as one remembers, the potion with which Baglioni seeks to restore the lovers is contained in an exquisitely made silver vase which "was wrought by the hands of the renowned Benvenuto Cellini," and which is, unlike Rappaccini's gift of deadly power, "well worthy to be a love gift." Nor must we forget that Roderick Elliston of "Egotism," when freed of his intolerable alienation, makes the symbolic gesture of writing a story. This is in the nature of an effort of understanding which completes his redemption, for in his story ("The Christmas Banquet") he acknowledges finally, by means of a creative act, the misery of isolation and the community of man even in misery. Roderick's development is thus the reverse of Ethan Brand's, and he becomes an "artist" when he ceases to be a cold egoist and turns instead into a sympathetic observer of other human beings.

It is indeed clear that we must make a distinction among Hawthorne's tales of isolated men and not confuse them in a single interpretative thesis. In his drama of solitude and society, the solitary man is not always the villain. The critical scales often turn the other way—as happens in most tales of the artist. If to lose hold of "the magnetic chain of humanity" is to fall into the unpardonable sin, for the exceptional man— the man of unusual gifts, of imagination, of high sensitivity— conformity to certain kinds of society promises a sort of spiritual death. This is precisely the dilemma of Hawthorne's artists. They live in a society which combines the Puritan mistrust of art with the emphasis on practicality and utility of both the early New England code and latter-day American life. It is a society in which the artist has no recognized place unless it be the one traditionally reserved for the Black Man. Nor is the general drabness of life conducive to artistic inspiration. The single occasion in Drowne's life when he ceases to be a mechanical woodcarver and becomes a real artist is provided when a noble Portuguese lady in exile, whose statue he is commissioned to carve, adds a touch of color to the routine dreariness of the town. As Copley, the painter, says to Drowne: "No wonder that she inspired a genius into you, and first created the artist who afterwards created her image." Hawthorne's own comment is that "in every human spirit there is imagination, sensibility, creative power, genius, which, according to circumstances, may either be developed in this world, or shrouded in a mask of dulness until another state of being." But the comment of the "Puritan of the old stamp" on Drowne's solitary artistic experience is different. "One thing is certain," he observes, "Drowne has sold himself to the devil."

In Drowne's world, as in that of Owen Warland, artistic activity is incompatible with the popular conception of social utility. The latter is dominated by Peter Hovenden, the practical man of "unimaginative sagacity, by contact with which everything was converted into a dream except the densest matter of the physical world." Hawthorne dramatized the conflict between the rival claims of art and practical utility, not only by pitting his artists against the demands of society but by placing the conflict in the center of the protagonist's own divided life. His artists, unlike those of James, are hardly ever artists only. Almost all of them have claims to a more useful occupation. Oberon of "The Devil in Manuscript" is training to be a lawyer. The painter of "The Prophetic Pictures" belongs outwardly to the recognized and lucrative profession of portrait painting and is, in that capacity, accepted as a perfectly respectable member of society. Owen Warland is a watchmaker as well as an "artist of the beautiful," and Drowne carves figureheads for seagoing vessels. The hero's choice is thus immediately personal. He can either follow the true bent of his genius and face excommunication or he can conform to the accepted code of utility and remain "shrouded in a mask of dulness until another state of being." Drowne, of course, continues to make mechanically decorative images after his one triumphant artistic achievement. But Owen Warland, who insists on devoting himself to his vision, loses the regard of Peter Hovenden, the retired watchmaker, the love of Hovenden's daughter, and finally also the product of his art.

Thus a certain kind of isolation is the necessary fate of the artist, in the world of Hawthorne's fiction as in his own world. It is not willfully sought but it is inevitably incurred. Hawthorne, however, saw in art itself the true answer to this dilemma. Art could be a form of communion without conformity, a means of remaining true to one's spiritual and artistic vision without divorcing oneself from "the magnetic chain of humanity." For what makes people cease "to partake of the universal throb" is not physical isolation but spiritual coldness, while art is based upon human sympathies and is thus an expression of one's otherwise unestablished relation with the community. We know that writing fiction was Hawthorne's own attempt, as he puts it in the preface to *Twice-Told Tales*, "to open an intercourse with the world." We can say the same of Owen Warland, since, after his rejection by the world, it is his art which saves him from the disintegrating sense of alienation. The artistic impulse itself is reawakened in him by his sympathy for nature and spiritually sustained by his love for Annie. Moreover, although she has turned him down and although he is aware that "the world, and Annie as the representative of the world" will never fittingly appreciate his artifact, it is for her and for her world that he fashions it and it is to them that he finally offers it.

What one has to realize, then, is that in Hawthorne the artist is isolated by society rather than alienated from humanity. If the painter of "The Prophetic Pictures" is condemned, as Drowne and Owen Warland are not, it is because he is cold and obsessed and not because he is an artist. What leads to damnation is not isolation by itself but isolation which ends in the warping of human sympathies. The artists are damned by a narrow-minded and utilitarian society only, whereas the truly damned characters are the obsessed— the bigoted zealot, the cold egotist, the man who lusts for power, the exploiter of human souls—those people, in short, whose obsessions have supplanted their sympathies.

Escaping the nightmare of a totally alienated existence through love of woman, by means of a place in the family community, and, for individuals of imagination, through the sympathy of art—these are the themes of the stories that I have considered so far. They are aspects of one major theme of community. With regard to the enforced isolation of the artists, it is perhaps worth while to cite Hawthorne's comment in the Notebook for 1840 upon the long period of his own retired life: "And now I begin to understand why I was imprisoned so many years in this lonely chamber, and why I could never break through the viewless bolts and bars; for if I had sooner made my escape into the world, I should have grown hard and rough, and been covered with earthly dust, and my heart might have become callous by rude encounters with the multitude." It is a remarkable comment on the actual society of men that isolation from it should be the only means available to the sensitive individual for protecting his integrity, and that for him there should be no way of acknowledging his sense of community with mankind except through art. It is indeed the picture of a society without any essential sense of community, a society whose deepest drives are the isolating ones. Against these forces, Hawthorne's imagination reacted by exploring the inescapable community of man at all imaginable levels of human experience, often at the level of its lowest common denominators. In a Notebook entry for 1836 he outlined a plan for a "new classification of society" whereby human beings, instead of being divided into "rich and poor, high and low," were to be classified on the basis of sorrow, disease, and sin. "Then proceed to generalize and classify the whole world together, as none can claim utter exemption from either sorrow, sin, or disease; and if they could, yet Death, like a great parent, comes and sweeps them all through one darksome portal—all his children."

The Reverend Leonard J. Fick, writing on "Hawthorne's Theology," very correctly points out that in this passage Hawthorne "fails to distinguish between sin and disease, or between sin and sorrow."[15] But Hawthorne was not thinking of doctrinal accuracy when he wrote it. Here, as elsewhere, he made use of certain universal categories to show how, in the face of the ultimate forces of life, all men are bound

15. Leonard J. Fick, *The Light Beyond: A Study of Hawthorne's Theology* (Westminster, Maryland, Newman Press, 1955), p. 77.

together by their common weakness. Although he never wrote one single story with this germ for a plan, we can see the ideas developed in three separate stories: "Lady Eleanore's Mantle," "The Christmas Banquet," and "Young Goodman Brown." Sorrow is the bond which unites the miserable guests in "The Christmas Banquet" and unites also the banqueters of one year with those of the succeeding years. These people are miserable enough, but the truly miserable man, the guest who seems apparently happy but who appears year after year, is the one who can feel nothing, not even sorrow, and who is thus excluded from companionship even in this "mystic fraternity." In "Young Goodman Brown" sin is the basis of a universal communion from which neither priest, nor governor, nor any ordinary man or woman—not Faith herself to whom Brown is wedded—can claim exemption. "Welcome, my children," says the majestic figure of Satan to Brown and Faith, "to the communion of your race. Ye have found thus young your nature and your destiny." Communion of the human race is precisely what Lady Eleanore, the English noblewoman, denies: "She seeks to place herself above the sympathies of our common nature," as Doctor Clarke says, "which envelops all human souls. See, if that nature do not assert its claim over her in some mode that shall bring her level with the lowest!" This leveling claim of nature turns out to be disease. When she arrives in America, her first action is to step over the prostrate form of Jervase Helwyse, who loves her and of whom she thus makes a footrest while she extends her hand to the governor: "and never, surely, was there an apter emblem of aristocracy and hereditary pride trampling on human sympathies and the kindred of nature, than these two figures presented at that moment." Jervase Helwyse appears before her again at the governor's ball, and, in a final attempt to save her from inevitable retribution, offers her a goblet of wine, begging her at the same time "to take one sip of this holy wine, and then to pass the goblet round among the guests. And this shall be a symbol that you have not sought to withdraw yourself from the chain of human sympathies." But, disdaining the communion cup, Lady Eleanore wraps herself the more closely in her gorgeous mantle "so as almost to shroud herself within it." It is this same mantle, the symbol of her pride, which becomes also the means of humbling it, for it has been embroidered by a London seamstress dying of smallpox. It becomes the source of the plague which, spreading in all directions, compels "rich and poor to feel themselves brethren then," and death indeed, as Hawthorne had said in his Notebook, makes all men his equal children.

In Hawthorne, thus, as in the elder Henry James, the sense of community is to be established precisely where it is denied —in the deepest consciousness of the individual. Visionaries and moralists of a society which claimed freedom from all external and repressive institutions, their focus falls inevitably on individual regeneration. But was the moral transformation whereby man recognized his fellowship with man destined to occur only in the extreme situations of intolerable alienation, grief, and death? Could society not be altered so that this sense would operate in normal circumstances, attitudes, and relationships? In other words, was it possible to achieve a regenerated community this side of paradise? Hawthorne explored the possibility in two great novels. But it also enters the theme of some of his tales. For instance, "Earth's Holocaust" describes the execution of a great program to purify the world by fire—"whether in the time past or time to come is a matter of little or no moment." In a huge bonfire lit on one of the broadest prairies of the West are flung heraldic devices, crowns and coats-of-arms, royal parchments and patents—all that "species of nonsense [which] has fairly lived out its life." It is the sort of nonsense indeed which was the source of Lady

Eleanore's pride and from which America had freed herself. The reformers then proceed to destroy the symbols of all the other existing institutions: marriage licenses, the gallows, Bibles, armaments, and even the accumulated literature of the past. But, as the narrator's grave companion says, "there is far less both of good and evil in the effect of this bonfire than the world might be willing to believe." For, as someone observes when arms and ammunitions are being consigned to destruction, "When Cain wished to slay his brother, he was at no loss for a weapon." Indeed, no amount of external reformation can create a regenerated society unless the change involves a comparable moral transformation. Unless, says Satan exultingly, speaking of the human heart, "unless they hit upon some method of purifying that foul cavern, forth from it will reissue all the shapes of wrong and misery—the same old shapes or worse ones—which they have taken such a vast deal of trouble to consume to ashes. I have stood by this livelong night and laughed in my sleeve at the whole business. Oh, take my word for it, it will be the old world yet!"

The new world does not have to be physically new. The scene for it need not be an untouched Arcadia. Nor does every spotless Arcadian scene promise a new beginning for humanity. Hawthorne believed that an altered moral consciousness was the key to a change in human relationships, and that transformation in human relationships was, in turn, the only secure index of social transformation. Thus in "The New Adam and Eve," reversing the usual schema of utopian fantasy, he does not place his characters on an undiscovered land but inducts them into a world where the Day of Doom has destroyed all traces of human life but left undisturbed "the abodes of man, and all that he has accomplished, the footprints of his wanderings and the results of his toil, the visible symbols of his intellectual cultivation and moral progress—in short, everything physical that can give evidence of his present position." In other words, the new Adam and Eve are not our representatives translated into a novel setting, but rather new human beings coming to terms with our own familiar surroundings; and if Hawthorne conceives of them as the prospective progenitors of a new humanity, it is because they represent a new relationship, based upon love, and a new consciousness which is burdened neither with the old sense of sin nor with the spirit that underlies trade, speculation, acquisitiveness, and other manifestations of "the world's artificial system."

In reading *The Scarlet Letter* it is necessary to remember that this is a book about and not of seventeenth-century New England. There is a danger, that is to say, of confusing the subject of the novel with the novelist's attitude, especially because the latter involves an irony which often assumes the innocent guise of approval. In many ways Hawthorne was undoubtedly the heir of the Puritan tradition, but he was also one of its severest critics.[16] His criticism, more searching and sustained than that of Fenimore Cooper before him, has at times the damaging effectiveness, without the invective, of the Smart Set's guerrilla attacks in the twentieth century. For instance, his comment on the portraits in Governor Bellingham's house—"as if they were the ghosts, rather than the pictures, of departed worthies, and were gazing with harsh and intolerant criticism at the pursuits and enjoyments of living men"—recalls Mencken's quick-fire definition of

16. Insofar as Hawthorne's personal attitudes are relevant here, one can compare the following statement, reportedly made by him shortly before his death, with the traditional Puritan austerity: "Why has the good old custom of coming together to get drunk gone out? Think of the delight of drinking in pleasant company and then lying down to sleep a deep strong sleep." (M. A. De Wolfe Howe, *Memories of a Hostess*, Boston, Atlantic Monthly Press, 1922, p. 63.) One can look at the statement perhaps as the dying allegorist's parable of the good life as an interlude of cheerful companionship before total oblivion.

Puritanism as "the haunting fear that someone, somewhere may be happy."[17] One can also see in the description of the Puritan children's two favorite pastimes of playing at going to church and scalping Indians, a parallel to the jest that the Pilgrim Fathers first fell upon their knees and then upon the aborigines. Unlike Cooper, Hawthorne never made the fate of the Indians his theme, but all the same, like the older writer, he felt and often expressed a sense of compassion for the depredations suffered by that race. To take the most striking example, this feeling enters poignantly the account of the history of American civilization, as Hawthorne gives it in "Main Street," finding a climax in the terse observation: "The pavements of the Main Street must be laid over the red man's grave." The same sketch, however, offers the well-known and more balanced statement of Hawthorne's attitude toward the American Puritans: "Let us thank God for having given us such ancestors; and let each successive generation thank Him, not less fervently, for being one step further from them in the march of ages."

Hawthorne himself was several thankful generations away from the Pilgrim Fathers. Actually he lived in the same generation with Emerson. But to state in this manner the distance that separates him from the subject of his novel can be misleading. Unlike Emerson, he was not cut off from the Puritans by the impassable peak of a novel and exciting theory of the cosmos. Nor did he view them as Cooper did—across the limitless spaces of the Hudson River. His attitude toward his subject suggests a complex relation rather than an intractable and artistically sterile distance. On account of his personal temperament, his artistic sensibility, and his family history, he could approach the seventeenth century as an insider, retaining at the same time the outsider's ability and freedom to

17. H. L. Mencken and George Jean Nathan, "Clinical Notes," *American Mercury*, 4 (1925), 59.

judge and evaluate. Like so many great works of literature—
Arthur Koestler's *Darkness at Noon* is a notable modern
example—*The Scarlet Letter* is a searching criticism of the
world with which it deals precisely because it takes its stand
firmly within that world.

Consider, for example, the central fact around which Hawthorne builds the curious pattern of his novel. The all-
pervasive sense of sin is as important here as it was in the life
and thought of the first Puritans. But we must not forget on
the other hand that the artist who evokes it is a man of
radically different sympathies, the author, among other
things, of "The New Adam and Eve." There is a passage in
this story which it is worth while to cite in detail because it
provides an explicit statement of the attitude that shapes the
moral action of *The Scarlet Letter*. I am referring to the passage where, during their puzzled wandering through the land-
marks of old humanity, the precursors of the new order arrive
at an edifice which is described as both a prison and a
hospital, serving as an emblem of that attitude of punitive
correction toward sinners which was the hallmark of Puritan
polity. The prisonhouse is now deserted because the Day of
Judgment has swept all human beings from the face of the
earth and "a new trial has been granted in a higher court
which may set judge, jury, and prisoner at its bar all in a row,
and perhaps find one no less guilty than another." The new
Adam and Eve, "so fresh from their Creator's hand," stand
baffled before the mystery of this edifice. They have no means
of discovering that it was

a hospital for the direst disease which could afflict their
predecessors. Its patients bore the outward marks of that
leprosy with which all were more or less infected. They
were sick—and so were the purest of their brethren—
with the plague of sin. A deadly sickness, indeed! Feeling

175

its symptoms within the breast, men concealed it with fear and shame, and were only the more cruel to those unfortunates whose pestiferous sores were flagrant to the common eye. Nothing save a rich garment could ever hide the plague spot. In the course of the world's lifetime, every remedy was tried for its cure and extirpation except the single one, the flower that grew in heaven and was sovereign for all the miseries of earth. Man never had attempted to cure sin by Love. Had he but once made the effort it might well have happened that there would have been no more need of the dark lazar house into which Adam and Eve have wandered.

This direct authorial comment can serve as a preface to Hawthorne's image of seventeenth-century New England society in *The Scarlet Letter*. One can, moreover, see the age to which such a comment belongs by setting beside it the following statement from Emerson's "Man the Reformer": "This great, overgrown, dead Christendom of ours still keeps alive at least the name of a lover of mankind. But one day all men will be lovers; and every calamity will be dissolved in the universal sunshine." Of course, the effectiveness of Hawthorne's novel arises not from any general doctrine but from the rich particularity with which he explores a definite historical phase of society as well as the fate of individuals in it. It is characteristic of his temper and times again, however, that he should set out on his evaluation of the Puritan settlement by conceding its importance as a utopian experiment. "The founders of a new colony," we read on the first page of the novel, "whatever utopia of human virtue and happiness they might originally project, have invariably recognized it among their earliest practical necessities to allot a portion of the virgin soil as a cemetery, and another portion as the site of a prison."

This seeming concession, however, strikes also the first note of Hawthorne's criticism. The prison in the action of the novel, as in "The New Adam and Eve," being a place for the correction of sinners, the point of Hawthorne's irony in linking it with the cemetery is not to deny the belief in the inevitability of sin but rather to endorse it, and thereby to focus his concern wholly on the problem of human response to this central fact of life. Here as elsewhere, then, Hawthorne is using Puritan metaphysics as a basis for the criticism of Puritan ethics. What *The Scarlet Letter* calls in question is a scheme of regeneration which on the one hand allots to sin the universal status of death and on the other reserves for it the special shame of the prisonhouse. In this novel, as much as in *The Blithedale Romance*, Hawthorne does not oppose the given theory by an alternative theory of his own. His method in each case is to make the theory double up on itself by proposing to it the test of a crucial human situation which falls well within its assumptions. *L'affaire Hester* becomes thus the appropriate test for seventeenth-century New England: the case of a fallen woman brought before the tribunal of a community which believes all humanity fallen. One does not have to go to "Young Goodman Brown" to see the critical use Hawthorne makes of the Puritan belief in universal sin. Toward the end of *The Scarlet Letter*, he observes that Dimmesdale's dying in the arms of a sinful woman had struck his admirers as a noble gesture, a way of demonstrating to the world "how utterly nugatory is the choicest of man's own righteousness," a parable enacted by the man of God to impress on the people "the mighty and mournful lesson, that, in the view of Infinite Purity, we are sinners all alike." But the incredulity of these witnesses with regard to the true nature of Dimmesdale's action is not surprising, for, as Hawthorne says earlier in the novel: "The sainted minister in the church! The woman of the scarlet letter in the market-place! What imagination would have been irreverent enough to surmise that the same scorching stigma was on them both!" The irony of the situation is that the noble parable of theory should be the shameful fact of life, that the obvious implications of the lesson should be so disregarded in practice, and that the divine insight into the impossibility of human righteousness should lead not to a sense of humility but to bigoted self-righteousness and moral blindness.

Nor does the bond of sin extend only to the chief personages in the drama. It unites likewise all the members of the community. "Had Hester sinned alone?" Hawthorne asks in chapter 5, and goes on to describe how, though she struggles against such mysterious power, Hester's experience has given her the ability to recognize fellow sinners instinctively, and how, in token of such recognition, the emblem of sin on her bosom throbs sympathetically in the presence of magistrate, minister, sanctified matron, and spotless maiden alike. Hawthorne's criticism, at times muted and at others rising into open denunciation and satire, is directed fundamentally against the denial of this innate sense of human communion. If sin is the postulated basis of life, should its open manifestation be treated with understanding and compassion or with inhuman chastisement? The answer of the Puritan community to this question—posed concretely in their midst by Hester—is to put her upon the pillory, to make her bear permanently the stigma of her shame, and finally to excommunicate her. The most terrible part, the truly inhuman aspect, of Hester's fate is not that she is punished publicly but that her punishment takes the form of isolating her from the rest of the community. Even while she is standing in the center of the crowd in the marketplace, the letter A has "the effect of a spell, taking her out of the ordinary relations with humanity, and enclosing her in a sphere by herself."

The Scarlet Letter presents thus a highly complex variation on Hawthorne's general theme of human isolation and human community. In the drama of society and solitude which is enacted here, there is no doubt about the side on which the novel aligns our sympathies. Hester Prynne's isolation is inflicted upon her rather than willfully sought by her; and if it does not warp her moral personality, the reason is that she seeks throughout her life to re-establish a relationship with other human beings on a new and more honest basis—in other words, she is isolated by society but not alienated from humanity. The blame for her tragic predicament falls heavily on the Puritan arbiters of her destiny. Even in terms of their own stern theory of sin, her excommunication, if one uses the metaphor of "The New Adam and Eve," amounts to the banishment of a leper from a leper colony. But in reality the author's judgment of Hester is very different from that of the Puritan community. While not disputing the sinfulness of her deed, he presents her also as a source of new life and moral vitality and as a woman of the tenderest human sympathies in a cold and intolerant society. He provides her adultery with a background of long bondage in a loveless marriage, and invests the passion which leads to it with "a consecration of its own."

Hawthorne, in fact, uses the very symbol with which society identifies Hester, as a means of reversing its view of her. To the Puritans, with their allegorical habit of mind and their interpretation of life as though it were a Morality play, the meaning of the A is clear. But not so to a humane critic of the Puritan view of life. In an allegory the hidden meaning is easy to discover; indeed it is the allegory itself which superficially conceals it. The purpose of allegory is to strengthen, by an exercise of fancy, the received doctrine and the shared moral code. Symbols, on the contrary, put accepted meanings into doubt, introduce new ones, and finally create a radically different alignment of sympathies. Thus, while Hester

179

becomes the sympathetic heroine of the novel, the society which persecutes her is revealed as not only bigoted and joyless but essentially evil; for to it belongs, equally with Chillingworth but without Chillingworth's personal justification, the unpardonable sin of violating in cold blood the sanctity of a human heart. Such indeed is the moral import of the inquisitorial scenes in the marketplace where the entire community has assembled to make a public spectacle of Hester's private sin. The iron-visaged good women of the settlement pour malice and abuse on her. The grim beadle, who leads her to the pillory through the remorseless crowd, calls down a "blessing on the righteous Colony of the Massachusetts, where iniquity is dragged out into the sunshine!" And, as for the governor, the magistrates, and the ministers, "out of the whole human family, it would not have been easy to select the same number of wise and virtuous persons, who should be less capable of sitting in judgment on an erring woman's heart, and disentangling its mesh of good and evil, than the sages of rigid aspect towards whom Hester Prynne now turned her face. She seemed conscious, indeed, that whatever sympathy she might expect lay in the larger and warmer heart of the multitude." Not one of these judges sees any virtue in her refusal to reveal the name of her lover. Even the kindly old John Wilson berates this token of her loyalty as unregenerate hardness and obstinacy; while the unrecognized lover himself, with curious moral hypocrisy, calls upon her from his elevated stand with the other dignitaries, to denounce the companion of her sin and not deny to him "the bitter, but wholesome, cup that is now presented to thy lips!" The effect of the scene—of its cruelty and the general absence of pity and understanding in it—is heightened rather than dispelled by the occasional soft words of the young mother, the one sympathetic observer in the hostile crowd, who tries ineffectually to remind her neighbors that Hester's suffering does not need this added inhumanity to make it an adequate atonement for her sin.

Here, then, planted at the outset of the novel, is Hawthorne's image of New England society, a society which claimed to have based itself on the highest principles of moral idealism but which turns out at the first test to be utterly lacking in the elementary Christian virtues of love and compassion. Its program of regeneration is in reality a mask for repression, and its intolerance and bigotry are worse than those of the European society from which it has, on that very account, separated itself. What its rulers seek assiduously is not the establishment of a republic of brotherly love but rather ruthless power over men. Their hypocrisy, the consequence of the wide divergence between their ideals and the practical aims of their enterprise, is insinuated everywhere, most strikingly in the contrast between the Puritan profession of austerity and the magnificence of the governor's residence which "might have befitted Aladdin's palace, rather than the mansion of a grave old Puritan ruler." Rich garments too are "readily allowed to individuals dignified by rank or wealth, even while sumptuary laws forbade these and similar extravagances to the plebeian order." This is indeed not the proclaimed city upon the hill—the refuge and sanctuary of oppressed generations and the future hope of mankind. On the contrary, the true hope of humanity lies in seeking refuge from rather than in it. "Begin all anew!" as Hester urges Dimmesdale in the forest. "Hast thou exhausted possibility in the failure of this one trial? Not so! The future is yet full of trial and success. There is happiness to be enjoyed! There is good to be done! Exchange this false life of thine for a true one."

The challenge to break away from organized society is there in Hawthorne as much as in Cooper. It provides the backbone of the dramatic conflict in *The Scarlet Letter*. That this challenge is not successfully executed is due to what one can only

call Hawthorne's greater historical and psychological realism
—a realism which recognizes that the protagonists, Dimmesdale particularly, are themselves encumbered with the spirit
of that same society against which they find themselves in
rebellion. This is a tragic novel which ends in failure, waste,
and death but which, like all true tragedies, affirms the very
values that go down in defeat. The moral victory belongs to
Hester. The future she talks about so passionately in the
passage I have cited above is of course primarily her own
domestic future. But nevertheless she comes to understand
that such a future is intimately connected with the future of
the whole society, and that true relationships cannot exist in
the family unless they are also established in the civil community at large.

Hester's unavailing attempt to reconstruct her life forms
the substance of the novel's action after her banishment from
society. Although she is free to leave the colony altogether,
she does not do so, but instead takes her stand at the farthest
edge of the settlement. The reason for this, as given in chapter
5, is twofold. In the first place, while society has cast her off,
she herself has not lost hold of the magnetic chain of
humanity: "The chain that bound her here was of iron links,
and galling to her inmost soul, but could never be broken."
The deeper reason—the reason which, with her own consciousness of sin, she trembles to acknowledge even to herself
—lies in the more intimate bond of love. "There dwelt, there
trode the feet of one with whom she deemed herself connected
in a union, that, unrecognized on earth, would bring them together before the bar of final judgment." Her relationship
with the civil community is perforce of a marginal character.
Being an outcast, and with her own judgment of society's
institutions, she neither seeks nor is allowed a full place in it.
Whether as a skillful embroiderer or a sister of mercy
at scenes of grief and misfortune, her attitude is one of

unobtrusive and undemanding sympathy. She is charitable to all alike, though, as Hawthorne says, the recipients of her kindness often bit the hand from which they received it.

By far the more interesting part of the novel, however, deals with the story within the story: the drama of broken family relationships within the larger drama of the protagonist's relation to society. The remarkable thing about the structure of *The Scarlet Letter* is the controlled integration of these two aspects of the theme, and the manner in which it connects the dominant principles of one sphere with the failure of human relationship in the other. The broken circuit of the family community thus reflects the absence of the magnetic chain of love and compassion in the civil community. The inner drama itself is accordingly enacted on two different scenes: the public stage of the marketplace and the more private one of the forest; the uniformly spaced actions on the scaffold of the pillory paralleling the short, consecutive chapters which describe first Hester and Pearl, then Hester and Dimmesdale, and finally all three together in the primeval woods. Of the two characters intimately bound up with Hester, Arthur Dimmesdale, the key figure in the tragedy of her personal life, is wholly committed to the public order which has banished her; while Pearl, the born outcast of society, owns no allegiance except to the private law of family affections. Between themselves they represent the two sides of the heroine's tragically divided world. It is a conflict whose development makes Pearl the final judgment on Dimmesdale and the society to which he belongs, even as she finally becomes the one solace of Hester's life. To Hester herself comes not happiness but the gift of understanding through pain and suffering.

During the first pillory scene, Pearl, true to the law which has brought her into existence, holds up her hand plaintively toward Dimmesdale, who, removed from the mother and child, is ensconced upon the seat of judgment. If in the conflict thus dramatized the minister is disloyal to the family community, it is not entirely from fear of the social establishment. His cowardice—the "anguish of pusillanimity," as Henry James calls it[18]—arises rather from the workings of the Puritan order within his own consciousness. His sense of personal sin is overwhelming to the point of moral blindness. By keeping him from joining Hester and Pearl on the public scaffold, it leads him to add hypocrisy and falseness to sin. In him we find again that morbid concern with self, that unrighteous egotism, which evades all issues of human responsibility by subtly transferring them to some clandestine register maintained between God and the individual soul. "He thus typified the constant introspection wherewith he tortured, but could not purify, himself." Because he is false to his primary social duty, because he is oblivious of his duty to Hester and Pearl—because, in short, he has withdrawn into himself and lost hold of the chain of human relationships—his is the inevitable fate reserved for such action in Hawthorne's universe: the whole world seems to him false, even nonexistent, and he himself "becomes a shadow, or, indeed, ceases to exist."

It is to escape the torture of such feeling that Dimmesdale ascends the pillory one night under cover of darkness. When Hester and Pearl join him and the three stand holding hands, it seems as if "the mother and the child were communicating their vital warmth to his half-torpid system. The three formed an electric chain." However, "subtle, but remorseful hypocrite" that he is, he knows that his action will remain as hidden from the world as his sin. Being committed so deeply to the society from which he is hiding his true self, there can be no

18. Henry James, "Nathaniel Hawthorne," *Library of the World's Best Literature*, ed. Charles Dudley Warner (New York, R. S. Peale and J. A. Hill, 1897), *12*, 7056.

redemption for him unless his confession is as public as Hester's had been earlier. "Thou wast not bold!—thou wast not true!" as Pearl mockingly reminds him. "Thou wouldst not promise to take my hand, and mother's hand, to-morrow noontide!"

This is the background one must keep in mind while approaching the magnificent forest scenes in the novel. Hester's action in seeking an interview with Dimmesdale is prompted primarily by her concern for his almost complete disintegration. Her compassion and loyalty, her taking the blame for his wretchedness upon herself, are in sharp contrast with his total self-absorption. She is compassionate even to Chillingworth who, it must be said, rewards her at least with ample understanding and a certain measure of sympathy. However, although her initial purpose is only to acquaint her lover with the true identity of Roger Chillingworth, the manner in which these scenes develop—and the human challenge that is developed with them—makes *The Scarlet Letter* a tragedy rather than simply a tale of unrelieved suffering. It is here too that Hester attains the full stature of a tragic heroine, who suffers, to be sure, but suffers with spirit and not entirely without hope. Her courage and vitality revive Dimmesdale from his long period of spiritual and moral numbness. With the insight and freedom she has so painfully won, she succeeds in relieving her lover from the torture of his morbid apprehensions, both of this world and the next, and in showing him the true path to redemption. "Heaven would show mercy," she says, "hadst thou but the strength to take advantage of it." And, as for the dreaded settlement and the men of iron who inhabit it: "Is the world, then, so narrow?" There is the pathless wilderness or the broad pathway of the sea—either of which will lead them to a new freedom.

The important thing here is to realize how fully the novel aligns our sympathies with Hester, and how completely it endorses, as a means of both heavenly and earthly redemption, her plan of withdrawing from the stern Puritan colony. As soon as the decision is made, Dimmesdale feels an unaccustomed sense of exhilaration, while Hester's beauty reappears in all its oriental splendor.

> And, as if the gloom of the earth and sky had been but the effluence of these two mortal hearts, it vanished with their sorrow. All at once, as with a sudden smile of heaven, forth burst the sunshine, pouring a very flood into the obscure forest, gladdening each green leaf, transmuting the yellow fallen ones to gold, and gleaming adown the gray trunks of the solemn trees. The objects that had made a shadow hitherto, embodied the brightness now. The course of the little brook might be traced by its merry gleam afar into the wood's heart of mystery, which had become a mystery of joy.

It is interesting to read this scene in the light of Emerson's statement (quoted earlier) contrasting dead Christendom with the universal sunshine of love. Nor must we forget the metaphorical meaning of sunshine in Hawthorne's own tales: its association with eternity in "The Minister's Black Veil" and, in "Egotism," its being the type of "the radiance of the Creator's face, expressing his love for all the creatures of his hand."

The ambiguity of Hawthorne's treatment of the forest reflects, as in the case of the scarlet A, the divergence between possible attitudes toward it. In itself, as is obvious from the passage quoted above, it possesses no predetermined character, either for good or for evil. It is a moral *tabula rasa*. As Hawthorne says a little later while speaking of Pearl: "The great black forest—stern as it showed itself to those who brought the guilt and troubles of the world into its bosom— became the playmate of the lonely infant, as well as it knew how." To the Puritans it appears undoubtedly a dark and gloomy place, but that is only a reflection of their own confined and joyless view of life, for, as Hawthorne says in an earlier chapter in describing Pearl's fanciful personification of natural objects to people her solitary existence: "The pine-trees, aged, black, and solemn, and flinging groans and other melancholy utterances on the breeze, needed little transformation to figure as Puritan elders." To the lovers, on the other hand, the forest provides a blissful prospect of refuge, just as the brook, mournful under the shade of Puritan gloom, symbolizes to them the joyful mystery of life.

The lawless wilderness is thus lawless only insofar as it is beyond the reach of the established law. To the little family community seeking to flee the intolerant Puritan society, it is what it had earlier been to the Puritans themselves: a haven of freedom and the possibility of starting a new life. That Hester and Dimmesdale finally choose the other alternative, the alternative of going back to the comparative freedom which even the Old World offers, is because in view of Dimmesdale's weak health they judge it more suitable than the hazardous task of working among the Indians in the wilderness. But the possibility of escape remains only a possibility. And it is just as well: to start a new life in the world there must first be born a new moral consciousness. Hester and Dimmesdale are far from being the Adam and Eve of a new order. Dimmesdale belongs wholly to the faith whose "pressure" is essential to his peace, "supporting, while it confined him within its iron framework." Unlike Hester, he has not undergone any "experience calculated to lead him beyond the scope of generally received laws . . . At the head of the social system, as the clergymen of that day stood, he was only the more trammelled by its regulations, its principles, and even its prejudices." He certainly is not the man to take advantage of either Heaven's or Hester's proffered mercy. The challenge of her plan, for all his temporary sense of exhilaration and freedom, has in effect a further disintegrating influence upon him. In contrast with her revived hope and firm dignity, his behavior during the walk back to the settlement is that of a man whose outlook on life has been not altered but merely unsettled. After years of sanctimonious piety he suddenly lapses into needless and blasphemous profanity. When Hester sees him again after the secret interview, he has reverted to his old self. Marching at the head of the procession, "he seemed so remote from her own sphere, and utterly beyond her reach . . . so unattainable in his worldly position, and still more so in that far vista of his unsympathizing thoughts, through which she now beheld him! Her spirit sank with the idea that all must have been a delusion, and that, vividly as she had dreamed it, there could be no real bond betwixt the clergyman and herself." The one thought of "this exemplary man," wholly self-absorbed again, is to preach the Election Sermon so well that the world may say of him ever after that he left "no public duty unperformed, nor ill performed!" In short, after resolving, like Huckleberry Finn, to go to hell rather than desert his loyalty to the private world—which is also his foremost moral duty—Dimmesdale returns piously to die on the public and well-beaten road to heaven.

The Scarlet Letter is a profound comment on the breakdown of human relationships in the society of the seventeenth century—a society which perhaps carried the seed of the dislocations more readily observable in our own. The force of individualism, which exerted itself on many spheres of experience, was at once its special glory and the cause of alienating man from man in it. Moreover, whether or not it was the age of dissociated sensibility, as presented in *The Scarlet Letter*, it reveals the beginnings of a disintegration in the individual psyche: a tendency for the life of the body, the mind, and the soul to fall apart, somewhat like the broken and isolated lives of Hester, Chillingworth, and Dimmesdale. There is in it a lack of that wholeness of life which Emerson took for his theme in "The American Scholar" and which has been noted more recently by W. B. Yeats in the following lines of his "Among School Children":

> Labour is blossoming or dancing where
> The body is not bruised to pleasure soul,
> Nor beauty born out of its own despair,
> Nor blear-eyed wisdom out of midnight oil.

It is a measure of Hawthorne's historical and psychological insight that he recognized that the effort to achieve a well-integrated community life in such a world must lead to tragedy. The social principles of the Puritans, laudable in their idealism, become in reality a travesty of Christian aspirations. Hester's attempt to achieve a more wholesome family community ends in failure. What is left at the conclusion of the novel is a vague hope that, with her father's public acknowledgment of her, the curse is lifted from Pearl's alienated existence, and that in some distant land she "would grow up amid human joy and sorrow, nor forever do battle with the world, but be a woman in it." She will realize, in other words, the future that Hester had dreamed of in her interview with Dimmesdale. As for the tragic heroine herself, she gains the understanding that love cannot come to fruition in a world divided against itself, that the fortunes of the family community are intimately bound up with the character of the civil community in which it exists, and that, for the full realization of human happiness: "As a first step, the whole system of society is to be torn down, and built up anew."

According to Hawthorne, then, the professed idealism of seventeenth-century Americans was finally irrelevant to their practical accomplishment. They were to be admired more for their driving and successful energy. Their purpose—the purpose to which they applied this energy—was not to establish a Commonwealth of brotherly love. It was to build edifices, of law and order as well as stone and mortar—the former more repressive than the ones they had left behind, the latter seeking to rival the remembered splendor of England, and both using the modes and materials of the Old World. This critical comment on the decisive beginnings of American civilization, marginally suggested in *The Scarlet Letter*, moves into the center of Hawthorne's second novel.

The House of the Seven Gables explores the cultural past of the country in economic terms. Here it is economic conflict, rather than the tension between sin and love, which divides the community and the family. Notwithstanding this difference in the main focus, however, Hawthorne's concern in either case is fundamentally ethical, and from this standpoint he suggests in both novels the underlying relation between the religious motivation and the economic drives of Puritan polity. If in *The Scarlet Letter* he takes time off to describe Governor Bellingham's mansion in ironic detail, in the later novel the history of the Pyncheon house, which now holds the center of the stage, has for its base a curiously mixed episode of religious persecution and material purpose. As Hawthorne presents it, the superstition about witchcraft is not only a part of the war against Satan in the New World, it is the convenient instrument of a covetous policy, and is used as such against Matthew Maule, the original owner of the envied plot of land and the plebeian adversary of Colonel Pyncheon who wants the site for his projected family mansion. When Maule is denounced as a wizard by the Puritan community, Colonel Pyncheon plays the foremost part in securing his execution, and such is the outcry fomented against the poor man that it seems "almost a religious act to drive the plough over the little area of his habitation." The dying wizard—defiant to the end—enjoys a revenge of sorts by shouting at his enemy the famous prophecy of doom: "God will give him blood to drink!"

The history of the cursed house, or the working out of Maule's curse in the fortunes of the Pyncheons over a period of two centuries, forms the narrative of the novel. Insofar as it represents an imaginative recreation of the history of American civilization, from the Puritanism of the seventeenth to the democracy of the nineteenth century, the remarkable thing about it is the manner in which Hawthorne sees it as a process of retribution stemming from some original moral lapse, an evil of continued potency though outwardly forgotten in the general run of prosperity. This can be interpreted of course as the transference of the idea of original sin from the spiritual to the temporal history of man. Nevertheless, it is worth while to note how closely Hawthorne's exploration of the history of the land parallels in this respect Cooper's preoccupation with the same subject in the Little-page Trilogy. In Cooper the original wrong, as I have attempted to establish, is the wrong done to Indians; whereas in *The Seven Gables* the wrongfully dispossessed man is the plebeian artisan rather than the colorful chieftain. Hawthorne, that is to say, deals with class from the outset, while Cooper, who begins with race, has to dress the expanding democratic challenge of the nineteenth century in Indian costume in order to make the point. The outline of moral action in either case, however, turns upon the sacrifice of idealistic principle to material expediency, and the devil in both is blind cupidity.

Maule's curse has the effect, among other things, of making the well of sweet water in the Pyncheon house hard and brackish, and generally of poisoning at the source the life-stream of the Pyncheon generations. His more substantial revenge, however, is that his numerous metaphorical progeny

—the lower orders of the rising democracy—take possession of the vast lands originally granted by patent to the Pyncheons' ancestor; and it reaches a triumphant climax when Holgrave, who is more literally Maule's lineal descendant, inherits, together with Phoebe, the Pyncheon estate itself. This story is, in other words, Hawthorne's parable of leveling democracy in America. One notices here again that in his drama of the American past the balancing factor is not the farther past of Europe but the future of America. This is not to say that the democratic development of the early nineteenth century engaged the full range of his sympathies or exhausted for him the whole prospect of possibilities. On the contrary, his attitude toward it is deeply ambivalent. Nor is this ambivalence a matter of hesitating between the Pyncheons and the Maules. It arises from Hawthorne's facing, or rather his not facing enough, the problem of the merged future of the Pyncheons and the Maules—the problem, in other words, of the future of democracy itself.

As between Hepzibah and Clifford on the one hand and Holgrave on the other, Hawthorne's artistic sympathies are divided, it is true, but not in a manner which leaves his meaning in doubt. In his own family history he could see both the ancestral elevation of the Pyncheons and the recent obscurity of the Maules who had lost themselves in the nameless crowd, "laboring on the wharves, or following the sea, as sailors before the mast." But he was a good democrat, and, unlike Cooper, he was not committed on personal grounds to uphold established privilege, whether of class or family, against the challenge of the times. Moreover, his sensibility responded firmly to all that is fresh and vigorous, and where Cooper saw advantage in hereditary status he recognized the possibility of decay. Thus, notwithstanding a certain measure of compassion for the broken lives of the abortive aesthete and his scowling sister, Hawthorne fully endorses the change in favor of Holgrave. Nor does he betray the moral force of his action, as Cooper does, by loading the dice against the Maules. He does not present the fabulous Pyncheon title to the Eastern lands as a sacred document, and he does not consider the Maules unprincipled villains because they ridicule "the idea of any man's asserting a right—on the strength of mouldy parchments, signed with the faded autographs of governors and legislators long dead and forgotten—to the lands which they or their fathers had wrested from the wild hand of nature by their own sturdy toil." To him this is not lawlessness, as it is to Cooper's Littlepages, but the development of democratic law. Where a similar recognition is obscured in Cooper by the special pleading of a case, Hawthorne makes his Pyncheons see the inevitability of their historical destiny and thus invests them with a spirit of tragic acquiescence. As Hepzibah, who has been reduced to the necessity of opening a grocery store, concludes after enumerating Holgrave's lawless ways and his "wild and disorganizing" views, "I suppose he has a law of his own!"

Hawthorne thus saw this democratic reversal of fortune as an inevitable and salutary change. He did not, however, regard it as the last word in social endeavor. It was more than just but less than millennial. His imagination had a curious way of simultaneously affirming and questioning the millennial possibilities of human life in this world. He countered skepticism with hope, and hope with criticism. To him the achievement of a perfect society, if possible at all, was possible only in an endlessly deferred future. Thus, as he says of Holgrave: "As to the main point,—may we never live to doubt it!—as to the better centuries that are coming, the artist was surely right. His error lay in supposing that this age, more than any past or future one, is destined to see the tattered garments of Antiquity exchanged for a new suit." It was this very claim of renewal, or regeneration, on the part of the

193

Puritan past, which Hawthorne had tested in *The Scarlet Letter*. It was again this claim which he tested in the communitarian experiment of *The Blithedale Romance*. In *The Seven Gables*, which links the two epochs, its criticism centers on the democracy represented by Holgrave.

This young man is Hawthorne's portrait of the new democratic individual, and he is far from being a wholly sympathetic character. There is something about him which is "not sinister, but questionable." His art, insofar as it can be called by that name, is a skill, more mechanized than Drowne's carving of wooden figureheads but essentially of the same class. It is a useful profession, and one, moreover, which "was of no more importance in his own view, nor likely to be more permanent, than any of the preceding ones." Like his many previous occupations, he has taken up photography on account of its exciting novelty. The chief distinctions of his character, as given in the chapter entitled "The Daguerreotypist," are his coldness, his self-reliance, his omnivorous appetite for superficial but extensive experience, his inexhaustible vitality, and "that personal ambition, hidden— from his own as well as other eyes—among his more generous impulses." It is this secret dynamo of ambition which propels him into his numerous eccentric theories of human welfare and finally reveals them all as a humbug. His true utopia is personal success, and his idealism essentially a matter of the personal million. When he achieves both at the end of the novel, he abandons his altruistic theories with a quiet smile.

The conclusion of *The Seven Gables* has left most critics dissatisfied. As F. O. Matthiessen says in the course of an excellent analysis of the novel: "Yet in the poetic justice of bestowing opulence on all those who had previously been deprived of it by the Judge, Hawthorne overlooked the fact that he was sowing all over again the same seeds of evil."[19] While

19. Matthiessen, *American Renaissance*, p. 332.

this is a penetrating comment on what has happened in effect, one wonders if the seeds of evil were being sowed again by Hawthorne or by the society which he was representing. In other words, there is a question here of how completely the novelist identifies himself with Holgravian democracy. Within the given drama, as Matthiessen recognizes, the ending is not only poetically but morally just. With regard to the future, Hawthorne was far from regarding the democratic reversal as the final answer to the problem of social regeneration. The proof of this lies not in what happens but in the ironic distance he consistently maintains with regard to the lucky daguerreo-typist. As I read Holgrave's character, he is only partially presented as the hope of the future. More largely he is its symptom. Nor is the question mark posed by the ending of the novel, entirely overlooked by Hawthorne. As he says earlier about Holgrave, after an explicit statement of the young man's status "as the representative of many compeers in his native land":

> His career it would be difficult to prefigure. There ap-
> peared to be qualities in Holgrave, such as, in a country
> where everything is free to the hand that can grasp it,
> could hardly fail to put some of the world's prizes within
> his reach. But these matters are delightfully uncertain. . . .
> The effervescence of youth and passion, and the fresh
> gloss of the intellect and imagination, endow them with
> a false brilliancy, which makes fools of themselves and
> other people. Like certain chintzes, calicoes, and ging-
> hams, they show finely in their first newness, but cannot
> stand the sun and rain, and assume a very sober aspect
> after washing-day.

This is a particularly strong comment on the tawdry nature of the democracy represented by Holgrave. In its warning about the uncertainty of the future it is similar to the fears expressed by Cooper and the elder James that the bright dawn of democratic hope might end in a clouded noon. Of course, Hawthorne had no ready-made answers to this problem. All he claimed, together with his hope in a better future for society, was the privilege of evaluating the efforts in that direction that his culture made available to him. This is one of the threads which links his three American novels, even as the idealistic drive toward social regeneration linked the American imagination over the period which they cover. *The Seven Gables* provides in this sense the narrative bridge between *The Scarlet Letter* and *The Blithedale Romance*. It also bridges historical diversity by isolating specifically the other important constant of American culture: that species of practical energy which manifests itself in materially imposing but morally dubious achievement. The thread of continuity here lies in the lineal descent of Judge Pyncheon of the nineteenth century from Colonel Pyncheon of the seventeenth, with a connection between Colonel Pyncheon and Governor Bellingham on the one hand and between Judge Pyncheon and Hollingsworth on the other. The last of these characters is, however, the most complex representative of the general type —at once a hero and a villain. In him, indeed, the two streams of idealism and energy meet in a disastrous confluence.

In *The Scarlet Letter* Hawthorne had noted the utopian aspect of the Puritan migration to New England. In *The Blithedale Romance* he presents the utopian experiment of Brook Farm as an extension of the Puritan tradition. The backward glance of comparison runs like a rich thread through the pattern of the latter novel, making explicit the significance which the American romancer saw in this otherwise quixotic enterprise.

The day on which the visionaries assemble at Blithedale— to begin "the life of Paradise anew"—is bleaker and less encouraging than the day of the Pilgrims' landing as described by William Bradford. How conscious Hawthorne's narrator is of the suggested parallel we notice when, seated by the blazing hearth of the farmhouse at the end of the tempestuous journey, he reflects that "the old Pilgrims might have swung their kettle over precisely such a fire as this" and that, though Blithedale was hardly a day's walk from the old city, "we had transported ourselves a world-wide distance from the system of society that shackled us at breakfast-time." The Blithedalers are careful to distinguish the moral idealism of their motivation from the guiding principles of other contemporary communitarians. When Miles Coverdale reads the works of Fourier during his convalescence, he concludes that the world was mistaken in equating Blithedale with Fourierism "inasmuch as the two theories differed, as widely as the zenith from the nadir, in their main principles." Hollingsworth, to whom Coverdale puts the case, dismisses the Frenchman in an impassioned speech which is a curious amalgam of Hawthorne and the elder James. Fourier, Hollingsworth declares, "has committed the unpardonable sin; for what more monstrous iniquity could the Devil himself contrive than to choose the selfish principle,—the principle of all human wrong, the very blackness of man's heart, the portion of ourselves which we shudder at, and which it is the whole aim of spiritual discipline to eradicate,—to choose it as the master-workman of his system? To seize upon and foster whatever vile, petty, sordid, filthy, bestial, and abominable corruptions have cankered into our nature, to be the efficient instruments of his infernal regeneration!" Since "the selfish principle" at the base of organized society is also the chief reason for the Blithedalers' withdrawal from it, in denouncing Fourier, Hollingsworth is stating by implication their own different purpose. The irony here, however, lies in the fact—which will be noted more fully later—that this criticism of Fourier remains the ultimate comment on Hollingsworth himself. The true importance of the Blithedale experiment, as Hawthorne presents it, is that it embodies the visionary hope for mankind which was coeval with the American settlement itself. Miles Coverdale puts the claim for it explicitly when he opens a later chapter, "Eliot's Pulpit," by saying: "Our Sundays at Blithedale were not ordinarily kept with such rigid observance as might have befitted the descendants of the Pilgrims, whose high enterprise, as we sometimes flattered ourselves, we had taken up, and were carrying it onward and aloft, to a point which they never dreamed of attaining."

In many ways Hawthorne was, as Mrs. Q. D. Leavis says, the unwilling heir of the Puritans. But this is far from being true with regard to the tradition of idealism which was a part of his inheritance. On the contrary, he affirmed it in the only serious way in which an artist can affirm tradition: by becoming its critic. It must be said in passing that as far as the actual experiment of Brook Farm is concerned, Hawthorne's motives in joining it were as mixed as those of his ancestors in coming to America. On the one hand, there was the practical expectation of a comfortable livelihood for himself and Sophia. On the other, there was a good deal of simple faith in the theory behind the venture—enough faith, at any rate, to induce him to stake a thousand dollars from his meager resources on its success. Brook Farm, as he says in the preface to the novel, was "essentially a day-dream, and yet a fact," and indeed, in the curious episode of his association with it, one finds it difficult to separate the hard-headed Yankee from the wild-eyed dreamer. Perhaps, like Coverdale, he hoped that in the long run "between theory and practice, a true and available mode of life might be struck out."

However, be his personal motivation what it may, the important thing to realize is that Brook Farm presented Hawthorne with an appropriate subject for his theme. In "Earth's

Holocaust," the fantasy which describes an attempted re-generation, he had observed that it mattered little whether the attempt was made in the time past or time to come. The contours of the action were indeed hidden in the whole history of America. *The Scarlet Letter* had dealt with it at its very source in the seventeenth century. In *Blithedale* Hawthorne brought the action up to date. Here again was an embodiment of the archetypal American experience: with-drawal from a corrupt society to form a regenerate com-munity. The basis for regeneration had of course shifted from theological to economic theory; social morality was no longer embedded in metaphysics. In this sense Hawthorne was mark-ing realistically enough the shift in tradition that had occurred over the centuries. As I have pointed out in chapter 1, al-though in America, unlike Europe, the communitarian tradition developed in unbroken continuity from its chiliastic source in the seventeenth century, the experimenters of the nineteenth century were communitarians first and sectarians only in the second place—or not at all. Moreover, it was no longer confined to alien groups. Ripley's community was both native in composition and secular in purpose.

It is to emphasize the action of withdrawal and to under-line the exercise of that radical choice which America was supposed to have made permanently available to mankind that the novel opens in society, with Coverdale about to take the plunge which he later compares to the Pilgrims' world-wide leap across the Atlantic. In the temporary movement of the story back to society, which occurs in the middle of the novel, we get some richly evoked scenes of Boston life. This is the most detailed body of social description in Hawthorne, and it comes very close to the best manner of European fiction. Hawthorne is not, however, a "social" novelist, and this presentation is the background rather than the milieu of the action, which explores not a social problem but the possibility of repudiating organized society in its entirety. The subject is not Boston life but rather the drama of Boston and Blithedale, or the American dialectic between actual society and ideal community. The theme is not reform but social regeneration.

While the Blithedalean visionaries acknowledge their kinship with the American Puritans of the seventeenth century, their own enterprise arises primarily from a repugnance to the principle of economic individualism, from the fact that society has come to be organized exclusively on the basis of the force which had caused the failure of Bradford's communitarian experiment but which Bradford had accepted as an inevitable factor of God's dispensation for the New World. Of course the Blithedale community has other avowed objectives, like the belief in agriculture as the true foundation of the good life. This, however, constitutes the ridiculous part of their venture, and is treated uniformly as such by Hawthorne. It is indeed the chief target of the mild but persistent comedy in which Silas Foster, together with the pigs and the manure dump, serves to point out the reality behind the masquerade, while Miles Coverdale, like Shakespeare's Touchstone, performs the function of more articulate comic exposure. Hawthorne, as much as Melville, faced but overcame the nineteenth-century temptation toward the Arcadian relapse. It is true that outdoor life helps both Priscilla and Coverdale to add sunburn to their cheeks. But, as Coverdale observes:

> The peril of our new way of life was not lest we should fail in becoming practical agriculturists, but that we should probably cease to be anything else. . . . The clods of earth, which we so constantly belabored and turned over and over, were never etherealized into thought. Our thoughts, on the contrary, were fast becoming cloddish. Our labor symbolized nothing, and left us mentally sluggish in the dusk of the evening. Intellectual activity

is incompatible with any large amount of bodily exercise. The yeoman and the scholar—the yeoman and the man of finest moral culture, though not the man of sturdiest sense and integrity—are two distinct individuals, and can never be melted or welded into one substance.

Hawthorne is exposing here again the fallacy of the virgin scene: the assumption that a new and regenerated life demands the total repudiation of man's accumulated moral and material achievement, and that, as soon as the heritage of the past is abandoned, regeneration begins of its own accord. In a later chapter, while describing the exciting bustle of city life, Coverdale goes on to say how all this "was just as valuable, in its way, as the sighing of the breeze among the birch-trees that overshadowed Eliot's pulpit." When in the same chapter he observes a scene of simple domestic affection, being fresh from the discords he has witnessed at Blithedale, he reflects that he had not "seen a prettier bit of nature" during his summer in the country than the actors in that scene had shown him here "in a rather stylish boarding-house."

One should be careful, however, not to divert the ridicule that Hawthorne reserves for the Arcadia to other aspects of the community idea. As a matter of fact, though he presents Blithedale in its single corporate image, he clearly distinguishes between the different values involved in its broad spectrum. For instance, he does not debunk the issue of the equality of the sexes as he does the cult of agriculture. His attitude toward it is ambiguous in the sense that he accords to it the dignity of a serious though not one-sided argument. It is true that even the ardent feminist Zenobia gives in to Hollingsworth's view that should women ever dream of straying from their natural subservience to man, the male sex must "use its physical force, that unmistakable evidence of sovereignty, to scourge them back within their proper bounds!" But as Coverdale reflects a moment later, is such submission to male egotism a token of woman's true nature or is it "the result of ages of compelled degradation?" Together with this goes the further reflection that "women, however intellectually superior, so seldom disquiet themselves about the rights or wrongs of their sex, unless their own individual affections chance to lie in idleness, or to be ill at ease." Thus, while Zenobia's side of the case is presented as unquestionably superior to Hollingsworth's Nietzschean bombast, the whole issue of feminist reform is seen as a secondary question—an unfortunate consequence of the general distortion of human relations in society. With regard to the primary cause of such dislocations—which is indeed the cause of the Blithedalean withdrawal—Hawthorne leaves us in no doubt. Early in the novel, while commenting on the first day's assembly at Blithedale, Coverdale observes:

> If ever men might lawfully dream awake, and give utterance to their wildest visions without dread of laughter or scorn on the part of the audience,—yes, and speak of earthly happiness, for themselves and mankind, as an object to be hopefully striven for, and probably attained,—we who made that little semicircle round the blazing fire were those very men. We had left the rusty iron framework of society behind us; we had broken through many hindrances that are powerful enough to keep most people on the weary tread-mill of the established system, even while they feel its irksomeness almost as intolerable as we did. We had stepped down from the pulpit; we had flung aside the pen; we had shut up the ledger . . . It was our purpose . . . [to show] mankind the example of a life governed by other than the false and cruel principles on which human society has all along been based.

> And, first of all, we had divorced ourselves from pride, and were striving to supply its place with familiar love.... We sought our profit by mutual aid, instead of wresting it by the strong hand from an enemy, or filching it craftily from those less shrewd than ourselves (if, indeed, there were any such in New England), or winning it by selfish competition with a neighbor; in one or another of which fashions every son of woman both perpetrates and suffers his share of the common evil, whether he chooses it or no.

Whatever one may say of Blithedale and its members as things eventually turn out, there is no question about the force with which the vision of an ideal community is presented here. Nor is there any ambiguity about the distribution of sympathies as between the values avowed by Coverdale and those which govern the "iron framework of society." The visionaries stand—in theory at least—upon the principle of human brotherhood as against the predatory competitiveness of the established system. Blithedale itself, as we shall see, is finally judged in terms of its own professed values and not by the standards and norms of society. It is only when, and insofar as, the visionaries themselves turn out to be men of iron masquerading in Arcadian costume, that Blithedale is dismissed as a humbug—as false as society but more hypocritical. But this process of criticism—of exposing the same basic drives twice over and of showing the corrupted rebel as more reprehensible than the original villain—does not lead to a reversal of values involved in the challenge. It makes for a more clear-sighted affirmation. Nor does the novelist, as distinct from the characters who are all more or less ironically presented, abandon his position with regard to "the common evil" of exploitative individualism which every person in society either suffers from or perpetrates. Hawthorne's attitude, it must be said, does not involve the repudiation of individual freedom and choice. On the contrary, like the elder James, he insists on the primacy of the moral person in all social arrangements. But the individualism he champions is not incompatible with, but rather tends toward and finds its richest fulfillment in, the human community.

Since the story is mainly concerned with the fortunes of the Blithedale community, the image of the surrounding society occupies of necessity a marginal position. Yet this is strictly true only in a physical sense. In reality, the main characters of the story, who are all communitarians, carry with themselves, more or less visibly, the outwardly repudiated social values and attitudes—like old earth clinging to tufts of transplanted grass. It is this fact which makes *Blithedale* an exploration of the dialectical rather than simply the oppositional relation between actual society and the aspiration toward a better community life. But, apart from this, one of the most remarkable feats of the novel is the manner in which the two peripheral characters—old Moodie and Westervelt—are made to suggest concretely certain sinister forces working in the depths of the social world. Although one would at first sight suppose them to belong wholly to the machinery of romance, even their connection with the central theme of *Blithedale* is close enough for one to conclude that Hawthorne's apologia in the preface with regard to the introduction of the communitarian experiment into the romance should be treated in the same light as Mark Twain's celebrated warning against finding a moral in *Huckleberry Finn*. Where Hawthorne maintains cautiously that the whole treatment of Brook Farm is "altogether incidental to the main purpose of the romance," one feels the whole romance is in reality a characteristically modulated projection of the main society-community theme.

In *The Seven Gables* Hawthorne had observed that in nineteenth-century America, "amid the fluctuating waves of our social life, somebody is always at the drowning-point." This process and the consequent sense of insecurity are exemplified in *Blithedale*—more starkly and less sentimentally than in the case of Hepzibah Pyncheon—by old Moodie: the grandee of yesterday become the pauper of today; Fauntleroy turned into "a gray kennel-rat." This is a motif which recurs in a good deal of later American fiction, the career of George Hurstwood in *Sister Carrie* being a case which readily comes to mind. Hawthorne's method, however, is one of poetic, or "romantic," evocation rather than the "realistic" accumulation of minute detail, and his purpose is not so much to show the impassable gulf between classes as to point out the morally untenable nature of those distinctions which separate man from man in society. It is only in this sense that the fact of the relation between Zenobia and Priscilla becomes more meaningful than a mere contrivance of romantic plotting, for the sisterhood that is avowed at Blithedale but denied in society is not a playful masquerade as Zenobia seems to think; it is a reflection of the true nature of things.

In Westervelt, who is also connected with Zenobia and Priscilla, the projected force is one of secret power. The relation between him and the poor seamstress Priscilla is not unlike that between Ethan Brand and Esther, and mesmerism is to that extent presented as a peculiarly sinister variation of exploitative science. It makes "a delusive show of spirituality" but is "really imbued throughout with a cold and dead materialism." Westervelt represents in this sense the final degradation of the Puritan tradition. However, just as Hawthorne had explored the social implications of Puritan theology, he uses here the new psychic phenomenon to embody a sociological insight. These subtle transferences and suggested correlations are characteristic of Hawthorne's complex fictional method. Westervelt is in many ways the polished gentleman, a representative of the social type in which

Coverdale sees a partial reflection of his own pre-Blithedale existence. But he is also a wizard the gold band around whose false teeth reveals him somehow as a "moral and physical humbug." Yet his power, though exerted invisibly, is real enough. In its remote control it suggests the exploitative power which technology was putting into the hands of men: the power to bring individuals into total bondage while leaving them outwardly free and untouched. Westervelt's human shape is thus "a necromantic, or perhaps a mechanical contrivance, in which a demon walked about." He, too, affirms faith in a golden future and speaks publicly of the dawning era "that would link soul to soul" in "mutually conscious brotherhood," but he speaks of it "as if it were a matter of chemical discovery." As against the brotherhood of voluntary love, which is based upon the magnetic chain of human sympathy, Westervelt's mesmeric union is enforced bondage, destructive of true individuality as well as true community.

The brotherhood of love and mutual sympathy, which is lacking or perverted in an individualist social system, is precisely what the Blithedale community has taken for the foundation of its life. It is likewise the basis of Hawthorne's criticism of Blithedale itself. What the novel finally calls in doubt is not the values avowed by the visionaries but their means, materials, and ultimately the depth and sincerity of their professions. Zenobia is a dilettante who, until she meets Hollingsworth, expects from Blithedale nothing worse than a naughty frolic and hardly anything better than a pleasant interlude in rusticity. She takes the experiment as a stage set for an unaccustomed personal role, and a curious theatricality accompanies her doings at Blithedale right up to the manner of her suicide. Coverdale is at heart a well-meaning sybarite who has joined the community out of boredom with an aimless life, although the sense of direction and purpose he develops while there is a different matter. He and Zenobia share between themselves the accusation that the Veiled Lady levels at Theodore in Zenobia's own legend: "Dost thou come hither, not in holy faith, nor with a pure and generous purpose, but in scornful scepticism and idle curiosity?" For his detachment and lack of faith Coverdale indeed suffers the same fate as Theodore does for not saving from her bondage the girl he eventually loves: he relapses into a purposeless life haunted by his lost dream. Zenobia pays for her scorn and impure motives by a gruesome death.

The one person at Blithedale who lacks neither faith nor energy is Hollingsworth. But his faith is not the faith in a regenerate community, and his energy, like that of the Puritan magistrates with whom he is explicitly compared, drives him into a moral blindness of unique opacity. Unlike the dilettantish triflers, he is in deadly earnest, and he is a true builder rather than a dreamer of schemes. What he seeks to build, however, is not a regenerate community but an enduring edifice for the treatment of criminals. His monomaniacal preoccupation with crime is the nineteenth-century equivalent of the Puritan absorption with sin. If Coverdale testifies to the ineffectuality of nineteenth-century American idealism, Hollingsworth remains a permanently frightening symbol of what happens to a visionary scheme when it is geared to an individual's ruthless egotism and overwhelming energy. As Hawthorne insists in several places, Hollingsworth's plan of criminal reform was motivated by an initially noble impulse. But he has fallen into the reformer's occupational disease of monomania—a danger which Emerson noted in "New England Reformers": "Do not be so vain of your one objection. Do you think there is only one? Alas! my good friend, there is no part of society or of life better than any other part." Hawthorne, a true visionary of the hopeful American years, had the same objection to reformist zeal; and Hollingsworth's scheme becomes truly criminal when, in pursuit of its success,

he subverts the nobler purpose of total regeneration embodied in the Blithedale community, destroying in the process
also the faith and happiness of its other members. The key
chapter for understanding the developments which lead
eventually to the failure of the community, is the one appropriately entitled "A Crisis." It is here that Hollingsworth
repudiates the communitarian idea, and we realize how he
has used the experiment as a covert base for his own operations. He has made arrangements with Zenobia, on morally
dubious grounds, for the financial support of his reformist
enterprise. Nor is he prepared to accept Coverdale's suggestion that he reveal his design to the other members of the
community. On the contrary, he invites Coverdale, too, to
become his collaborator and join in the subversion of the
Blithedale experiment. "And have you no regrets," Coverdale
inquires, "in overthrowing this fair system of our new life,
which has been planned so deeply, and is now beginning to
flourish so hopefully around us? How beautiful it is, and, so
far as we can yet see, how practicable! The ages have waited
for us, and here we are, the very first that have essayed to
carry on our mortal existence in love and mutual help!
Hollingsworth, I would be loath to take the ruin of this enterprise upon my conscience." To which the indomitable man
replies: "Then let it rest wholly upon mine!" When Coverdale
refuses to join him finally, rather than tolerate a friend who
does not share his own fanatical purpose Hollingsworth
repudiates the bond of personal friendship too.

This man of iron thus possesses all those attributes that
Hawthorne had enumerated in *The Seven Gables* as constitut-
ing the essential moral continuity between the Puritan of the
seventeenth century and his descendant of the nineteenth.
Like the members of that persistent clan, he is brutal in
personal relations and dishonest in public ones, "laying his
purposes deep, and following them out with an inveteracy of

pursuit that knew neither rest nor conscience; trampling on the weak, and, when essential to his ends, doing his utmost to beat down the strong." His altruistic professions notwithstanding, Hollingsworth reveals in himself finally the same egotism, selfish principle, or ruthless individualism which the Blithedalean visionaries identified as the "common evil" of the established system. In *The Seven Gables* Hawthorne had said that the truth about a public man is often best discovered in a woman's view of him, and in *Blithedale* it is indeed a disillusioned Zenobia who gives utterance to the moral obliquity of Hollingsworth's character. "It is all self!" she declares in one of the climaxial scenes of the novel. "Nothing else; nothing but self, self, self! The fiend, I doubt not, has made his choicest mirth of you these seven years past, and especially in the mad summer which we have spent together. I see it now! I am awake, disenchanted, disinthralled! Self, self, self!"

Thus at Blithedale, too, instead of brotherhood there is selfhood, instead of faith there is skepticism, and instead of love there is fresh antagonism. It is not that, as Coverdale puts it, the Blithedaleans stand in a position of "new hostility, rather than new brotherhood" with regard to the society at large; because, as Coverdale himself adds, this could not fail to be the case so long as they were in "so pitiful a minority." Their estrangement from society is inevitable in "proportion with the strictness of our mutual bond among ourselves." The criticism of the Blithedale community therefore lies not in its hostile relation to the surrounding social system but rather in the absence of the promised bond within itself and in the divergence between its theory of mutual sympathy on the one hand and its reality of fresh antagonisms and mutual suspicions on the other. When Coverdale returns to Blithedale toward the end of the novel it has become a grim battlefield, with Hollingsworth resembling a Puritan magistrate holding an inquest of life and death in a case of witchcraft. The succeeding scenes enact Zenobia's tragedy, which, as Mark Van Doren says, is trash.[20] But it seems to me that Van Doren misses the whole force of this calculated vulgarity, for the point is precisely that the community, built on a premise of high idealism, should resolve itself finally into the same old story of love, jealousy, and sensational suicide. Zenobia's fate only illustrates the true tragedy of Blithedale.

The great test of the experiment's human worth is of course Priscilla. It is not for nothing that Coverdale is made to put the question of Blithedale's success or failure to her avatar as the Veiled Lady in the opening chapter. Unless the visionaries can save this daughter of poverty from her bondage, their enterprise will be a mockery of their principles. It is, indeed, Hollingsworth who declares: "As we do by this friendless girl, so shall we prosper." After vanishing from her enslavement to Westervelt, she has arisen, as Zenobia says in her legend, among this knot of visionary people to await her new destiny. What volumes of meaning this conveys with regard to the hope that was associated with the whole experiment of America! But the visionaries deliver Priscilla back to Westervelt, Zenobia being the chief instrument of her renewed bondage. A long line of critics has taken Hawthorne to task for not revealing the precise nature of Zenobia's relation with Westervelt. To me it seems that the ambiguity with which he surrounds their connection detracts nothing from, but rather adds to, the intended effect of obscure but intimate collusion. It is a collusion in which Hollingsworth is somewhat vaguely but quite unquestionably implicated, for, when Coverdale asks Priscilla in town if Hollingsworth knows where she is, the girl replies that she has come at his bidding. Coverdale himself, though honest, plays the limited role that

20. Mark Van Doren, *Nathaniel Hawthorne*, American Men of Letters Series (New York, William Sloane Associates, 1949), pp. 189–90.

befits his self-appointed position as chorus to the action.

Blithedale is thus not the regenerate community it professes to be. It is a company bound together, as the younger Henry James said in words that might have come from his father, rather by "its mutual suspicions and frictions, than by any successful surrender of self."[21] It has repeated rather than eliminated the cardinal sin of the outwardly repudiated society. "Alas," the narrator says at the end of the novel, "what faith is requisite to bear up against such results of generous effort!" Hawthorne had taken for his theme the exploration of such generous effort over the whole field of American history. Faced with the corruption which inevitably overtook the visionary schemes, it is not surprising that, like Cooper, he seems to conclude that nothing like social perfection is possible upon this earth. But, like Cooper again, he knew that it was foolish to expect perfection before its time. Because his faith was matched by his historical understanding, he did not become cynical. He realized that the nineteenth century belonged to gold-toothed wizards and narrow-minded reformers, and, what is more, the visionaries were themselves imbued with the spirit of their age. Blithedale was accordingly doomed from the outset, not only to failure, but to unreality. As Coverdale says of the experiment from the perspective of his retreat to Boston: "But, considered in a profounder relation, it was part of another age, a different state of society, a segment of an existence peculiar in its aims and methods, a leaf of some mysterious volume interpolated into the current history which time was writing off."

Set out of its time and place, the community remains thus only a noble and anticipatory gesture of hope. There is, however, no unreality about the values it affirms even in failure. The true measure of these values is neither Hollingsworth nor Zenobia. They constitute the destructive element. One must

21. Henry James, *Library of the World's Best Literature*, *12*, 7058.

look elsewhere—to Priscilla and Coverdale—for their tragic affirmation. Whatever her ultimate destiny, it is only at Blithedale that Priscilla comes into her proper heritage of freedom, happiness, dignity, and even love—such as it is. With regard to Coverdale, though his end is not very different from his beginning, we must not overlook the development that lies in between. After he sheds the more frivolous part of his skepticism together with his illness, he is reborn into a new existence. He is not, it is true, converted to the Arcadia of pigs and masquerades. Nor does he by any means abandon the serious part of his critical attitude toward the enterprise. The important change lies in the new sense of community which he acquires and which gives meaning to his otherwise empty life. He returns to Boston only because of the break with Hollingsworth and the consequent feeling of excommunication. How much he still belongs inwardly to Blithedale, however, we see from the tumultuous excitement with which he returns to it and the deep response with which he greets its distant glimpse: "In the sweat of my brow I had there earned bread and eaten it, and so established my claim to be on earth, and my fellowship with all the sons of labor. I could have knelt down, and have laid my breast against that soil. The red clay of which my frame was moulded seemed nearer akin to those crumbling furrows than to any other portion of the world's dust. There was my home, and there might be my grave." Years later the middle-aged Coverdale voices the same sentiment: "Often, however, in these years that are darkening around me, I remember our beautiful scheme of a noble and unselfish life; and how fair, in that first summer, appeared the prospect that it might endure for generations, and be perfected, as the ages rolled away, into the system of a people and a world! Were my former associates now there, —were there only three or four of those true-hearted men still laboring in the sun,—I sometimes fancy that I should direct my world-weary footsteps thitherward, and entreat them to receive me, for old friendship's sake."

To seek an affirmation of visionary hope, Cooper had read American history backward. Hawthorne, who started with the past, had moved up to his own time, and from there referred the faith in a sane community life to some possible future age. "More and more I feel that we had struck upon what ought to be a truth," as Coverdale says. "Posterity may dig it up, and profit by it."

5. Herman Melville:

THE NEW-WORLD VOYAGEUR

It is with fiction as with religion: it should present
another world, and yet one to which we feel the tie.

— *The Confidence-Man*

Writing to Hawthorne on July 17, 1852, Melville acknowledged receipt of *The Blithedale Romance* published three days
earlier. Although he had not had time to go far into the book,
he thought his friend had "most admirably employed materials which are richer than I had fancied them." He especially
welcomed the novel as a timely "antidote to the mooniness
of some dreamers—who are merely dreamers," adding,
after another quick dash: "Yet who the devel [sic] aint a
dreamer?"[1]

Like so many of Melville's remarks on Hawthorne, this
brief comment tells us something about Melville himself and
a good deal about the American mind of the time generally.
A dreamer exposing the mooniness of mere dreamers is not a
bad reading of Hawthorne's attitude. Nor is the observation
contained in the rhetorical question an unjustified assertion

1. *The Letters of Herman Melville*, ed. Merrell R. Davis and William
H. Gilman (New Haven, Yale University Press, 1960), p. 153.

about the visionary cast of the mid-century imagination—an imagination which, liberated from the cramping orthodoxies of religion, economics, and society as well as the geographical limitations of man's horizon, enjoyed a renaissance-like freedom to speculate on the problems of human destiny in the very teeth of discouraging obstructions, both of the visible and the invisible world. That Melville obviously included himself among the spite-of-the-devil dreamers might appear surprising. When he wrote this letter to Hawthorne, he had just finished tracing the doom of moral idealism in *Pierre*. His work during the succeeding five years was to consist of *Israel Potter*, a narrative of betrayal and disillusionment; *The Confidence-Man*, an unrelieved satire on the social reality of nineteenth-century America; and such tales of despair as "Bartleby," "Benito Cereno," and "The Encantadas." These are all stories which suggest the quality of an unshakable nightmare rather than the expression of any visionary hope. In them Melville concerned himself with the exploration of the dark places of human life and civilization.

But, on the other hand, it must not be forgotten that the man who went on to create the blasted landscape—morally as stunted as it is geographically sterile—of the treacherous Galapagos Islands started his career with a peep at the earthly paradise of the Typees. Partly based on experience but mostly imagined, this first book was Melville's testament to one important aspect of what Lascelles Abercrombie calls "the general circumstance" of the poet's time. The epic poet, as Abercrombie says, "has a definite function to perform. We see him accepting, and with his genius transfiguring, the general circumstance of his time; we see him symbolizing, in some appropriate form, whatever sense of the significance of life he feels acting as the accepted unconscious metaphysic of his age."[2]

2. Lascelles Abercrombie, *The Epic: An Essay* (London, Martin Secker, 1922), p. 48.

The sojourn among the South Sea Islanders was indeed the nineteenth-century mariner's version of a gesture often celebrated in American life and literature. It was his equivalent of the communitarian experiment at Plymouth, of Crèvecoeur's projected journey to the Indian tribe, and of Coverdale's pilgrimage to Blithedale. Fanciful as these actions are—some looking forward and others back—they all have a serious side to them. In one way or another all of them arise from the background of the given civilization of the time and embody the American theme of rejection and quest. In the course of a short span of years Melville's imagination was to seize upon the other factors that constituted, together with this one, "the accepted unconscious metaphysic of his age." But first in *Typee* he evoked his dream world of an ideal community—evoked it with suitable and decisive reservations, to be sure, but also with a good deal of simple and passionate faith.

In these tragic times—they are still very much the times of Herman Melville—we quite naturally assume greater wisdom in works of unrelieved gloom than in those of unmixed hope. It is not certain which of these two oversimplified attitudes is more and which less complacent, for it is as possible to be disturbed by hope as it is to be lulled by despair. But Melville's fiction is guilty of neither reduction. As he says of the tortoise—the presiding genius of the Galapagos Islands—in "The Encantadas":

> if you put them on their backs you thereby expose their bright sides without the possibility of their recovering themselves, and turning into view the other. But after you have done this, and because you have done this, you should not swear that the tortoise has no dark side. Enjoy the bright, keep it turned up perpetually if you can, but be honest, and don't deny the black. Neither

should he, who cannot turn the tortoise from its natural position so as to hide the darker and expose its livelier aspect, like a great October pumpkin in the sun, for that cause declare the creature to be one total inky blot. The tortoise is both black and bright.[3]

Even in the fresh and youthful *Typee* Melville's dream of the ideal possibilities of life is not naive. It does not fail to take into account the grimmer realities of man's nature and the nature of the world he lives in. Likewise in his later work, when blackness has moved into the center of the universe, he acknowledges the brightness that is the other side of life. The acknowledgment is by no means equally explicit in all cases. More often the ideal finds an inverted expression in the very intensity of its denial in the actual. This is the enduring aspect of Melville's theme which D. H. Lawrence noted when he said that Melville "never quite put the knife in the heart of his paradisal ideal. Somehow, somewhere, somewhen, love should be a fulfilment, and life should be a thing of bliss. That was his fixed ideal."[4] Lawrence, needless to say, did not wholly approve of idealism. As he says in concluding his essay on *Typee* and *Omoo:*

> Melville was, at the core, a mystic and an idealist.
> Perhaps, so am I.
> And he stuck to his ideal guns.
> I abandon mine.[5]

Whether or not Melville should have stuck to his ideal guns, we can all have our opinions. But I think no one can deny that he never quite abandoned them. For all his

3. Unless otherwise stated, the edition used for quotations from Melville is *The Works of Herman Melville*, 16 vols. London, Constable, Standard Edition, 1922–24.
4. Lawrence, *Studies in Classic American Literature*, pp. 206–07.
5. Ibid., p. 212.

relevance to our own time, he was the poet of a more hopeful age. It is customary these days to approach Melville's early work from the perspective of the despair which overtook and virtually silenced him; to search his sunnier productions for somber hints. Seen in this way, the most important thing in *Typee*, for example, becomes that hurried glimpse at the end into the skeletal remnants of a furtively conducted cannibal ritual. My own procedure is going to be the reverse of this. Following chronology—both in reading as well as in perspective—I propose to emphasize the earliest theme and then to pursue its mutations until it is submerged in and beyond *Moby-Dick*. This is the theme that Lawrence calls the "paradisal ideal" of love and that I have called the ideal community. Into it enters the antipodal concept of "civilization"—what Melville called in *Redburn* "snivelization." This social drama, it must be said in order to keep the record straight, takes place within the larger and, for Melville, the more dominant theme of the nature and challenge of metaphysical reality; but with this I shall be only marginally concerned.

Before turning to the novels I should like to point out that, among the American writers of this period, while Melville invites the closest comparison with Hawthorne, there are aspects of his work which are more akin to Cooper. His essay on Hawthorne's *Mosses* testifies loudly to the common preoccupations of these two writers: the recognition of the "great power of blackness" and the probing "at the very axis of reality." Melville came to Hawthorne rather late, but the influence was instantaneous and profound. With regard to Cooper, however, the acquaintance goes farther back and the stimulus was more leisurely. Cooper's works were, as he says in a letter, "among the earliest I remember, as in my boyhood producing a vivid, and awakening power upon my mind."[6]

6. *The Letters of Herman Melville*, p. 145.

Melville shared with Cooper a more aggressive Americanism than that of Hawthorne. To him, as to the older writer, the mystique of democracy extended far beyond the Anglo-Saxon world and embraced all peoples and races in one brotherhood of humanity. The patrician Cooper perhaps patronizes a little in this matter, whereas it comes more naturally to Melville with his experience of forecastle democracy. Nevertheless, interracial "civic friendship" is a constant theme in both novelists, even as it links their work with that of Mark Twain later in the century. Melville's South Sea Islanders owe a great deal to Cooper's portrayal of American Indians, and his heathen Apollos remind us at every step of such characters as Chingachgook and Uncas. His world is peopled as densely with savages and barbarians as that of the Leatherstocking Tales. It is a significant fact that, whereas the actual crew of the *Acushnet* was composed of twenty-one Americans, three Portuguese, and one Englishman,[7] the crew of the whaling boat as we have it in *Moby-Dick* is a motley crowd drawn from almost all the nationalities of the world, not to mention those of the nether world. This acculturation was somehow connected in Melville's imagination with the meaning of democracy, and in this respect he was as hopelessly ungenteel and as hopefully American as Natty Bumppo or Whitman. It was also connected, once again as in the case of Natty and Whitman, with the religious feeling of all humanity's oneness before God. Reviewing Parkman's *The Oregon Trail* in 1849, Melville took exception to the historian's contemptuous attitude toward the American Indians, reminding him that even the civilized nations had, at one time or the other, passed through a stage of savagery. "We are all of us—Anglo-Saxons, Dyaks, and Indians—sprung from one head," he added, "and made in one image. And if we regret

7. Lewis Mumford, *Herman Melville* (New York, Literary Guild of America, 1929), p. 43.

this brotherhood now, we shall be forced to join hands hereafter."[8]

One must also mention here the great American fact of space—the endless expanse of elements which, is as likely to happen when a people is brought face to face with it,[9] yields mystic intimations of the vastness and inscrutability of the universe and becomes the occasion for meditations on the nature of metaphysical reality. In this sense, the sea, and especially the Pacific, was to Melville what the unexplored West was to Cooper. Melville's use of the American continental imagery in describing the open sea has been noted by several commentators. This is paralleled by Cooper's sea imagery in evoking the spirit of the American wilderness. One can notice this most remarkably in the first chapter of *The Pathfinder*, which opens with the following sentences: "The sublimity connected with vastness is familiar to every eye. The most abstruse, the most far-reaching, perhaps the most chastened of the poet's thoughts, crowd on the imagination as he gazes into the depths of the illimitable void." The chapter then goes on to describe the primeval forest in terms of tempests, whirlwinds, water-spouts, waves, breakers, oceans of leaves, and sails at sea. Cooper, of course, always hurried on from such scenes, as from a rich backdrop, to the more pressing concerns of his story, while in Melville "the illimitable void" is very often an undetachable part of the human story itself. A similar comparison—a comparison between literary pioneering and the full exploitation of the discovered resources—can be made with regard to the apprehension of the spirit which informs the untamed elements. As I have attempted to point out, in Cooper the conception of

8. *Literary World*, March 31, 1849. Quoted by Willard Thorp, *Herman Melville: Representative Selections* (New York, American Book Company, 1938), p. cii.

9. I am thinking mainly of the Vedic literature produced by the Aryans after their migration to the Indian subcontinent.

nature as the temple of the Lord did not always preclude that deeper insight which reveals it also as the embattled arena of mutual destructiveness. For this we can even go back to the "optimistic" Crèvecoeur who, in the latter part of the *Letters*, turns to the contemplation of the nature of man as well as the nature of nature, and concludes in a very unoptimistic key that "men, like the elements, are always at war."[10] In Melville this insight is not confined to random hints but assumes its proper proportion as the "horrible vulturism of earth." The importance of this recognition, arising directly from the contemplation of observed natural phenomena, should be taken into account as at least a partial source of that "power of blackness" which is common both to Melville's and Hawthorne's vision, but which in Hawthorne's case stems more directly from his Calvinistic inheritance. However, while conceding the importance of this aspect of nature in Melville's imagination, one should go on to note that it is nature again in *Moby-Dick* which stands disclosed, not perhaps as the temple of the Lord, but certainly as the sanctum sanctorum of imperturbable love.

Finally, like Cooper, Melville turned to certain modes of primitive life in order to gain a perspective on what James Baird, in his recent discussion of literary primitivism, has called "the cultural failure" of the nineteenth-century Western world.[11] This failure meant, among other things, the breakdown of traditional forms of community life and the emergence of an increasingly sterile egocentricity. Human beings in Melville's work, as in Cooper's, share the predatory tendency of the natural world as well as its ultimate capacity for love. But the individualist society whose writers they were

10. See above, p. 23.
11. James Baird, *Ishmael* (Baltimore, Johns Hopkins Press, 1956). Mr. Baird's discussion provides admirable explication of the nature and function of oriental thought and symbol in Melville's work.

encouraged the former and obscured the latter. As Stubb indicates to Pip when that inept Negro sailor falls overboard: "though man loved his fellow, yet man is a money-making animal, which propensity too often interferes with his benevolence." Was the fact of self-interest, formulated here in the second mate's characteristically offhand manner, the ultimate truth about man in society? Ishmael and Queequeg would say no. Years earlier, faced with similar perplexity at the spectacle of civilized humanity, Crèvecoeur had turned to the tribal Indians and wondered what it was in "their social bond" which made it so "singularly captivating, and far superior to anything to be boasted of among us."[12] Melville outdid the "romantic" American farmer by actually living among cannibals and making a whole book out of the experience. But the question he asked himself was the same.

Even after a century *Typee* remains in some ways an angry young book. But that does not tell the whole story of its effectiveness. If this account of a brief Polynesian sojourn seems weightier than the narrative of beachcombing vagabondage in *Omoo*, the chief reason lies in the fact that its criticism of Western civilization is balanced by an alternative concept of social organization. It is a fiction which, like religion—to use Melville's own words quoted in the epigraph—presents "another world, and yet one to which we feel the tie." It is a singularly disarming if unsophisticated attempt on the part of a young writer to engage, in terms of readily available experience, a problem which is still among the profounder social problems of the West: the problem of "community lost and community to be gained."[13] It is true that in this first book Melville traveled half the circumference of the globe, and a couple of millennia backward in time, from the

12. See above, p. 27.
13. See above, p. 149 n.

American civilization of the day, to discover his ideal community. In his later work he was to bridge the spatial and temporal gap between the two sides of the drama, and to give a fugitive and fleeting expression to the community theme in the contemporary world of the here and now. But this fact does not make *Typee* an exercise in literary escapism; it only places it in the American imaginative tradition of total repudiation and radical quest. In terms of the values involved, this peep at Polynesian life does not turn away from the issues that are raised; it faces them squarely.

As a work of imagination, *Typee* can be compared with two distinct kinds of fictional narrative. In the first place, there is a whole body of literature—usually of second-rate writing and no thematic pretensions—which takes the reader out of this world and into an imaginary realm where the sun always shines and the rain never falls—never at least in such a way as to remind the reader of his wet feet. The whole purpose of this literature is to induce temporary forgetfulness of life and its problems. It has nothing to do with known human and social realities; in Melville's terms, there is no recognizable tie between the world it creates for us and our own world. At the other extreme from these Shangri-las there is the serious kind of imaginary construct of which a notable example is Samuel Butler's *Erewhon*. The pretended unreality of such a realm is only a strategic device. Whether the reader is carried into it by means of a dream, an allegory, a boat, a balloon, or some other mode of literary transportation that happens to be handy, he is in truth hardly moved an inch from the reality he knows, be it of manners, morals, social institutions, or whatever it is that the writer wishes to reform. Butler's "Nowhere" is England still, but England with some of its institutions turned upside down in order to shock the reader into a concern for their abuses. For instance, consider what is perhaps the most effectively contrived inversion in Butler's satire: the Erewhon code which requires disease to be punished but which maintains that crime is an unfortunate accident for which the afflicted criminal deserves not blame but sympathy and condolence. The purpose here obviously is not to hold up the Erewhonian community as an ideal in any sense; it is merely to confront us with the recognition that crime is after all a sort of disease and that society should accordingly treat it in a more humane spirit. Such imaginary structures are thus wholly satire-determined. To revert to Melville's words, they present not another world but our own in another light.

Typee, needless to say, shares the impulse that lies behind both these kinds of fiction. It is full of angry, if not very artful, denunciation of civilization and its institutions. On the other hand, its portrayal of the Happy Valley is not altogether innocent of a Shangri-la–like quality of perpetual sunshine and exotic glamor. In this sense Melville was obviously exploiting simultaneously, though not without honest reservations, the taste for tropic-island bewitchment as well as the Rousseau-esque myth of aboriginal perfection. But there is more to this book than the use of these best-selling devices; there is all its seriousness. As William Ellery Sedgwick has said: "Of course it will be insisted by critics of a certain stamp that in this contrast between civilized and savage life Melville is still following 'a long and ample tradition, both literary and philosophical,' namely, the exaltation of the Noble Savage at the expense of his civilized opposite. True as this may be, it is not the whole truth nor the most interesting part of it. If there is a literary convention here there is the pressure of personal responses to animate it."[14] To this one can add that over and above the animation of personal response, there are behind *Typee* the force and confidence of an

14. William Ellery Sedgwick, *Herman Melville: The Tragedy of Mind* (Cambridge, Harvard University Press, 1944), p. 26.

important American tradition, as also the contemporary ferment that made this an age of millennial expectations. Melville's personal formulation of it apart, preoccupation with the theme of perfect community was at this date shared by a large number of American dreamers. George Ripley, for instance, hailed the novel in the *Harbinger* for its portrayal of an "ideal society" whose perfection is based on the fact that "there is *abundance for every person*, and thus the most fruitful cause of the selfishness and crime of our enlightened and philosophic situation does not exist there. Here is the lesson which the leaders of this nineteenth century may learn from the Typee."[15]

The most important thing about *Typee*, then, is its social theme, and this theme turns out to be the traditional American theme of a corrupt civilization at one end—one end of the globe in this case—and the dream of a simple and well-integrated community at the other. The inhabitants of the valley are not altogether the creatures of a satirical purpose. They are not Americans standing on their heads. Unlike Erewhon, Typee does not treat its criminals better. There are no criminals in Typee. Nor are there a hundred other social evils with which the civilized narrator is only too familiar. This state of affairs, as we shall see, arises primarily from the fact that life in Typee is based upon fundamentally different social principles. It exhibits an organization that makes harmony in human relations not a state of exalted virtue but simply a matter of the ordinary every-day course of things. In this connection it is worth while to note that Melville, unlike a true celebrator of the Noble Savage, is far from depicting each individual of the Polynesian tribe as a paragon of moral perfection. Like Cooper, or more like Natty Bumppo, he too

15. Hugh W. Hetherington, *Melville's Reviewers: British and American: 1846–1891* (Chapel Hill, University of North Carolina Press, 1961), p. 52.

distinguishes firmly between "gifts" and "nature," and points out time and again how, underneath the different and decisive customs of the country the inhabitants of the valley share the usual impulses, more developed perhaps in one direction and less in another, which belong to the common nature of humanity everywhere. If the savages offer points of contrast with civilized men, they also offer points of comparison. Mehevi at the Ti, for instance, does the honors of the house with the warmth and hospitality of an English squire; like the gentlemen of Europe the men of Typee indulge their mirth freely after the cloth is drawn and the ladies retire; the women are as lavish with cosmetics and ointments as women anywhere in the world; and, more importantly, as Melville observes in connection with a local mausoleum, both the superstitions and the faith of the Typees afford "evidence of the fact, that however ignorant man may be, he still feels within him his immortal spirit yearning after the unknown future." Nor, at the other extreme, are the savages innocent of violence and bloodshed, though such impulses are wisely channeled into carefully regulated wars.

Their physical perfection apart, Melville admires the Typees finally not for individual merit but for being a harmonious community. The principle of their social organization is their true distinction and the decisive point of contrast between them and civilized men. It is the source of their virtue and the reason for Melville's extenuation of their vice. Melville, it must be remembered, was evoking the picture of the Happy Valley across a span of unusually disillusioning experience with various forms of civilized society: civil and military, afloat as well as ashore. As Sedgwick has pointed out: "In *Typee* there are two perspectives. There is the perspective of the story proper, or of the events at the time they happened; and there is the broader perspective of the book as a whole, in which the events of the story and their circumstances are seen at a distance of four years across all the light and shadow of Melville's experience in the interim."[16] Melville himself makes this plain when he declares that "after passing a few weeks in this valley of the Marquesas, I formed a higher estimate of human nature than I had ever before entertained. But alas! since then I have been one of the crew of a man-of-war, and the pent-up wickedness of five hundred men has nearly overturned all my previous theories."

One should accordingly refrain from looking with easy complacency upon the idealization of Typee. The overdrawn brightness of its image only reflects the darkness of civilized society in Melville's mind. The two images in fact mutually interpret each other. Though the valley of the Typees itself is comparatively untouched by contact with outsiders, civilization is judged in the book in terms of its effect upon other Polynesian peoples. Melville is far from claiming that the natives of these islands cannot derive immense advantage from being moved out of their Stone Age ignorance and lethargy. He is advocating not primitivism, but humanity. "Let the savages be civilised," he declares, "but civilise them with benefits, and not with evils; and let heathenism be destroyed, but not by destroying the heathen. The Anglo-Saxon hive have extirpated Paganism," he adds, pointing to the parallel in his own country, "from the greater part of the North American continent; but with it they have likewise extirpated the greater portion of the Red race."

The process of civilizing the Polynesians is spearheaded by ruthless army commanders, canting missionaries, and rapacious tradesmen, and the fruits of civilization for the natives consist of degradation and exploitation. As Melville observes with some irony about the state of affairs in the Sandwich Islands:

16. Sedgwick, *Herman Melville*, p. 24.

Behold the glorious result!—The abominations of Paganism have given way to the pure rites of the Christian worship—the ignorant savage has been supplanted by the refined European! Look at Honolulu, the metropolis of the Sandwich Islands!—A community of disinterested merchants, and devoted self-exiled heralds of the Cross, located on the very spot that twenty years ago was defiled by the presence of idolatry. What a subject for an eloquent Bible-meeting orator! . . . Nor until I visited Honolulu was I aware of the fact that the small remnant of the natives had been civilised into draught horses, and evangelised into beasts of burden. But so it is. They have been literally broken into the traces, and are harnessed to the vehicles of their spiritual instructors like so many dumb brutes!

Add to the destructiveness of this form of Christian-capitalist civilization the desolation caused by invading European armies and, as Melville says, who "can wonder at the deadly hatred of the Typees to all foreigners after such unprovoked atrocities? Thus it is that they whom we denominate 'savages' are made to deserve the title." It is indeed in this change from the feeling of universal love to one of distrust and hate that Melville locates the worst legacy of a corrupt civilization: "When the inhabitants of some sequestered island first descry the 'big canoe' of the European rolling through the blue waters toward their shores, they rush down to the beach in crowds, and with open arms stand ready to embrace the strangers. Fatal embrace! They fold to their bosoms the vipers whose sting is destined to poison all their joys; and the instinctive feeling of love within their breasts is soon converted into the bitterest hate."

It is against this background—the background of "the vices, cruelties, and enormities of every kind that spring up in the tainted atmosphere of a feverish civilisation"—that we must regard Melville's idealization of the Typee valley. This civilization is represented more concretely, though not extensively, by the ship *Dolly*, which the narrator, presumably like other "long-haired, bare-necked youths," had been forced to join by "the united influences of Captain Marryat and hard times." In this book Melville does not dwell much either on the representative capacity of the ship or on shipboard usage. Nevertheless, it is obvious that, whether or not the sailors' expectation of adventure has been fulfilled, their poverty has remained unalleviated. As a matter of fact, the ship has only exposed them further to tryanny and inhuman neglect. In this connection one can contrast the captain of the *Dolly*—the remote and vengeful "Lord of the Plank"—with the Typee chieftain Mehevi who, though a sovereign in his own right, is so unattended by any ceremony and so close to the common inhabitants of the valley that the narrator remains for a long time unaware of his true status. It is to protest against the conditions aboard that the two sailors decide to risk falling among notorious savages rather than have any further truck with the repudiated vessel. Familiar as this gesture is in American fiction, we must notice further that the narrator and his companion Toby belong, characteristically enough, to that class of men "who never reveal their origin, never allude to home, and go rambling over the world as if pursued by some mysterious fate they cannot possibly elude."

The mysterious fate in this particular case involves a hazardous journey through certain chasms, ravines, and gorges beyond which, as the runaway sailors are convinced, lies the desired sanctuary of the Happy Valley. The writing here is remarkable in its combination of symbolical overtones with the raciest and most straightforward narrative of physical adventure. As has been observed before, this journey constitutes a sort of descent into inferno—a Ulyssean detour to find the way home. The passage through the outlandish regions—described in chapter 7 in terms of death-like coldness, appalling darkness, and infernal torment—marks a process of dying, or a process of being born anew, or simply a necessary preparation for the different world that awaits the fugitives. When at last they view the sunny expanse of land toward which they have so painfully struggled over a period of several days, it is greeted as a revelation of Eden itself: "Had a glimpse of the gardens of Paradise been revealed to me, I could scarcely have been more ravished with the sight." *Typee* is undoubtedly a sea yarn, suitably stretched here and there as all sea yarns are, and handsomely overlaid with literary and other cliches. But it is also the first book of a great imaginative genius who started on his career at a time when his culture's experience was beginning to assume an articulate form—the form of an apprehensible and meaningful action. For all its lack of sophistication, or perhaps because of it, *Typee* captures with revealing simplicity one aspect of this action: the dialectical movement between a corrupt civilization and an ideal community, or the opposition between the dream and the reality of society in America. It is this over-all rhythm of the book which distinguishes its theme from its travel-diary method, and which constitutes its claim to serious consideration.

Having arrived in Paradise, what did Melville and Toby find there? They found sunshine and breadfruit; healthful aboriginal savages and long-haired beautiful women; nudity, dancing, and only occasional drapery of white tapa; ease and indolence, and quantities of sleep; in short, all that makes living among cannibals worth the risk. These were also the conditions that finally led Melville to despair and made him long for a speedy release from this subhuman existence. Such exotic novelties, however, do not exhaust the meaning that Melville projected into the image of Typee. He also recognized in this valley certain admirable possibilities, a social situation of which he gives a full account in chapters 17 and 27. The narrator begins in the earlier of these two chapters by saying that, having reconciled himself inwardly to an indefinite period of stay in the valley, his ailing limb seemed to heal suddenly and he entertained hope of a quick and complete recovery. "In the altered frame of mind," somewhat like Miles Coverdale after his illness at Blithedale, he now looks upon the surrounding world with fresh insight: "every object that presented itself to my notice in the valley struck me in a new light, and the opportunities I now enjoyed of observing the manners of its inmates tended to strengthen my favourable impressions." He is disposed to believe that he has found his way into the "Happy Valley" and that beyond its mountains there is "naught but a world of care and anxiety." Contrasting the Typee community with the society he has known, he is ready to extenuate even the worst abuses of the former. With regard to cannibalism, for example, he records at more than one place the horror and revulsion aroused in him by this primitive rite. This of course falls within the first of the book's two perspectives noted by Sedgwick. But we must not forget the other, the broader perspective in which the image of Typee is flatteringly refracted through Melville's experience with civilization. In this light he argues that cannibalism—"a rather bad trait"—is practiced only on the declared enemies of the tribe, whereas in civilized societies innocent men are tortured and executed with the utmost cruelty and for no apparent reason. "The fiend-like skill we display," he concludes in a passage reminiscent of Swiftian savagery, "in the invention of all manner of death-dealing engines, the vindictiveness with which we carry on our wars, and the misery and desolation that follow in their train, are enough of themselves to distinguish the white civilised man as the most ferocious animal on the face of the earth." His "remorseless cruelty," he goes on to add, can be seen in the penal institutions of "our own favoured land"; in particular the treatment of criminals "whom we mason up in the cells of our prisons, and condemn to perpetual solitude in the very heart of our population."

In Typee, on the other hand, no one is ever brought to trial and there are no lawyers or law courts. Like America, it enjoys an abundance of natural resources, but these are universally and equally shared. Hence there are no destitute widows, no starving children, no beggars, and therefore also no "cold charities." Liberty of conscience, merely promised in the narrator's own country, prevails here without limitation or hindrance. There is neither civil nor domestic disharmony of any sort: no foreclosures of mortgages, no debts or debtors' prisons, no bolts, bars, or padlocks, no jealousies in love and no divorce. The prevailing polyandry results in no discord, and "wedlock, as known among these Typees, seems to be of a more distinct and enduring nature than is usually the case with barbarous people. A baneful promiscuous intercourse of the sexes is hereby avoided, and virtue, without being clamorously invoked, is, as it were, unconsciously practised." Of course, the Typees, like the rest of humanity, are a warring people, but their battles, unlike those of a society based upon predatory competition, are not internecine. Surely, the narrator observes, "if our evil passions must find vent, it is far better to expend them on strangers and aliens, than in the bosom of the community in which we dwell. In many polished countries civil contentions, as well as domestic enmities, are prevalent, at the same time that the most atrocious foreign wars are waged. How much less guilty, then, are our islanders, who of these three sins are only chargeable with one, and that the least criminal!"

The harmonious community life of the Typees is characterized chiefly by the absence of three institutions. In the first place, money plays no part in the social relationships of these people: "That 'root of all evil' was not to be found in the valley." Likewise, there is no repressive police machinery, and, more important than these two, no property in land. In connection with private property, Melville's narrator makes the important distinction that was being blurred by Cooper's Littlepages around the same time in the history of American fiction. In chapter 27 he makes it clear that there was no "community of goods" in Typee and that, on the contrary, "personal property" was held inviolate and was in no case encroached upon by the inhabitants. But he observes that there is a vast difference between personal property and what he calls the "investment of 'real property'" or "real estate." "Whether the land of the valley was the joint property of its inhabitants, or whether it was parcelled out among a certain number of landed proprietors who allowed everybody to 'squat' and 'poach' as much as he or she pleased, I never could ascertain. At any rate, musty parchments and title deeds there were none on the island; and I am half inclined to believe that its inhabitants hold their broad valleys in fee simple from Nature herself; to have and to hold, so long as grass grows and water runs."

The question to which the narrator is led inevitably by this state of affairs is the one which was most pertinent to the fortunes of his own tradition, the tradition of a people who had sought to form a pure community in freedom from all repressive social institutions but who had found themselves developing instead into an anti-society of isolated individuals permanently warring against each other. How, he asks in more than one place, did the Typees manage, "without the aid of established law, to exhibit, in so eminent a degree, that social order which is the greatest blessing and highest pride of the social state?" If "the better principles of our nature, cannot exist unless enforced by the statute-book, how are we to account for the social condition of the Typees?" His answer is quite characteristic of the visionary cast of the whole body of imaginative literature with which I have been dealing. "Civilisation," he says, "does not engross all the virtues of humanity"; there are some natural capacities which, with its emphasis on individualism, property, and money, it has not even tried. Every man harbors a "fraternal feeling" toward other men and all human beings desire to act "in concert and good fellowship." Free from the motives which vitiate human relationships in civilized societies, the harmonious life of the Typees is based precisely upon these feelings.

> During my whole stay on the island I never witnessed a single quarrel, nor anything that in the slightest degree approached even to a dispute. The natives appeared to form one household, whose members were bound together by the ties of strong affection. The love of kindred I did not so much perceive, for it seemed blended in the general love; and where all were treated as brothers and sisters, it was hard to tell who were actually related to each other by blood.

Here, then, is Melville's image of the ideal community: the image of a sort of prelapsarian Blithedale. Like Miles Coverdale, the narrator of *Typee* also abandons the community in order to return eventually to society or civilization. The reasons for this action are quite simple. On the level of the story, it is quite natural that, after tasting of this alien Paradise, the adventurous sailor should want to go back home to his mother. Moreover, while in Typee, he cannot hope to procure medical attention for his illness. It is not true, as D. H. Lawrence seems to imply, that his diseased limb gets progressively worse in Typee and heals immediately on his return to shipboard in *Omoo*. But it is true that his illness is a projection of psychological dis-ease, for it gets better or worse as he resigns himself to his existence in the valley or revives hopes of escape from it; and herein lies the more important motivation for the escape. To reconcile oneself to Typee is to comfort oneself falsely with an impossible primitivism. Typee is at best a picture of "community lost"—lost for good reasons—and not the image of "community to be gained." To a man of the nineteenth-century Western world, it is more than happy but also less than human. The Typees do not hunt the whale, whether we interpret that symbol in economic, technological, intellectual, psychological, or spiritual terms. However painful it may prove to be, it is a necessary part of human destiny to accept the challenge of the Leviathan. By contrast, the somnolent Typees are content to make fire by rubbing two pieces of wood for hours on end, and the movement of their inward life is characterized by similar childishness.

So Melville makes his narrator leave the Happy Valley, but neither reconciled to civilization nor in repudiation of the social values which he has observed and endorsed in Typee. The idea of community—of people forming one harmonious household—continues to be a persistent, though not equally central, theme in Melville's succeeding novels.[17] And as for his continued denunciation of civilization, one has only to turn to *Omoo*.

Omoo continues the narrative of Melville's Polynesian

17. For the persistence of this idea—in the statements of various characters, in authorial comment, and in incident—throughout the whole body of Melville's work, see R. E. Watters, "Melville's 'Sociality,' " *American Literature, 17* (1945), 33–49. My own treatment, more detailed on the one hand, is restricted on the other to those works where the idea of community possesses both thematic weight and structural importance. However, I am in agreement with Watters' general thesis, namely that Melville countered the transcendentalist approval of solitude and self-reliance by a "positive alternative": "the racial and social community of mankind, with its wealth of social virtues: love, sympathy, gratitude, friendliness, charity, kindness, companionship" (p. 49).

adventures from where he had left it off in *Typee*. More true
to the young sailor's actual experiences, it is the lightest and
sunniest of all his works. On coming aboard the *Julia*, his
recent stay in the Typee valley seems to him to possess already
"the strangeness of a dream." Back in the midst of his own
people and civilization—"so long my earnest prayer—with
home and friends once more in prospect"—he cannot help
contrasting the shabbiness and petty cruelties of this world
with the memory of the dream world he has left behind. Here
he is face to face again with the same callousness and imper-
sonality from which he and Toby had earlier sought refuge
among cannibals. The Captain, for instance, seeks to make a
"well man" of him, not because he feels any "compassion"
for him but only because he is anxious "to have the benefit of
[his] services as soon as possible." Remembering how the
Typees, notwithstanding their curious desire to retain him a
captive, had treated him with the kindliness and affection of a
member of the household, he feels "weighed down by a
melancholy that could not be shaken off."

The melancholy is nevertheless shaken off soon enough as
Melville gets involved in all the bizarre doings aboard the
Julia and as he starts finally on his picaresque wanderings
through the Tahitian group of islands in the rare company of
Doctor Long Ghost. The book soon develops into an account
to which one can apply the traditional categories of critical
approbation: a memorable portrait-gallery of character types,
arresting adventure, abundant humor, racy dialogue, and
competent narrative. Connecting all the incidents and scenes
—insofar as they are connected at all—is the general observation of a people deep in the process of being uprooted from
their cultural moorings. There is a great deal of pleasant
comedy here. As a notable instance, one can cite the description of Queen Pomaree's palace with its "incongruous assemblage of the most costly objects from all quarters of the globe"

lying cheek by jowl "beside the rudest native articles, without the slightest attempt at order":

> Superb writing-desks of rosewood, inlaid with silver and mother-of-pearl; decanters and goblets of cut-glass; embossed volumes of plates; gilded candelabras; sets of globes and mathematical instruments; the finest porcelain; richly mounted sabres and fowling-pieces; laced hats and sumptuous garments of all sorts, with numerous other matters of European manufacture, were strewn about among greasy calabashes half-filled with "poee," rolls of old tappa and matting, paddles and fish-spears, and the ordinary furniture of a Tahitian dwelling.

The process of nineteenth-century colonization, of which this is the lighter side, provides also considerable evidence of its more destructive aspects. To the Polynesians, as Melville had said in *Typee*, civilization has brought no benefits. On the contrary, missionaries, merchants, and soldiers have left everywhere a legacy of disease and devastation, and put the natives well on the road to complete extinction. Whether or not Melville had Cooper specifically in mind, he strikes in this book time and again that note of elegy on the death of a tribal community with which every reader of Cooper's work is familiar. For this one can turn especially to chapter 49, which ends with the recording of a native dirge marking the melancholy destiny of the Tahitian people, and which records also Pomaree's statement to the representatives of a missionary society—a statement strongly reminiscent of Cooper's Indian chiefs: "You have come to see me at a very bad time. Your ancestors came in the time of men, when Tahiti was inhabited: you are come to behold just the remnant of my people."

The breakdown of community values in Tahiti and their supercession by the values of civilization is evident in the degradation of human relationships, most notably in the corruption of the custom of *tayo* or selfless friendship. We know how Melville celebrated such relationship in novel after novel. In his copy of Shakespeare he never failed to underscore the slightest expression of the theme of friendship. It was to him indeed something more meaningful than the customary chumming up of fellow sailors. Like many other American writers of the century, he saw in it—at the level of the values involved—a human bulwark against the disintegration and isolation implicit in an individualistic and mercenary society. Accordingly, he notes with regret, on this score as much as any other, the destructive advance of civilization in Polynesia, for as he says in *Omoo*, among the Tahitians, "vitiated as they are by sophisticating influences, this custom [of *tayo*] has in most cases degenerated into a mere mercenary relation." It is only in a few remote and therefore uncorrupted villages that Melville and his companion find Typee-like oases of harmonious life and spontaneous affection: in Loohooloo, which seems like "a snug little community of cousins," and in Tamai, which forms "a happy little community, comparatively free from many deplorable evils to which the rest of their countrymen are subject."

Omoo, more than *Typee*, has the appearance of factual record and the directness of documentary method. Melville's next book, *Mardi*, also begins as a narrative of physical adventure, but develops, after chapter 40, into something very different. The change in plan arose from the fact that, as Melville explained to John Murray, his English publisher, having suffered from "the reiterated imputation of being a romancer in disguise," he had at last resolved to write "a *real* romance" and demonstrate how different such a work would be from *Typee* and *Omoo*. But, more important than this, while proceeding with his "narrative of *facts*" he began to feel "an incurible [sic] distaste for the same; & a longing to plume my pinions for a flight, & felt irked, cramped &

238

fettered by plodding along with dull common places,—So suddenly standing [abandoning?] the thing alltogether, I went to work heart & soul at a romance."[18]

This statement is important because facts and documentation, while undoubtedly restricting the play of Melville's creativity on the one hand, provided on the other a solid basis for his greatest fictional achievement: ballasting an imagination whose flights tend at times to leave reality altogether behind. In this sense he achieved a perfect artistic synthesis in *Moby-Dick* where, in his own words in that novel, "facts and fancy, half-way meeting, interpenetrate, and form one seamless whole." This, as Charles Feidelson has pointed out, constitutes the essence of his mature symbolistic method.[19] In his early work one can notice Melville groping his way toward it through a process of alternating rejections, abandoning fact for fancy and then fancy for fact, and yet moving gradually toward the final synthesis. The great divide in *Mardi* illustrates the first movement into the region of fancy. After chapter 40 the book is still concerned with facts, with matters of social and moral reality. By and large, however, fact and fancy do not "interpenetrate" to form "one seamless whole," but are connected (and divided) by many linear threads of allegory. The two are easily detachable, and the reader makes constant reference from the one to the other: checking Mardi against the world, Kolumbo against America, Maramma against Catholicism, Lombardo against Dante, and so on.

The allegorical Mardian voyages of the hero, Taji, and his companions, however, are precipitated by the desire to search for the lost Yillah, and what she stands for is by no means as easily ascertainable. Though insufficiently concretized, this Polynesian albino is a true artistic symbol insofar as her

18. *The Letters of Herman Melville*, p. 70.
19. Charles Feidelson, Jr., *Symbolism and American Literature* (University of Chicago Press, 1953), p. 176. See also pp. 166–75.

meaning is indeterminate, subsuming in itself many possible
meanings but exhausted neither by any one nor by all of
them. The journey after Yillah has been variously interpreted
as a quest for spiritual perfection, for the ultimate comprehension of universal mystery, for the fullness of human
experience, for ideal love, and for lost innocence. She symbolizes all these things perhaps, and more, including the
spirit of perfect social justice and harmony. To Yoomy the
poet especially she is the embodiment of the last, for, as we
shall see, he foretells whether Yillah will be found in a particular land or not by the social conditions obtaining in that
land.

Mardi is a highly complex (not to say complicated) work of
fiction. As Newton Arvin has pointed out, it revolves around
several more or less disjunct centers of reference: "There is an
emotional center, an intellectual center, a social and political
center; and though they are by no means utterly unrelated to
one another, they do not occupy the same point in space."[20]
Of all these possible areas of comment, my own discussion
will be confined to the social aspect of the theme, and even
here mainly to the images of Vivenza and Serenia: the society
of nineteenth-century America and the ideal brotherhood of
love. In the republic of Serenia Melville presents us again
with "another world, and yet one to which we feel the tie."
By comparison with the primitive community of the Typees,
however, the social state projected in Serenia is inspired
directly by the spirit of Christian ethics, and to that extent
Mardi approximates more closely still the religion-like visionary function assigned to fiction by Melville. But in the first
chapters of the novel the ideal of universal brotherhood is
invoked as much in the name of biblical mythology as of the
forecastle democracy of a shrinking world. All men are

20. Newton Arvin, *Herman Melville*, American Men of Letters
Series (New York, William Sloane Associates, 1950), p. 95.

kinsmen, Melville argues in a passage remarkable for its verve and fancy, "since in antediluvian days, the sons of God did verily wed with our mothers, the irresistible daughters of Eve. Thus all generations are blended . . . the nations and families . . . one and all, brothers in essence—oh, be we then brothers indeed! . . . The New Zealander's tattooing is not a prodigy; nor the Chinaman's ways an enigma. No custom is strange; no creed is absurd; no foe, but who will in the end prove a friend. In heaven, at last, our good, old, white-haired father Adam will greet all alike, and sociality forever prevail."

When, in the first chapter, the narrator decides upon deserting the living purgatory that is the ship *Arcturion*, the professed goal of his enterprise is the Kingsmill Islands—"loosely laid down upon the charts, and invested with all the charms of dreamland"—or, in other words, again a land of enchantment like the Typee valley. But even here, with perhaps no idea in the author's mind except to take his readers on yet another jaunt of Polynesian adventure, he dimly perceives an endless horizon further west of the islands and conjures up vistas "leading to worlds beyond." These worlds, as *Mardi* eventually settles down upon its drastically altered course, turn out to be thinly camouflaged pictures of the various nations and regions, political ideologies and social institutions, beliefs and customs, of our own world, with the imaginary land of Serenia crowning the evocations at the end. Serenia is the logical culmination of this set of images insofar as this Christian republic has realized in practice that ideal community of love which Melville invokes at the outset but which is violated, in one way or the other, by all the national societies encountered by the Mardian voyagers.

Dominora, or England, for example, has its good points as Melville is prepared to concede. But its "rapacious old monarch" Bello is, as his name suggests, an "indefatigable breeder of contentions and wars." In the interests of the doctrine of the balance of power—the "Equipoise of Calabashes"—he is forever interfering in European affairs. Dominora itself is plunged in domestic strife, and in a land that seems to promise abundance for everyone people are dying of starvation. Melville here presents a brief but effective vignette of the class conflict that marked the Chartist decade in England, with impoverished and brutally oppressed peasants and workers agitating for bread and being massacred by soldiers who "for hire betray their kith and their kin." The same story of rapacity and violence is repeated in Dominora's Eastern empire, where Bello's "World-End's garrison" keeps watch over his vast possessions and interests. Yoomy notes this fact as the voyagers pay reverence to the ancient lands of Orienda: "On the world's ancestral hearth, we spill our brothers' blood." To which the philosopher Babbalanja adds: "The march of conquest through wild provinces may be the march of Mind; but not the march of Love . . . Oh, curse of commerce! that it barters souls for gold." No wonder, though the voyagers wander far and wide in Dominora, "nowhere was Yillah found."

In Vivenza—the United States—things seem altogether different at first. The irrepressible Yoomy, catching his first glimpse of the land, exclaims joyfully: "Labour laughs in this land; and claps his hands in the jubilee groves! methinks that Yillah will yet be found." Even after the voyagers have had a closer look and experienced disillusionment at every step, the poet still exhibits a chastened hopefulness: "Yet," he says, "spite her thralls, in that land seems more of good than elsewhere. Our hopes are not wild dreams: Vivenza cheers our hearts. She is a rainbow to the isles!" Nor does that severe critic of Vivenza who remains anonymous, hesitate to concede in his open letter to the people of the Republic that theirs "is the best and happiest land under the sun." But this, as he goes on to point out, is due not to their own wisdom but to the revolutionary tradition of the Pilgrim Fathers and the facts of American geography.

As a matter of fact, Melville's evocation of the promise of America in *Mardi* is crowded with a whole symphony of echoes spanning three centuries of cultural history: echoes of his own vision of abundance for all in *Typee;* of that strain of hope eclipsed by apprehension which one encounters everywhere in the imaginative literature of the mid-century; of the visionary tradition handed down by the American Puritans; of Columbus' dream and prayer in the "Ave Maria" section of Hart Crane's *The Bridge;* and of the great concluding passages of Scott Fitzgerald's *Gatsby*. Comparing the old world of Dominora with the new world of Kolumbo, Melville says of the latter and its prospective inhabitants:

> Did not their bards pronounce them a fresh start in the Mardian species; requiring a new world for their full development? For be it known, that the great land of Kolumbo, no inconsiderable part of which was embraced by Vivenza, was the last island discovered in the Archipelago.
>
> In good round truth . . . Vivenza was a noble land. Like a young tropic tree she stood, laden down with greenness, myriad blossoms, and the ripened fruit thickhanging from one bough. She was promising as the morning.
>
> Or Vivenza might be likened to St. John, feeding on locusts and wild honey, and with prophetic voice crying to the nations from the wilderness. Or, child-like, standing among the old robed kings and emperors of the Archipelago, Vivenza seemed a young Messiah, to whose discourse the bearded Rabbis bowed.
>
> So seemed Vivenza in its better aspect.

Several chapters later this is followed by an invocation

combining national hopefulness with a social idealism that
embraces the whole of humanity:

> Kolumbo;—last sought, last found, Mardi's estate, so
> long kept back;—pray Oro, it be not squandered foolish-
> ly. Here lie plantations, held in fee by stout hearts and
> arms; and boundless fields, that may be had for seeing.
> Here, your foes are forests, struck down with bloodless
> maces.—Ho! Mardi's Poor, and Mardi's Strong! ye, who
> starve or beg; seventh sons who slave for earth's first-
> born—here is your home; predestinated yours; Come
> over . . . fathers of the wedded tribes to come!—abject
> now, illustrious evermore:—Ho: Sinew, Brawn, and
> Thigh.

But this hopefulness only serves as the background to the
critical image of American society, for, as the Mardian
voyagers observe, reality in Vivenza has already belied the
dream. Babbalanja—expressing the sort of apprehensiveness
that was being voiced around the same time also by Cooper,
Hawthorne, and the elder James—declares that Vivenza's
"climacteric is not come; hers is not yet a nation's manhood
even; though now in childhood, she anticipates her youth,
and lusts for empire like any czar." The same warning with
regard to the future is contained in the anonymous scroll
which, taking note of the fact that the country, once oppressed
by Dominora, is now emulating Dominora's example of
acquisitive expansionism, prophesies that she will not long
remain as liberal as she is now. The vaunted liberty of the
land is already a matter of illusory appearance. "There is not
so much freedom here as these freemen think," Babbalanja
observes somewhat in the manner of Hawthorne's canny
commentators, a statement elaborated in the scroll which
declares that it is not "the prime end, and chief blessing, to be
politically free. And freedom is only good as a means; is no

end in itself. . . . freedom is more social than political." And as for the twin claim of equality: "Civilization has never been the brother of equality." Nor does Vivenza afford any evidence of the values of mutual love and brotherhood. Its inhabitants do not form a living human community. Their social union is superficial, limited, and negative. They resemble, as Melville suggests by means of an extended simile which occupies a whole chapter, a mollusc-like confederacy of self-sufficient individual units—isolated cells, each oblivious of the rest, and the whole body politic neither showing nor sharing any common purpose except when threatened by external aggression.

The disillusionment of the voyagers becomes total in the slave-holding southern part of Vivenza. Though they had at times "heard whisperings that promised an end" to their wanderings, now even Yoomy abates "his sanguine hopes." "Here," he cries, "labour has lost his laugh!" Thus "as in Dominora,—so, throughout Vivenza, North and South,—Yillah harboured not." Was the quest for Yillah, then, doomed to failure? Would the world never achieve a state of perfect social justice and harmony? "Are all our dreams, then, vain?" as Yoomy exclaims on leaving Vivenza. "Is this no dawn of day that streaks the crimson East! Naught but the false and flickering lights which sometimes mock Aurora in the north! Ah, man, my brother! Have all martyrs for thee bled in vain; in vain we poets sang, and prophets spoken!"

Melville's answer to this question is Serenia. The answer is as characteristic of the mid-century imagination as the question itself—both couched in visionary terms and neither concerned with the mechanics of political power and social change. Serenia is the ideal community of love and universal brotherhood. Inspired by the precepts of Christ (Alma), its principles are in harmony with human wisdom also. Coverdale, we remember, had observed that, though Blithedale ended in failure, it embodied what ought to be a truth. Here, too, while King Media insists in the beginning that the "social fabric" of Serenia "must soon fall to pieces" because it is "based upon the idlest of theories," the Serenian guide argues: "Right reason, and Alma, are the same; else Alma, not reason, would we reject. The Master's great command is Love; and here do all things wise, and all things good, unite." Eventually the Mardian voyagers are convinced of Serenia's practicability, and all but one of them come to believe that they have at last succeeded in their quest. The philosopher's doubts are resolved, the historian regards Serenia as the final consummation of the world's history, and the poet as the fulfillment of all human dreams. The statesman leaves the republic only in order to convert his own land to its principles. The change of faith which they experience—the moral transformation of the individual—is postulated here, as elsewhere in the literature of the period, as the necessary and sufficient basis for the practical realization of the envisioned social theory.

Taji alone leaves Serenia with his quest unanswered. In other words, here, as in *Typee*, Melville makes his protagonist abandon the ideal community, and perhaps for reasons not entirely dissimilar. The world of Serenia, although conceived in religious rather than secular terms, also precludes the possibility of certain kinds of intellectual and spiritual experience, including the experience of flying in the face of the gods and assuming undisputed command as the captain of one's soul—if only to exercise the paramount choice of nihilistic abdication: the glory and the tragedy of absolute individualism from the renaissance to our own time. Taji is warned by his companions that certain kinds of knowledge are attainable to God alone and that all human search must end eventually in Serenia. But he asserts that he is "the hunter that never rests! the hunter without a home! She I seek still flies before; and I will follow, though she lead me beyond the reef; through sunless seas; and into night and death." For him Yillah—white, like Moby-Dick—has come to represent the ultimate mysteries of the universe, and he himself has become the embodiment of unalloyed individual Will. In this respect Melville's demigod recalls another mythic sailor-hero of the nineteenth century: Tennyson's Ulysses, with whom he shares the indomitable "will / To strive, to seek, to find, and not to yield." Like Tennyson's Ulysses again, but unlike that of Homer's, Taji is not homeward bound but rather poised away from home and friends and ready to be washed down by the gulfs in a pursuit that goes beyond "the utmost bound of human thought."

In *Redburn*, Melville's next work, there is a passage which seems incongruous with the general tenor of the book. Here we find evoked again, in characteristic terms, the beatific vision of America as the prospective land of universal brotherhood:

> Settled by the people of all nations, all nations may claim her for their own. You cannot spill a drop of American blood without spilling the blood of the whole world. . . . We are not a nation, so much as a world; for unless we may claim all the world for our sire, like Melchisedec, we are without father or mother.
> For who was our father and our mother? Or can we point to any Romulus and Remus for our founders? Our ancestry is lost in the universal paternity . . . We are the heirs of all time, and with all nations we divide our inheritance. On this Western Hemisphere all tribes and people are forming into one federated whole; and there is a future which shall see the estranged children of Adam restored as to the old hearthstone in Eden.

The other world beyond this, which was longed for by the devout before Columbus' time, was found in the New; and the deep-sea lead, that first struck these soundings, brought up the soil of Earth's Paradise. Not a Paradise then, or now; but to be made so at God's good pleasure, and in the fulness and mellowness of time.

But this vision remains only a matter of words, for it is not suggested by what the youthful sailor has seen of the world on his first voyage but arises rather in despite of his harrowing experiences. How distant the promised "fulness and mellowness of time" are from actuality can be seen from his apostrophe to Adam and Eve on beholding the spectacle of human misery in Liverpool: "Adam and Eve! If indeed ye are yet alive in heaven, may it be no part of your immortality to look down upon the world ye have left. For as all these sufferers and cripples are as much your family as young Abel, so, to you, the sight of the world's woes would be a parental torment indeed."

In *Redburn* Melville is back in the realm of "fact" and wholly concerned with civilized society. Although relieved by a certain strain of wry and at times savage humor, it is from end to end a grim book. The voyage that begins with the suicide of a drunken sailor at one end and the spontaneous combustion of the corpse of another at the other end is overcast with a sense of treachery, betrayal, and, for the first time, real evil. The world that is projected here exhibits a total negation of the values embodied in Serenia, the *Highlander* being without parallel in Melville's fleet of imaginary vessels in that it lacks even the minimal fellowship of forecastle brotherhood. It is only toward the end of the book that this oppressive situation is somewhat relieved by the friendship between Redburn and Harry Bolton. Bolton is the narrator's

English counterpart: a "gentleman" fallen upon evil days in an insecure world.

The initiation of a friendless boy into a corrupt society is the theme of *Redburn*. The civilization he encounters is the civilization of Dominora and Vivenza again, but this time concretized in a tightly controlled prose that ranks with Melville's best. Captain Marryat and hard times, it seems, are again the prime movers of the resolution that sends the boy to sea, although the accent falls heavily in this book all along upon hard times. The world seems "bitter cold as December, and bleak as its blasts" as Wellinborough Redburn sets out on his first voyage, armed with *The Wealth of Nations*, to retrieve his family's fortunes. The writing, especially in the first five chapters, is so packed with suggestiveness that Redburn's hardships seem to reflect the hard times in the world at large, and one wonders if the blighted hopes he talks about are his country's or only his own. Adam Smith, however, proves as unhelpful as the stupid Jack Blunt's talismanic "Dream Book," and the boy returns home as penniless as when he went. But it is not poverty alone that makes Redburn's situation so painful and his voyage so oppressive. It is rather the Ishmael-like aloneness that he experiences both in America and on board the ship.

Melville's image of civilized society has an occasional lightness of touch which helps to bring out the full power of its more pervasive somberness. Recalling his earlier enthusiasm for the luxurious freedom of the Typee valley, we have here Larry's ecstatic praise for the savages of "Madagasky" and his assertion of their superiority over "snivelized" men. His "illiberal insinuations against civilisation," however, are amply borne out when Redburn is greeted in Liverpool by an unbroken and lurid wilderness of warehouses, poverty, and suffering. Casting aside as useless his prosperous father's outdated guidebook, the young sailor takes a harrowing excursion through the Dickensian underworld of urban England. The Liverpool he discovers is not the city of well-appointed hotels and old monuments, but a Sodom-like maze of dark alleys infested with beggary, crime, misery, and all conceivable kinds of vice. He encounters scores of ragged old women scraping heaps of rubbish for food, and, in a particularly gruesome passage, describes a woman and her three children slowly dying of starvation while everyone to whose attention he calls their situation turns away unconcerned. The same story of callousness is repeated later when, on the return voyage, an epidemic breaks out among the Irish emigrants and even a known doctor among the cabin passengers refuses so much as to step inside the steerage—an occurrence that makes Melville conclude: "We talk of the Turks, and abhor the cannibals; but may not some of *them* go to heaven before some of *us?* We may have civilised bodies and yet barbarous souls."

The evil of the society at large, as the case of the emigrants suggests, is only re-enacted on board the *Highlander*. As already mentioned, the ship's company lacks completely that spirit of fellowship which Melville usually associated with common sailors. Of course here, too, the picture is relieved by such comic episodes as young Redburn's offering the snuff box in a friendly way to the second mate, and his putting on his best suit of clothes to make a social call on the captain. The comedy of such gestures, directed as it is chiefly at Redburn's Sunday-school idea of what the world is really like, is not entirely lacking in pathos. The preposterousness of his actions is indeed equaled only by his ignorance; but if the absurdity reflects his own simplicity, it also provides a commentary on the absence of such values as common kindliness, warmth, and compassion in the society in which he finds himself. There is something touching and not at all absurd in his hope that somewhere in the wide world he would surely find a friendly hand to help and guide him; that Captain Riga, for instance, "would be attentive and considerate to me, and strive to cheer me up, and comfort me in my lonesomeness. I did not even deem it at all impossible that he would invite me down into the cabin of a pleasant night, to ask me questions concerning my parents, and prospects in life . . . or give me a slate and pencil, and teach me problems in navigation."

It being his first voyage, one understands that Redburn should have expected tokens of friendliness from "the proud gods and commodores of this earth." He gets over such foolishness soon enough, but what makes his situation truly painful is the absence of the slightest sense of community among his fellow sailors. Their treatment of him is only partially motivated by his Sunday-school gentility. They are a set of depraved and brutalized men, and Redburn's "incipient love" toward them ends almost immediately in bitter disillusionment. Their collective spirit of evil finds its supreme embodiment in Jackson, the consumptive sailor who is like Ahab in his vengeful hatred of the whole world and like Claggart in his particular malice toward Redburn. Thus, unlike the Ishmael of *Moby-Dick*, who finds a sustaining community on the *Pequod*, Redburn becomes an outcast among his fellow sailors. His own attitude toward them, however, does not lack that spirit of understanding and compassion whose absence has dehumanized them so completely. While he detests them with the full passion of his youth and innocence, he also realizes that, if they represent the evil of the world, the world itself has brutalized them into it. He even feels compassionate toward Jackson, in whom he recognizes "more woe than wickedness": "and his wickedness seemed to spring from his woe; and for all his hideousness there was that in his eye at times that was ineffably pitiable and touching; and though there were moments when I almost hated this Jackson, yet I have pitied no man as I have pitied him."

Redburn also realizes that there is but a thin line that divides the isolation of a castaway from the inhuman malevolence of a Jackson, and he prays that, in a world of castaways, he himself may stay on the human side: "at last I found myself a sort of Ishmael in the ship, without a single friend or companion; and I began to feel a hatred growing up in me against the whole crew—so much so, that I prayed against it, that it might not master my heart completely, and so make a fiend of me, something like Jackson."

It is as an Ishmael that Melville's narrator makes his first appearance in the work that came next: *White Jacket*. The protective garment which gives him his name here sets him apart from the rest of the crew. As Howard Vincent has pointed out, the two chief symbolical meanings of the jacket are the idea of self-sufficiency and the desire to keep the paradisal vision safe from rude contact with reality. Its wearer "wants self-sufficiency, and in this sufficiency to remain aloof from—or above—his fellow sailors." What he is "trying to hold and protect" is "the paradise now almost lost."[21] With the help of this insight one can see how *White Jacket* marks a further stage in the development of Melville's theme. His narrator here is the same man who had first evoked the ideal of the Happy Valley in *Typee* and Serenia in *Mardi* and who had then proceeded to describe its total negation in the civilized society of *Redburn*.

The civilization represented by the *Neversink* is the civilization of *Redburn* again. Of course the action in *White Jacket* is confined to shipboard, but the ship itself embodies the whole world in microcosm. The allegorical status of the man-of-war is declared boldly in the subtitle, labored somewhat heavily in the last chapter, and stated explicitly at several points in between. "But we have seen that a man-of-war is

21. Howard P. Vincent, "'White-Jacket': An Essay in Interpretation," *New England Quarterly*, 22 (1949), 307, 308.

but this old-fashioned world of ours afloat," as Melville says in one place, "full of all manner of characters—full of strange contradictions; and though boasting some fine fellows here and there, yet, upon the whole, charged to the combings of her hatchways with the spirit of Belial and all unrighteousness." It is a brutal and corrupt world, engendering everywhere all sorts of vices and iniquities. Hierarchic in structure, and based upon a rigid caste system, it is lorded over by a narrowing spiral of officers headed by the czar-like Captain and Commodore. The ranks are sharply divided by inequalities in work, and there is one law in practice for the sailors and another for the officers. Running through the book, like a constant refrain, is the observation of class antagonism: "the people" (always underlined) on the one hand, and, on the other, a social entity variously designated as "officers," "tyrants," or "oppressors."

Against all these things, so markedly offensive to the spirit of democracy, Melville protests vigorously, taking his stand on the principles of the Declaration of Independence. But there is a deeper side to the critical image of civilized society as it is projected in *White Jacket*. This is conveyed by the very concept of the world as a man-of-war and refers to its innate tendency to breed mutual antagonisms and violence. The governing code of this world is embodied in the Articles of War—a document that has replaced the old commandment "Thou shalt not kill" by an equally universal and categorical imperative of its own: "Shall suffer death." Nor is it only during the time of actual warfare that the sailors are liable to incur its rigorous penalties. It is read out to them every month, as a sort of morning prayer, and, as Melville says in concluding chapter 70—where he plays with some heavy-handed irony upon "the pure, bubbling milk of human kindness, and Christian charity" displayed by this "Sermon on the Mount"—"the Martial Law" does not relax "its gripe" in peace or war, but is likely, even after death, to "hunt you straight through the other world, and out again at its other end, following you through all eternity."

In *Typee*, as I have already noted, Melville maintained that savage societies were superior to civilized ones, inasmuch as the latter, in addition to waging atrocious foreign wars, were marked by constant strife and violence within "the bosom of the community." As is obvious, the antagonism that Melville dwells upon in *White Jacket* is precisely this civil antagonism —the war within a nation rather than the war of nations. What we have here is the image of a society divided against itself, with the spirit of suspicion and hatred animating each separate cog in the machine. The most explicit statement of the general violation of community aboard the *Neversink* appears in the chapter entitled "The Social State in a Man-of-War," where Melville begins by enumerating all the evils— flogging, stealing, smuggling, gambling, etc.—that he has previously described at length in separate chapters. He then observes that these do not "comprise the whole catalogue of evil. One single feature is full of significance." This feature turns out to be the calculated antagonism between the sailors and the marines, the true function of the latter in a man-of-war being to stand guard over common seamen and to awe them into submission. "Know, then, that what standing armies are to nations, what turnkeys are to jails, these marines are to the seamen . . . Their muskets are their keys." The consequent division—"the mutual contempt, and even hatred, subsisting between these two bodies of men—both clinging to one keel, both lodged in one household"—is considered the most politic basis for maintaining social order and security: "Checks and balances, blood against blood, *that* is the cry and the argument."

Nor is this domestic contention limited to the sailors and the marines. It permeates the entire "household." "What applies to the relation in which the marine and sailor stand toward each other . . . will," as Melville goes on to add, "in degree, apply to nearly the entire interior of a man-of-war's discipline. . . . Through all the endless ramifications of rank and station, in most men-of-war there runs a sinister vein of bitterness, not exceeded by the fireside hatreds in a family of step-sons ashore. It were sickening to detail all the paltry irritabilities, jealousies, and cabals, the spiteful detractions and animosities, that lurk far down, and cling to the very kelson of the ship."

Against this one can set Whitman's declaration of faith in *Song of Myself*:

And I know that the spirit of God is the brother of my own,
And that all the men ever born are also my brothers . . .
And that a kelson of the creation is love . . .

A similar affirmation is Melville's answer to the deep antagonisms working in the depths of the society he pictures in *White Jacket*. He, too, declares his faith in love and brotherhood, embodying these values in the small maintop community that functions as a human oasis within the otherwise morally sterile world of the *Neversink*. "We main-top men were brothers, one and all; and we loaned ourselves to each other with all the freedom in the world." The moving spirit of this community is the "matchless and unmatchable Jack Chase." Himself a part of "the people," as he declares in his argument with the "poetical" Lemsford, he is a true popular hero. Versatile, cultivated, and lovable, he is a defender of the rights of man and the liberties of the world, having deserted his ship once to fight in the cause of freedom in Peru. Unlike Jackson of *Redburn*—who held the sailors in a bondage that corroded "in their secret hearts" and set man against man— Jack Chase inspires a bond of love and fellowship. He is the leader of the spirit of community which prevails among the maintop men. During the Cape Horn theatricals, his spirited rendering of Percy Royal-Mast moves even the officers to "confess a human brotherhood" with the sailors, although the transformation in their case is short-lived and they soon ship "their quarter-deck faces again." This episode can perhaps be taken as a light-hearted commentary on the power of art—on both its scope and its limitation as an instrument of actual social change.

However, though neither Jack Chase nor his men cause any alteration in the state of the world at large, the values they represent act as a thematic counterweight to the image of actual society on the *Neversink*. It is the existence of the maintop community and the awareness of its possibility that account for the hopeful attitude of the narrator in this book. In *Redburn* his encounter with civilization had made him an Ishmael. Here he achieves a sense of belonging, and when, toward the end, he struggles out of his jacket at the pain of death, he is, as it were, reborn into a full consciousness of the new values: "We main-top men are all aloft in the top; and round our mast we circle, a brother-band, hand in hand, all spliced together. . . . Hand in hand we topmates stand, rocked in our Pisgah top." But however hopeful the vision of the future, the narrator realizes that, in the world of present reality, their community possesses no permanence, that it is their last night on the maintop, and that the five hundred other sailors have already retreated inland "not, alas! in battle array, as at quarters, but scattered broadcast over the land."

The theme of community in *White Jacket* is allied on the one hand with the idea of class struggle, and all but submerged on the other by the numerous reformist appeals which form the main burden of the book. The use of the marines to oppress "the people" recalls the Mardian picture of Chartist England where Bello's soldiers "for hire betray their kith and their kin," while the other shipboard abuses are such as Dickens himself might have taken for his subject. Indeed the Navy—with its "close cribbing and confinement"—provided Melville with a conception of society common enough in English fiction but rarely entertained by the imaginative writers of this period in America. The Martial Law that governs the *Neversink* makes the narrator say to himself: "Hear you that, White Jacket! I tell you there is no escape." In other words, society, as conceived in *White Jacket*, cannot be repudiated effortlessly in the name of individual freedom or an ideal alternative. Ubiquitous and inexorable, its institutions are the most powerful determinants of the individual's destiny—even his moral personality. For, as Melville says, expanding an insight barely hinted at in *Redburn*, he will not pronounce authoritatively "upon the essential criminality of any man-of-war's man." The sailor is "not essentially criminal, but only made so by arbitrary laws," and depravity "in the oppressed" is "in a large degree, the effect, and not the cause and justification of oppression." The established order is thus an organic system, a system in which social causes become moral effects, and which therefore rules out the possibility of immaculate disinvolvement on the part of a few of its constituent members. It can be reformed by persuasion or changed by struggle directed from within it; but it cannot be ignored. Its dreamers cannot remove to a virgin scene and proceed forthwith to give practical shape to their social visions.

This recognition marks an important development in Melville's handling of the society-community theme. In *Typee* and *Mardi* the images of the actual and the ideal are spatially disjunct: each sovereign in its own right, like the kingdom of Satan and the kingdom of God. The two, if connected at all, are connected only by the protagonist's choice which alternates between repudiation and return. In *Redburn*, on the

other hand, there is no disjunction but there is no choice
either. The civilization it describes is uniformly marked by a
denial of all values except its own corrupt ones. *White Jacket*
projects for the first time the vision of a community of love
and brotherhood arising from within the existing society
itself. The common sailors who form it are a part of the real
world, but they are the forward-looking hopeful part. "We
are the pioneers of the world; the advance-guard, sent on
through the wilderness of untried things, to break a new path
in the New World that is ours." To this statement, *Moby-
Dick*—which maintains the same close relation between the
actual and the ideal—was to give a new resonance and a
largeness of meaning quite beyond the reach of the confined
martial world of *White Jacket*.

The idea that Americans were destined to be the pioneers
of a new order was, of course, as old as the settlement of
Plymouth colony. While it continued to be one of the more
inspiring of American ideals, by the beginning of the nineteenth century, its meaning had been extended into larger
areas than the ones contemplated by the Puritans. It now
stood for social, political, and technological as well as moral
advancement, and it involved a constant dislocation of settled
forms, though by no means the rejection of all the intellectual
and cultural values of the world's ancient heritage. Together
with this ideal of breaking new ground in new realms of
experience—the quest of "the hunter without a home," as
Taji puts it—went an exploration into the scope and limitation of transcendental individualism: the individual's dream
of becoming an all-powerful demigod and the opposite possibility of his being reduced to the helpless position of an
Ishmael. The idea of isolated Ishmaels and Ahabs was connected in its turn with an insight into the necessity of human
community.

Roughly analyzed as they are here, these elements constituted for the nineteenth-century American epic poet (in Lascelles Abercrombie's words) that "sense of the significance of life" which he felt operating "as the accepted unconscious metaphysic of his age." We can find a fragmentary expression of this metaphysic in all of Melville's early work, but it was only in *Moby-Dick* that he transfigured it by bringing together all its constituents and by giving them their proper place in one epic structure. At its primary level, Melville's narrative, like the practical energies of his generation, took for its field of operation man's struggle against the untamed elements. That such a subject should eventually develop to include, not only physical adventure, but also the exploration of metaphysical problems; that it should combine facts of economics with flights of speculation; that it should at one and the same time celebrate the glory and dramatize the tragedy of individual will—these and similar other achievements are a tribute to the breadth of Melville's genius. They represent nevertheless the artistic transmutation—the exploitation on a grand scale—of problems and possibilities implicit in his culture.

Crude as the statement may sound, *Moby-Dick* represents, in one of its many aspects, an attempt to resolve that Cod-God paradox which presented the American imagination with one of the central problems of American civilization. As I noted in the first chapter, this was essentially the problem of reconciling the material drives behind the colonization of the new continent with the moral-metaphysical vision that accompanied it. It would perhaps be too rash to say that Melville resolved the problem by investing the fish itself with divinity, and by altering in the process the traditional concept of God in the light of certain intuitions of pre-Christian speculative thought. But there is no doubt that in his symbolistic imagination the physical adventure of following the

Leviathan was indistinguishable from the metaphysical adventure of searching for the so-called ultimate realities of
life.

On the side of physical adventure, there are obvious con-
nections between Melville's epic and the contemporary phase
of American history; between the imaginary voyage of the
Pequod and the historical fact of continental conquest. For
example, we can follow Harry Levin's analysis of Melville's
imagery and see how the ocean itself can be regarded as a
metaphor for the American continent, and how as "the most
rugged of individualists, Ahab can be historically placed
among those captains of industry and freebooters of enterprise who, at the public expense, were so rapidly transforming
the country and the age."[22] It is also obvious that Melville's
theme was not the celebration but rather the tragic evaluation
of that exuberant and pervasive spirit in whose name so many
dubious activities—from military expansionism to the build-
ing of personal empires—were justified as the earthly revelation of providential design. The fate that attends the *Pequod*
is far other than the destiny which seemed so hopefully manifest to the nation as a whole. Having said so much, however,
one should also say that this interpretation, like many other
interpretations of *Moby-Dick*, seems curiously inadequate:
illuminating but reductory. To acknowledge the bewildering
complexity of this epic has become a commonplace of criticism—a customary ritual enacted for the privilege of commenting on it at all. Whether or not such acknowledgment is
necessary in the case of the many exhaustive and admirable
studies made in recent years, for me it is imperative. My discussion will be concerned eventually with disentangling but
one of the many thematic strands which enter into the luxuri-
ant pattern of this fiction. Since, however, the theme which I

22. Harry Levin, *The Power of Blackness* (New York, Knopf, 1958),
pp. 204, 212.

propose to discuss also featured in the larger cultural picture, it is worth while to pause a little longer on the relation between *Moby-Dick* and the national spirit of the century.

The inadequacy of viewing Melville's epic entirely in terms of historical facts can to some extent be remedied by taking into account what is perhaps a characteristic imaginative response to these facts: characteristic in the sense that, though by no means common, it is not confined to Melville either, but suggests, in its fusing of material circumstance with moral argument and metaphysical vision, derivation from the oldest of American traditions. This can be illustrated by considering at some length a curious contemporary document, a lecture delivered by the elder Henry James in the winter of 1850–51, at about the same time that *Moby-Dick* was being reconstructed into its final shape. Entitled "Property as a Symbol," the lecture begins as a grandiose justification of individual enterprise and material acquisition. As an example of what is meant by "property," James refers to John Jacob Astor, whose highly profitable fur trade had become an instrument for opening up the West. But it soon becomes clear that he is talking more about exploration, discovery, and scientific invention than about the amassing of personal fortune, and the lecture develops into a theological argument concerning the ethics of man's subjugation of the earth. The conclusion at which he arrives is that such human effort is justified only if it is made not for selfish materialism but in obedience to God's commandment and in the interests of the community.

More interesting than the conclusion is the thread of the argument itself; if, that is, one can disentangle a straight-enough thread from James' highly repetitive and declamatory prose. The initial question that he poses is disarmingly simple: why, he asks, do men pay deference to property while being ashamed of paying such deference? It is because property is only "representatively sacred";[23] it is sacred as a symbol. Since man represents the highest earthly embodiment of divine perfection, James argues, it follows "that the whole lower creation, or whatsoever is beneath man, must also be involved in him and express him. Man being the true creature or image of God, his empire must needs be universal. He must necessarily constitute the measure of all the inferior things of the universe. He must be the master key which shall fit all the wards of the lower creation, and make its mysteries intelligible." But nature will "typify the invisible things of man's spirit" only when "the face of nature has put on her most human expression, that is to say, when science shall have developed all her resources of use and ornament to man, then man shall see himself spiritually reflected in her, whether in all the unfathomable depth of his affections, or all the pomp and starry splendor of his intelligence, as he now sees his outward person reflected in a glass." Having reconciled technology with his own theology, James goes on to reveal the symbolic meaning of property by means of an appropriate reference to biblical mythology:

> Accordingly I am led by a rational inquisition to conclude, that Property symbolizes the perfect sovereignty which man is destined to exercise over nature. All the prestige which surrounds it, all the influence it exerts, springs from its symbolic or representative virtue, consists in the fact of its representing that complete lordship of nature which man is destined one day to realize. The opening page of the Mosaic cosmogony tells us that the divinely appointed destiny of man was to subdue the earth to himself, and to have dominion over the fish of the sea, over the fowl of the air, and over every living thing that moves upon the face of the earth.[24]

23. Henry James, *Lectures and Miscellanies* (New York, Redfield, 1852), p. 72. 24. Ibid., pp. 61–63.

James then goes on to give an account of those instrumentalities which are divinely implanted within creation to bring it to this happy end. In the first place, there is "the temper of mind which God begets" in man in order to impel him "to subdue the whole realm of the outward and finite to himself, to the service of his proper individuality, and so vindicate the truth of his infinite origin."[25] Looking forward to the later formulations of pragmatic philosophy, James maintains that human understanding is dependent on human action, and that it is not by contemplation of the universe but through the attempt to make it "freely subservient to the uses of his life," that man can become "rightly conscious of himself" or aware of his relation to "exhaustless divinity." "We know nothing in respect either to the nature or the intensity of our passions until they become developed in action. . . . *His* passions are the most potent who is most impelled to action by them."[26] On the other side, God has so ordered the physical forces of the universe, that by "the antagonism which nature presents" to man, "by the stringent limitation it imposes upon him, he is stimulated or piqued into incessant self-assertion, is evermore thrown back upon the instincts of his inward infinitude, until finally the veil of the temple is rent from top to bottom, and the holy of holies stands suddenly revealed." The ultimate metaphysical revelation—which, James believes will bear "the lineaments of an immaculate and omnipotent humanity"—is thus born out of the active matching of human and natural powers in the universe. It is through this process that man will attain his "final self-consciousness, his true self-knowledge, and in that his true knowledge of God."[27]

Property, then, is the outward symbol of all these momentous issues. But to go on to the social and ethical part of

25. Ibid., p. 63.
26. Ibid., pp. 64, 65.
27. Ibid., p. 66.

James' argument: "Property cannot be a final fact of history, cannot be a good in itself, cannot be a divine end in humanity . . . Property which can be acquired and alienated, is only a transient good, is but the symbol or shadow of a higher good, namely, man's inherent sovereignty over nature." Society only recognizes "the sceptre" of that "divine or perfect man . . . who has no outward or mercenary end to achieve, but is simply intent upon living up to his own ideal, or obeying the infinite divinity he finds within his soul."[28] Such an individual can apparently assume one of many practical avatars. If he is not an Astor, advancing in spite of himself the great cause of "sovereignty over nature," he can appear as "the inventor of the spinning-jenny" and be elevated by society above "all the saints of the Romish calendar *plus* if you please all those of the Greek."[29] But however perfect or divine, he is incapable of accomplishing by himself the appointed purpose of human destiny. Sovereignty over nature is a sovereignty "of which . . . society or fellowship among men is the indispensable means or instrument."[30]

It would certainly not do to labor too hard the correspondence between the theme of *Moby-Dick* and this theory of matter and metaphysics. For one thing, Melville's method does not lend itself easily to theoretical interpretation. Also, notwithstanding the marked similarity between the two views of human destiny, Melville conceives of it as essentially tragic. He is nowhere nearly as hopeful as Henry James is here. He is not at all confident that there is any divine assurance of success in the human struggle against the elements. If *Moby-Dick* celebrates the heroism of man's assault on the unknown powers of the universe, it is more in the spirit of the early renaissance which suspected something infernal, rather than

28. Ibid., pp. 69, 75, 79.
29. Ibid., p. 80.
30. Ibid., p. 68.

divine, in such an undertaking. Like Marlowe's Faustus, Ahab is in league with the agents of Lucifer. And, of course, nature in this novel is not merely an assemblage of vast physical forces. The interlocking imagery of the sea, the creatures of the sea, and, above all, the quintessential white whale project the unknown element in the universe on a more comprehensive scale. While it undoubtedly represents the physical challenge of man's precarious existence, the sea also embodies the idea of chance and the other incomprehensible features of the fate that presides over the human situation. On the one hand, the sea and the whale are, according to Melville's own comparisons, akin to the white Himalayas, the white polar regions, and the white milky way. On the other hand, in their inscrutability and their amoral purposiveness, they symbolize on a grand scale those forces which Thomas Hardy tried to objectify again and again in such evocations of nature as Egdon Heath and Little Hintock.

All these differences, important as they are, do not, however, obscure the significant common feature of Henry James' symbolical interpretation of what he calls "Property" and Melville's symbolical novel: that curious imaginative view which, in each case, conceives a solidly physical subject as a problem in metaphysics and in personal and social morality. It is a view which, while focused here upon contemporary subjects, reveals at the same time the persistent vitality of a tradition that goes back over two centuries to the earliest conception of the American settlement as a dramatic phase in the conflict of supramundane powers. Melville is, of course, concerned most concretely with whaling—with whaling as an industry, as an advance in technology, as an agency for the dissemination of new social and political ideals. But—like Henry James' fur-trade and spinning-jenny or like Bradford's beaver-skins—whale fishing in itself has no ultimate significance. It is a vehicle for the fulfillment of man's moral, social, and metaphysical destiny. Furthermore, we have in Melville's novel, as in James' essay, the idea that comprehension is dependent upon action, and that it is only at some stage in the course of his struggle against the visible forces of nature that man can hope to be confronted with the invisible realities of life. This is true of Ahab, who seeks to get at the mysteries that torment him by striking through the "pasteboard masks" of visible objects. But it is even more true of the contemplative Ishmael. For him also the Leviathan—"this antemosaic, unsourced existence"—symbolizes the problem of universal reality. His idea of the universe is, of course, very different from Ahab's. He does not see it so sharply divided between the good and the evil spheres, or even between the human and non-human ones. Eventually he comes very close to regarding it as one indivisible totality—a vast ambiguity of man, fish, and the elements, of good and evil. But while such an insight bears remarkable affinity to the viewpoint of oriental metaphysics, Ishmael achieves it not through oriental contemplation but through sustained action. Though he does not pursue Moby-Dick out of vengeance, yet pursue him he must if he is to comprehend him and to resolve the problem of the universe. This, according to his own confession in the opening chapter, is one of the chief motives for his whaling voyage. Books and museums can only help to outline the problem. But as he says much later: "Only in the heart of quickest perils; only when within the eddyings of his angry flukes; only on the profound unbounded sea, can the fully invested whale be truly and livingly found out." It is indeed precisely in such circumstances that a moment of illumination has previously come to him; the moment in "The Grand Armada" chapter when, to use Henry James' words, "the veil of the temple is rent, from top to bottom, and the holy of holies stands suddenly revealed." Ishmael's earlier experience of the "horrible vulturism of earth" is now supplemented by a vision of elemental fecundity, love, joy, and peace which animate the center of all existence. This fuller understanding gives him also a new insight into the reality of his own being, an insight which (though Ishmael does not explicitly note this fact) points out by contrast the tragic blindness of Ahab's view: "But even so, amid the tornadoed Atlantic of my being, do I myself still forever centrally disport in mute calm; and while ponderous planets of unwaning woe revolve round me, deep down and deep inland there I still bathe me in eternal mildness of joy."

Having said all this by way of a summary tribute to what is perhaps the most fascinating aspect of *Moby-Dick*, I must go on to consider the social side of Melville's theme. Here again the accent, as in the case of James' essay, falls heavily upon the great individual who is "stimulated or piqued into incessant self-assertion, is evermore thrown back upon the instincts of his inward infinitude" by "the antagonism which nature presents to him" and who is thus impelled to attack, to comprehend, and finally to establish human "lordship" over the powers that govern the universe. This is the sympathetic, heroic, Promethean side of Ahab's character, and he shares it with James' "divine or perfect man . . . who has no outward or mercenary end to achieve, but is simply intent upon living up to his own ideal, or obeying the infinite divinity he finds within his soul." But Ahab is far from being a "divine" or "perfect" hero. He is a greater man than Starbuck but not a better one—and this chiefly because he lacks the nobler motivation of his self-appointed task as well as a true comprehension of its implications for the rest of humanity. If he is a monomaniac, it is not because he has only one serious purpose in life. That is a part of his heroic greatness. His monomania is essentially a matter of his undeviating sense of personal wrong and personal vengeance, and this overmastering sense is in its turn the result of his total egocentricity:

the recurring fatal flaw in the literature of a culture where Calvinistic self-absorption had finally issued into action as the unfettered activity of isolated and self-sufficient individuals.

Ahab, in other words—in Henry James' words—fails to recognize that, whether he is seeking sovereignty over nature or an understanding of the supernatural, it is an enterprise of which "society or fellowship among men is the indispensable means or instrument." He fails to recognize, that is, the moral implications of such a recognition. Although to him the assault on Moby-Dick is a personal feud, even in the impiety of such colossal egotism he realizes of course that he has to depend on other people. But he curses the necessity for what he calls "mortal inter-indebtedness" and refuses to accept the obligations that go with it. Like Ethan Brand, he uses men— not "fellowship among men"—as the instruments of his purpose, and he has to plot incessantly to keep them subservient, since he knows that "of all tools used in the shadow of the moon, men are most apt to get out of order."

It is only toward the end that a sense of human community blossoms faintly in Ahab's parched soul. Awakened first by his compassion for Pip, the demented Negro boy, it finds its most moving and tragic expression in the brief interlude of mutual understanding and affection between him and Starbuck. The episode is too well known to be discussed at length here, but what one must note is the marvellous rightness of its placement in the structure: immediately before the point at which the whole action is precipitated into its climax by the sighting of Moby-Dick. This scene with Starbuck on a beautiful Pacific day marks the high point of the reader's sympathy for Ahab, and, by providing the clearest understanding of the protagonist's character, it ensures the proper arousal of the emotion of pity as well as terror in the impending catastrophe. Even Ahab himself goes to meet the final dispensation of his fate not perhaps with any enlarged understanding of why it is his fate but certainly with an insight into at least one great circumstance that has blasted his whole existence. This self-discovery is born, as in Ishmael's case, of the vision of joy and peace that the universe seems to have put forth on this beautiful day. Moved to tears, Ahab reviews the barren landscape of his forty adult years:

> When I think of this life I have led; the desolation of solitude it has been; the masoned, walled-town of a captain's exclusiveness, which admits but small entrance to any sympathy from the green country without—oh, weariness! heaviness! Guinea-coast slavery of solitary command!—when I think of all this; only half suspected, not so keenly known to me before . . . away, whole oceans away, from that young girl-wife I wedded past fifty . . . wife? wife?—rather a widow with her husband alive! Ay, I widowed that poor girl when I married her, Starbuck . . . Close! stand close to me, Starbuck; let me look into a human eye; it is better than to gaze into the sea or sky; better than to gaze upon God. By the green land; by the bright hearthstone! this is the magic glass, man; I see my wife and my child in thine eye.

Ahab's solitary condition has a great deal to do with his overmastering perversity, his brooding over himself to the point of monomania. In this sense, his "madness," though it takes a different course, proceeds from an experience essentially similar to the one that Pip undergoes. This simple minded Negro's brief immersion in the "heartless immensity" of the ocean epitomizes Ahab's life-long situation. It is true that Pip's dementia turns out to be innocuous, while Ahab's monomania spells disaster for the *Pequod*, but the decisive factor in the experience of the great captain is the same that unsettles the ordinary sailor's mind: the "intense concentration of self" caused by complete isolation. Be the man great or small, such "awful lonesomeness," as Melville puts it, "is intolerable."

The "desolation of solitude"—the tragedy of an existence devoid of human contact and relationships—was, however, a more pervasive feature of Ahab's society (on land as well as sea) than Ahab realized. He quite understandably connects it with a "captain's exclusiveness." But Hawthorne had shown its workings in the life of ministers and laymen, scientists and artists, and in such ordinary characters as Wakefield, who had also, while alive, widowed his wife. Melville's own Redburn had become isolated in the democratic forecastle. One need not, however, go outside *Moby-Dick* to realize the pervasiveness of the Ishmael situation, or, in other words, the importance of the theme of "solitude in the midst of society." The very opening sentence of the novel declares it together with the narrator's name. The narrator himself, though a lowly man, seems to have been as effectively cut off from any human sympathy "from the green country without" as Ahab was, for, as he tells us in the first paragraph, there is "a damp, drizzly November" in his soul.

The theme of community or "fellowship among men"—counterweight to the theme of isolation—is only briefly though powerfully expressed in the Pip-Ahab and Ahab-Starbuck episodes. It is more fully associated with Ishmael and, of course, with the very idea of a whaleboat. There is a difference between the basic conception of the world in a whaleboat and the martial undemocratic world of *White Jacket*. The spontaneous "sociality" that prevails on and between whalers, as Melville observes at some length and with a great deal of playfulness while describing the institution of "Gamming," stands in sharp contrast with the suspicious aloofness of merchant ships and the absence (natural enough) of "hearty goodwill and brotherly love" between men-of-war. But of more importance is the fact that whaling in its early days was, as Charles Olson has pointed out, "a collective, communal affair."[31] This fact is reflected in two early chapters of the novel: in the general explanation of the term "lay"; in the procedure that Ishmael, and later Queequeg, go through before their lays can be settled; and, most memorably perhaps, in the comic interlude between the irascible but honest Peleg and the miserly, sanctimonious Bildad who, among other god-fearing things, proposes the seven hundred and seventy-seventh lay for poor Ishmael. The sailors of the *Pequod* are thus not wage-earners but, in theory at least, prospective shareholders in the profits of the voyage, the size of their shares depending on their skill and usefulness. Whatever the nature of the enterprise, they have all a personal stake in its success.

In reality, however, whaling was a sweated industry, and the sailors got practically nothing apart from their board. Likewise, the idea of general democratic "sociality" was marked in practice by the great flaw that divided the cabin from the forecastle. Yet in the forecastle at least, we have the customary Melvillian association of America and democracy with universal brotherhood. The crew of the *Pequod* is made up of "Isolatoes" from "all the isles of the sea" who, though previously "not acknowledging the common continent of men," are now "federated along one keel" in one "Anacharsis Clootz deputation." It is in this spirit, and while engaged in one of the many common tasks involved in whaling, that Ishmael delivers himself of a plea for the immediate establishment of the millennium of love: "Oh! my dear fellow-beings, why should we longer cherish any social acerbities, or know the slightest ill-humour or envy! Come; let us squeeze

31. Charles Olson, *Call Me Ishmael* (New York, Reynal and Hitchcock, 1947), p. 21.

hands all round; nay, let us all squeeze ourselves into each other; let us squeeze ourselves universally into the very milk and sperm of kindness."

More concretely, however, the theme of community in *Moby-Dick* finds its expression in the values that govern the relationship between Ishmael and Queequeg. Ishmael, we remember, had decided to go to sea for several reasons not all of which were clear to himself. But the two which he articulates are the problem of the universe that was revolving in his mind and that was symbolized in his imagination by the great Leviathan; and the unbearable sense of being an outcast aroused by an unfriendly world and also perhaps a loveless home. The South Sea islander helps him to resolve both his problems, the metaphysical as well as the social. The friendship that unites the two men suggests an alternative to the values of the society which has made him an Ishmael. We remember that Redburn, when he found himself an outcast, had prayed that the despair of his situation might not lead him into inhuman callousness and fiendish hatred against the whole world. For the narrator of *Moby-Dick*, who faces the same danger, Queequeg represents the answer to that prayer. As this pagan harpooneer shares his bed and his earthly treasure with the friendless sailor, the latter's baseless apprehensions vanish together with his prejudice; until finally, in the process of recognizing his outlandish friend's innate humanity, Ishmael recovers his own. "I felt a melting in me," he says. "No more my splintered heart and maddened hand were turned against the wolfish world. This soothing savage had redeemed it. . . . his very indifference speaking a nature in which there lurked no civilised hypocrisies and bland deceits."

Queequeg's social philosophy, of which his friendship for Ishmael is a more pronounced and personal expression, is pithily summarized a little later in the book. This is occasioned by the incident in which the harpooneer saves the life of an atrocious "bumpkin" who, before falling overboard, had taken the tattooed savage to be a special incarnation of the devil and plagued him accordingly. As Queequeg lights his pipe with customary calmness after the rescue, the narrator translates his thoughts as follows: "It's a mutual, joint-stock world, in all meridians. We cannibals must help these Christians." This is also the lesson brought home by the hazards of whaling at every turn. That it is not lost on Ishmael we discover in "The Monkey-Rope" chapter where he describes how, when one sailor is engaged in cutting the floating whale, he is fastened by a rope to another on board. Thus tied to Queequeg on this occasion, he is impressed by his situation so "strongly and metaphysically" as to make him feel that his own "individuality" has "now merged in a joint stock company of two." If Queequeg should "sink to rise no more, then both usage and honour demanded, that instead of cutting the cord, it should drag me down in his wake. So, then, an elongated Siamese ligature united us. Queequeg was my own inseparable twin brother; nor could I any way get rid of the dangerous liabilities which the hempen bond entailed."

In reality, however, as things turn out, Queequeg is responsible not for dragging Ishmael down but for saving him from the general wreck of the *Pequod*. Father Mapple, it will be recalled, had preached with the full conviction of his Protestant belief: "Delight is to him whose strong arms yet support him, when the ship of this base treacherous world has gone down beneath him." But when the *Pequod* goes down, Ishmael is not saved by his own arms. It is Queequeg again who redeems him. Much earlier in the Spouter-Inn, when these two men had become "bosom friends," the savage had declared that "he would gladly die" for Ishmael "if need should be." But when the time for Queequeg's dying actually arrived and, after he had made all the necessary preparations, he suddenly recalled a duty he was leaving unperformed and so decided to stay alive a little longer. Whether or not the deathbed recollection has anything to do with the Spouter-Inn pledge, Queequeg's going through the pantomime of death without dying does eventually lead to his friend's being saved. It is his coffin, turned into a lifebuoy at his suggestion, that prevents Ishmael's drowning in the vortex of the *Pequod*.

What we have here, however, is not altogether a matter of physical support. As R. E. Watters has pointed out, the coffin is a "composite creation" which, like the doubloon or the white whale, functions as a symbol.[32] One of its many possible meanings is closely connected with the metaphysical part of Ishmael's problem: his search for an answer to the riddle of the universe. Queequeg, we remember, had engraved on the coffin the marks tattooed on his body, that hieroglyphic maze which, in its turn, represented "the work of a departed prophet" embodying "a complete theory of the heavens and the earth, and a mystical treatise on the art of attaining truth." This is not to suggest that Ishmael's being saved by the coffin means that the truth he has been seeking is contained in the inscription on its lid. The discovery involved here is rather that there is no single ultimate truth and that the universe in its totality is as mysterious as the departed prophet's treatise on it. This is a lesson in humility that Ahab never learns. Metaphysical voyaging, like the physical, cannot succeed through the unaided effort of single individuals—or even single cultures. The search for truth also postulates a "joint-stock world, in all meridians," for, where Father Mapple's belief fails, a pagan's wisdom may save. Ahab, in his defiance of the power that animates the universe (the spirit of fire in this case), had once confessed: "Come in thy lowest form of love, and I will kneel and kiss thee." Something like this vision of humility encountering love is evoked on the last

32. R. E. Watters, "The Meanings of the White Whale," *University of Toronto Quarterly*, 20 (1950–51), 168. See also pp. 166–68.

page of the novel, but the man who experiences it is not Ahab, but a redeemed Ishmael: "The unharming sharks, they glided by as if with padlocks on their mouths; the savage sea-hawks sailed with sheathed beaks."

When the *Pequod* sinks—driven to its end by the force of an egocentric will—it drags down with itself "a living part of heaven." One can say that a similar loss (not necessarily an artistic loss) marks the works succeeding *Moby-Dick*, for the vision of an earthly paradise rarely figures in their varied themes. Whether or not we follow D. H. Lawrence in interpreting the *Pequod* as the "symbol of this civilized world of ours,"[33] it is true that the tales which follow its catastrophe are the tales of a civilization that has floundered. Of course, unlike Ahab's whaler, civilizations are never sunk lock stock and barrel. One can even argue that they only flounder in the minds of such visionaries as have leveled their sights on too high a course. But what integrating factor, for the imagination at least, did American civilization possess except its myths and its visions?

Be that as it may, Melville's view of the world after *Moby-Dick* is marked by a singular absence of the earlier hopefulness. In place of the Happy Valley we now have the blasted shores of the Enchanted Islands, the latter name itself suggesting ironically the contrast between the two—between the anticipated vision and the experienced reality of the new land. It is a contrast to which Melville points unambiguously when, in the first sketch of "The Encantadas," he observes how the uniform sterility of the Galapagos is thrown into relief by bits of vegetation, "of sugar-cane, bamboo, and cocoa-nuts, washed upon this other and darker world from the charming palm isles to the westward and southward; all the way from Paradise to Tartarus." A similar dialectic lies, of course, at the center of the dyptich "The Paradise of Bachelors and The

33. *Studies in Classic American Literature*, p. 236.

Tartarus of Maids." Here the somewhat whimsical evocation of "paradise"— the peace and quiet of a life secluded from the world—serves as a preface to the second and larger part of the story which describes the bleak wasteland of a New England paper mill. "At rows of blank-looking counters sat rows of blank-looking girls, with blank, white folders in their blank hands, all blankly folding blank paper."

"The Encantadas," too, presents in part the image of society. Its characters are recognizable social types, and the wasteland spirit that broods over it is not confined altogether to the remote and treacherous Galapagos. Even at home, as the narrator says in concluding the first sketch, "in scenes of social merriment . . . I have drawn the attention of my comrades by my fixed gaze and sudden change of air, as I have seemed to see, slowly emerging from those imagined solitudes, and heavily crawling along the floor, the ghost of a gigantic tortoise."

If this story suggests the opposite of the social hopefulness that Melville had celebrated earlier, such characters as Bartleby seem to represent the flotsam and jetsam that has irrevocably broken down as a society. Indeed, the values that emerge from the tales of the '50s are individual innocence, individual integrity, individual fortitude, and redemption through individual suffering. At times of course, as in "Benito Cereno," there is no question of even such redeeming possibilities, and the world of reality seems "one total inky blot." The experience of the Civil War and its aftermath only served to intensify the vision of despair. "Melville," as Walter Bezanson says in the excellent introduction to his recent edition of *Clarel*, "was bitter about the loss of the social myth which he had often criticized but which had nourished his life and art."[34] As for *Clarel* itself, one can only repeat the concluding words of Bezanson's study: "The loss

34. Melville, *Clarel*, ed. Bezanson, p. cvi.

of faith is the basic assumed fact of the poem, and its largest problem is how to endure the overwhelming sense of a shattered vision."[35]

It was only at the end of his life and in his last tale that Melville found, as many of his readers agree, a new and quiet serenity. *Billy Budd* also incorporates the "sense of a shattered vision" but without being overwhelmed by it. Although so different from each other in theme and setting, Melville's last two major works, the long poem and the short novel, share a spirit of disillusionment that derives from the same phase of historical experience. If, as Bezanson observes, *Clarel* grew out of the postbellum decade, *Billy Budd*, as Norman Pearson has argued, is "related to the Civil War, that mutiny within a state whose implications had been a troubled concern of some of Melville's poetry."[36] But *Billy Budd*, for all its sadness and horror, is firmly rooted in a secure faith. Where the tortured sensibility of *Clarel* reflects its troubled times, the imagination at work in the story of the Handsome Sailor transcends history to reaffirm, without dogma, the value of the Christian myth of innocence, evil, and the necessity of redemptive suffering.

The affirmation involved in Billy's tragedy, however, is very different from the sort of hopefulness which had animated the early visions of the Happy Valley, Serenia, and the Main-top community in *White Jacket*. Although placed in a definite context of historical and social events, "with all this," as the author says, "the story has little concernment, restricted as it is to the inner life of one particular ship and the career of an individual sailor." The inner life of H.M.S. *Indomitable*, however, is not conceived in the same terms as the inner life of the *Neversink*. Here there is no question of

35. Ibid., p. cix.
36. Ibid., p. ciii. Norman Holmes Pearson, "Billy Budd: 'The King's Yarn,'" *American Quarterly*, 3 (1951), 105.

projecting the dialectic between a society founded upon the kelson of mutual antagonism on the one hand, and a harmonious community on the other. *Billy Budd* is the story of three persons—Billy himself, Claggart, and Captain Vere—individuals whose characters are sketched with great economy in the first seven chapters before the rest of the book turns with equal austerity to delineate the inner drama of their mutual relationships. The surrounding humanity, always a shadowy mass, plays perhaps a less important role than that assigned to the chorus in classical tragedies.

The tale's religious reference too has very little to do with the broad social ethics of Christianity embodied in the Republic of Serenia. The distinctive relevance of *Billy Budd* belongs indeed to a private sphere. This can be seen by holding it up against *White Jacket*, a book with which it offers so many comparisons on the surface that one cannot fail to note the deeper contrast. Billy Budd may be in some sense the redeemer of mankind, but unlike Jack Chase he is not the champion of the rights of man and the liberties of the world. With his hero's dramatic farewell to his old ship, the *Rights-of-Man*, in the first chapter of *Billy Budd*, Melville also formally takes leave of that democratic hopefulness which, together with a belief in the triumph of the Christian spirit of brotherhood, had earlier inspired his answer to the observed corruptions of civilized society. For the Handsome Sailor to demur against impressment would have been, in Melville's words, "as idle as the protest of a goldfinch popped into a cage." But Billy, of course, has no idea of protesting against either his removal from the *Rights-of-Man* or anything else implied in the fate of serving on a man-of-war. Unlike White Jacket and Jack Chase, he does not question the basic morality of a world governed by the Articles of War. He accepts it, and in so doing reveals a different order of heroism. No longer "that cynosure he had previously been," the new foretopman becomes eventually the cynosure of inward eyes. By vindicating the possibility of goodness and innocence in the face of suffering caused by "natural" depravity, his memory makes life endurable and spreads comfort over the moment of death.

The tragic acquiescence of *Billy Budd* is based upon the acceptance of the social vision as permanently shattered. The hopefulness it represents is perhaps the only sort possible after such acceptance, even as the heroism of the sacrificial lamb is the only sort of heroism possible in a world that is felt to be alterable no longer, but rather given over permanently to the necessity of martial expediency and fundamentally un-changeable laws. Billy's career exemplifies a way of achieving grace in a situation where man is, like the Handsome Sailor, "a goldfinch popped into a cage." This is perhaps why Melville's tale, sketchy and awkward in places as it is, speaks so intimately to a bewildered generation whose social hopes, like those of Melville's own generation, failed to survive the disillusionment of war-torn history.

6. Huckleberry Finn:

A SOUTHWESTERN STATEMENT

The boy [Huck] and the Negro slave form a family,
a primitive community—and it is a community of
saints.
　　　　　—Lionel Trilling, "Huckleberry Finn"

The Adventures of Huckleberry Finn marks in so many ways a
turning point in the history of American fiction. Its crucial
influence on subsequent writing in the country is widely
recognized today. Novelists who came after Mark Twain and
who recognized what he had done with his native idiom could
hardly write again as Cooper and Melville had done. He may
be called the George Washington of American letters because,
by investing the national language with the autonomous
dignity of a great work of art, he virtually created it. Since,
however, even the most radical shift in literature rarely involves a total break with tradition, but is more often a
regenerative development of it, to appreciate the true distinction of *Huckleberry Finn* we must see it in relation both to
what came after it and to what went before. We can exag-
gerate matters a little and remark with Hemingway that all
modern fiction derives from this single book. In doing so,

however, we must not imagine it to be a sort of literary Adam, a work which miraculously begot a fruitful line of fiction but which was itself unrelated to any previous kin. Nor is it enough to see its connection with the minor frontier tradition, the tradition of Southwestern humor. Twain's masterpiece belongs in a more important sense with the major novels that preceded it in the nineteenth century. Among other things, its theme is a fresh and distinctive restatement of the theme I have been considering in this study.

It is tempting, for instance, to use Trilling's comment quoted above[1] to argue that with *Huckleberry Finn* the story has come full circle to the very terms in which William Bradford had launched it into American literature almost two and a half centuries earlier. Bradford's narrative, it is scarcely necessary to recall, had also celebrated the heroic adventure of escaping from a corrupt society in order to establish "a community of saints" in the wilderness. In reality, however, the inspiring ideals of the community on the raft, when compared with those of the Puritan fugitives, are wholly secular in character. There is nothing of the saint about Huck or Jim unless we use the term as a common figure of speech to denote the contrast between them and the general run of surrounding humanity. Quite simply they are decent human beings, and their little world is better described as "a family" or "a primitive community." In other words, both Twain's protagonists and his ideal social construct are closer to those of Cooper and Melville than of William Bradford and John Winthrop. The Puritans leaders' idealism was derived from religious inspiration alone, while the nineteenth-century writers had behind them the added ideals of the Enlightenment and political democracy. Furthermore, whereas in the Eastern novelists the former source is still operative if not

1. Lionel Trilling, "Huckleberry Finn," in *The Liberal Imagination* (New York, Viking Press, 1950), p. 108.

vital, Twain's values are wholly social and political. *Huckleberry Finn* represents the final secularization of the society-community theme.

Of course Twain began writing after the Civil War. What he felt about the actual world of the sixties and seventies can be seen from the satirical evocation of postwar society in *The Gilded Age*—the novel in which Twain struck, according to William Dean Howells, his one and only blow in the cause of realism. Later developments, the combination of personal misfortune and a deepening sense of national tragedy, created in his mind those "symbols of despair" with which Bernard DeVoto has identified his last works. Out of this mood were born the nihilism and the ironclad mechanical determinism of such anxiety-bound phantasies as *What Is Man?* and *The Mysterious Stranger*. But somewhere in the middle period of his writing career Twain achieved the balanced vision that lies behind *The Adventures of Huckleberry Finn*. The anxiety and the criticism of social reality are present here. So is a certain deterministic coloring of the view. But this novel is informed by an idealism that belongs to an earlier period of American cultural history. As DeVoto has said: "When he [Twain] wrote fiction, he was impelled to write about the society in which his boyhood had been spent, and to write it out of the phantasies, the ecstasy, and the apprehension which he remembered from his boyhood. . . . Hannibal was the master condition of his fiction, and fiction was the instinctual part of his work. His artistic creativeness, his phantasy-making, was rooted in his boyhood."[2] Whatever one says of his other fiction, the great "phantasy" that went into *Huckleberry Finn* is of a piece with the dream of social possibilities that had figured in the works of writers who were mature men when Twain was still a boy. The "ecstasy" and

2. *Mark Twain in Eruption*, ed. Bernard DeVoto (New York, Harper, 1940), p. xvii.

the "apprehension" which colored the world of his boyhood and out of which he fashioned his masterpiece characterized also the workings of the older novelists' imagination. In Melville's case, as I have pointed out, the ecstasy of the forties had already yielded to confirmed apprehension in the early fifties, and, by the time the war broke out, he realized that the era of hopefulness had ended. But Twain, in recollecting the earlier society, recaptured with it the central tension of the earlier theme.

It has been remarked often that in *Life on the Mississippi* Twain left out of account that aspect of the world in a steam-boat which Melville had taken for his subject in *The Confidence-Man*. Twain's book provides indeed a wholly idyllic picture—a beautiful, nostalgic picture of the days gone by forever. Of course Twain recognized as well as Melville the seamy side of the Mississippi Valley culture. He introduces it in full measure into *Huckleberry Finn*, coming close to Melville's own terms in the description of the two confidence tricksters, the King and the Duke. The comparison of the two novels, however, brings out a more interesting point, for Twain's theme includes an affirmative motif that Melville had discarded over thirty years earlier. Where *The Confidence-Man* presents an unrelieved satire, *Huckleberry Finn*, like Melville's own early novels, balances the satire with the evocation of an alternative social construct based on radically different values than those of the surrounding society. Indeed, it is the com-munity on the raft, and the significance of this community, that distinguish the meaning of Twain's novel, not only from *The Confidence-Man* but from his own other works.

Mark Twain of course explored the persistent American theme of community in his own distinctive and epoch-making way. In Cooper it was intimately connected with the romance of the vanishing Indian tribes, and it involved, among other contradictions, a progression characterized by the backward

reading of history. Hawthorne, with his acute historical consciousness, projected it along a more or less direct line from
the seventeenth century to the nineteenth. In Melville we had
the primitive community variation again, together with the
added dimension of metaphysical voyaging. Twain, in his
turn, stated the theme in terms of his native Southwestern
tradition, clothing it with the life and substance of fresh,
first-hand experience, and, above all, pressing into its service
the miraculous invention of a new literary voice. The distinction of *Huckleberry Finn* lies in the double fact that it
gave new vitality to an old theme and thereby also a new
seriousness to the otherwise negligible tradition of frontier
humor.

There is a certain deceptive simplicity about Twain's novel
which makes it peculiarly liable to misinterpretation. For a
time readers more or less obeyed the author's prefatory order
to desist from searching the book for motive, moral, or plot.
Lately, however, critics have been making up for lost time by
reading too much—and in too many unwarranted directions
—into the novel. Where all seemed childishly simple before,
everything is incredibly complex now. Under the circumstances, any approach to *Huckleberry Finn* should, I believe,
take note of Leo Marx's excellent and timely warning. The
issue raised by this novel, Marx rightly points out,

> is not the kind of moral issue to which today's criticism
> readily addresses itself. Today our critics, no less than
> our novelists and poets, are most sensitively attuned to
> moral problems which arise in the sphere of individual
> behavior. They are deeply aware of sin, of individual
> infractions of our culture's Christian ethic. But my im-
> pression is that they are, possibly because of the strength
> of the reaction against the mechanical sociological

criticism of the thirties, less sensitive to questions of what
might be called social or political morality.[3]

To put it briefly, the question raised by *Huckleberry Finn*
is one of man's conduct toward man, or, in larger terms, the
moral basis on which a sane and civilized human society can
be built. As in the case of the earlier novelists, so in Twain's
case also the theme involves an examination of the existing
social order as well as the presentation of an alternative social
construct. That is to say, we have here again the familiar
structural and moral polarization of civilization and community. It is necessary to emphasize, even overemphasize,
this point, because to lose sight of either of the two poles
between which the narrative moves is to miss the inclusive-
ness of its theme. Accordingly, to Marx's warning about one
sort of current misinterpretation must be added a further
caution against oversimplifying the social issue posed by the
novel. *Huckleberry Finn* is not fundamentally a book about
Negro slavery. It is a common mistake, but a mistake nevertheless, to equate too closely the meaning of Huck's journey
down the Mississippi with the issue of Jim's escape from
slavery. Jim's freedom is undoubtedly an important part of
this meaning, but it is only a part, just as slavery itself is only
one aspect of the social order which Huck has decided to
repudiate in its entirety. It is often forgotten that Huck arrives
at this decision independently of Jim's flight and without
having given any thought whatsoever to the question of
chattel slavery. Before his meeting with the runaway slave on
Jackson's Island, his abolitionist sentiment extends only to
things like shoes, formal clothes, domestic hygiene, regular

3. Leo Marx, "Mr. Eliot, Mr. Trilling, and *Huckleberry Finn*,"
American Scholar, 22 (1953), 435. As is evident, I am extensively indebted to this essay. My differences with Marx are merely a matter of
relative emphasis.

hours, Sunday school, prayer books, and other such appur-
tenances of civilization. It is true that in the course of the
journey down the river, as Huck grows up, his critical eye is
turned on more important issues. But even in his maturest
judgment of the surrounding social world, the question of
slavery is overshadowed by the observation of such other
endemic and equally pervasive attributes of this world as its
cruelty, violence, hypocrisy, and acquisitiveness.

Huck's commitment to the slave's freedom is thus motivated by an ethic which includes but also goes beyond the
disapproval of slavery. It is the product of a moral sensibility
engaged with issues larger and more fundamental than those
suggested by any single social institution. On the one hand, it
dictates that unconscious sympathy between Huck and Jim
which predates, and eventually leads up to, the boy's conscious acceptance of the abolitionist's role. On the other, it
lies at the base of Huck's attitude toward the established
order—an attitude that matures but does not change, since
his adult experience only confirms his juvenile act of repudiation. The society which he had found merely irksome as a
child he comes to judge eventually as depraved and corrupt.

Huck's choice thus involves the whole question of human
society. His rejection of civilization and his acceptance of the
fullest responsibility in a contrasted social order constitute
the basic pattern of the novel. It is a pattern familiar enough
in American literature, as crowded with echoes from Cooper
and Melville as Huck's gesture of repudiation is with echoes
from similar symbolic actions on the part of earlier protagonists. Huck Finn is indeed the representative American hero
cast in the image of a Southwestern boy. A younger and more
entertaining Natty Bumppo as well as a less embittered
Ishmael, he asserts, like these two characters, the right to free
himself from civilization and its imperatives. But, as in the
case of the older heroes, such an assertion does not imply

lawless individualism. On the contrary, it marks the beginning of a moral process which leads eventually to the recognition and acceptance of the law of human community.

This is the theme that lies at the heart of the novel's organization. As is obvious, it is a theme whose implications are broader than those involved in the subordinate story of Jim's escape. To lose sight of this fact, to forget that Jim's story is only a part of Huck's more complex adventure, is to diminish the scope and intention of Twain's achievement. Furthermore, such a restricted reading of the book's meaning leads, in its turn, to an unjust evaluation of the inspired excellence as well as the limitation of its form. On the one hand, the reader is likely to miss the finely contrived balance of its structure, while, on the other, he faces the danger of exaggerating out of all proportion the importance of its one serious lapse. Some such weakness can be noticed indeed even in Marx's otherwise illuminating essay. Marx recognizes fully the larger focus of the novel. "The truly profound meanings of the novel," he observes, "are generated by the impingement of the actual world of slavery, feuds, lynching, murder, and a spurious Christian morality upon the ideal of the raft."[4] But the bulk of Marx's discussion is addressed, for understandable reasons, to a less profound level of the novel's meaning, and by stressing overmuch the flight-from-slavery aspect of its theme he arrives at certain unduly harsh strictures. One of these relates to the view he takes of the novel's ending. With Marx's taking Twain to task for the reintroduction of Tom Sawyer into the narrative, and for the bad taste of such a farcical denouement, no one can quarrel seriously. All one can do is to add one's own reasons for finding the final sequence unsatisfactory, since, seen from any except the most uncritical point of view, this episode represents a disappointing anticlimax. What I find unacceptable in

4. Ibid., p. 431.

Marx's account is the significance he accords to the agency Twain uses in bringing Jim's story to an end: the Negro's emancipation by an act of manumission. This would be a minor point were it not connected with a more important critical issue: the adequacy or otherwise of Twain's whole theme. Marx considers Miss Watson's deathbed freeing of Jim as one of the many clues that suggest a basic failure of vision. Applying to *Huckleberry Finn* Santayana's general comment on American humorists, he concludes: "To say that Clemens only half escaped the genteel tradition is not to say that he failed to note any of the creed's inadequacies, but rather that he had 'nothing solid' to put in its place."[5] For lack of an alternative conception of human society, in other words, Twain abandoned the implications of his insight. "The unhappy truth about the ending of *Huckleberry Finn* is that the author," as Marx says elsewhere in the essay, "having revealed the tawdry nature of the culture of the great valley, yielded to its essential complacency."[6]

Whatever may be the case with Twain's other works, these charges, I believe, are unmerited by *Huckleberry Finn*. I shall have occasion later to revert to them. Here I should like to begin by pointing out that Miss Watson's will is a fictional instrumentality quite unworthy of the sociomoral significance that Marx has read into it. If one sees Jim's manumission in the context of his heroic flight, and that flight as a segment of Huck's longer and unfinished journey, one sees it for what it is: a mere literary device, far less improbable and artistically more satisfactory than half-a-dozen other tricks used by Twain to round off various episodes in the book. The very unemphatic, almost casual, manner in which the fact of Miss Watson's will is reported is enough to show that it is no more than a contrivance used to bring about a denouement toward

5. Ibid., p. 438.
6. Ibid., p. 432.

which Jim's story has been moving but which cannot be achieved in any other way that would also be consistent with historical truth. If Twain yielded to anything here, it was only to literary convention; and that too with the greatest amount of caution against the customary complacency of happy endings. Dickens, for instance, would have found it impossible to resist the temptation of devoting a whole chapter to Miss Watson's conversion, complete with deathbed contrition, a general feeling of sweetness and amity all round, and the eventual change of heart. Twain not only spares us the shocking experience of such a scene; he does more. He leaves his young hero—the keeper of our conscience—unadopted, unconvinced, and essentially uncompromised.

To see Jim's manumission as a betrayal of the novel's central affirmation is to restrict that affirmation to the single issue of slavery. On such an assumption we should rightly reject as digressive interpolations all those portions of the book which amount to more than half its bulk but which bear no relation to the story of Jim's escape. In other words, we should judge the novel an episodic narrative barely saved from chaotic shapelessness by the often interrupted though linear thread of the journey down the river. For it is not only during the final Tom Sawyer episode that Huck neglects the urgency of Jim's situation. He does this repeatedly, in such instances as the lengthy Grangerford and Wilks episodes, not to mention other diversionary actions. In reality, however, these episodes are not narrative digressions but integral parts of the novel's meaning and form. They constitute one of the two poles which define dialectically the nature of Twain's theme.

This part of *Huckleberry Finn* is addressed to the investigation of actual society. Huck's periodic forays into the towns and hamlets studded along the banks of the river are like so many thrusts of discovery directed at the heartland of the Mississippi Valley civilization. The young boy's fresh and honest eyes provide Twain with the necessary instrument of satire—the instrument that rends the obscuring veil of familiarity from this world and lays bare its organic ugliness and inhumanity. It is the same world that Huck repudiates at St. Petersburg when the genteel confinement of his life in the house of Widow Douglas erupts into brutality and violence with the return of Pap and the failure of the judge's naive attempt to reform him. Seen now at an adult level of experience, it confirms the rightness of Huck's early decision on the one hand, and, on the other, leads up to and makes so much more meaningful the reaffirmation of the same resolve in the last words of the novel.

The two gestures which thus precipitate and conclude the action are not merely literal resolutions to flee physically; more significantly they are in the nature of enacted judgments on the civilization that motivates them. They indicate a visionary attitude which, as I have attempted to show in this study, is a distinctive characteristic of the American imagination: a revolutionary attitude that looks upon the given social order as corrupt beyond the possibility of honest compromise and therefore rejects the idea of ameliorative reform. Twain's view of contemporary Western civilization is indeed not very different from that of the other writers whom I have already discussed. For instance, what he says about it in *The Mysterious Stranger* comes very close to Melville's indictment of a hypocritical and mercenary Christianity in *Typee*. During Satan's revelation of the marching spectacle of human history, as he gives Theodor a glimpse of what lies beyond his own feudal period, they see "Christianity and Civilization march hand in hand through those ages, 'leaving famine and death and desolation in their wake, and other signs of the progress of the human race,' as Satan observed." "Two or three centuries from now," Satan goes on to add, "it will be recognized that all the competent killers are Christians; then the pagan world will go to school to the Christian—not to acquire his religion, but his guns."[7]

In this book, as I suggested earlier, Twain's view is colored by the later developments of American history. For instance, in what seems a reference to the country's imperialist adventure, Satan is made to reflect upon the spectacle of intensified bloodshed which he has prophetically revealed to Theodor. To what end, he asks, do men wage war? "Who gets a profit out of it? Nobody but a parcel of usurping little monarchs and nobilities who despise you; would feel defiled if you touched them; would shut the door in your face if you proposed to call; whom you slave for, fight for, die for, and are not ashamed of it, but proud." Basically, however, the feudal society of *The Mysterious Stranger*—with its superstition, ignorance, witch-hunting, compulsive conformity, intolerance, and brutality—is a satirical exposé of the familiar Southern world of Twain's childhood. Of course when he wrote this late satire, he identified these conditions as the permanent destiny of mankind in a fundamentally meaningless universe. It was intended to be a satire on the whole human race. But, as Bernard DeVoto has said: "When he wrote fiction, which is to say when the bases of his personality were finding instinctive expression, the human race was the race he had known in Hannibal."[8] In *Huckleberry Finn*, which deals directly with this scene and this period, his deterministic view is flexible enough to admit the meaningfulness of human choice, and his view of human society hopeful enough to permit the evocation of an alternative possibility. With regard to the actual civilization of the time, however, his satire is as savage as the satire of *The Mysterious Stranger*. Only here it is

7. The edition used for quotations from Twain is *The Writings of Mark Twain*, 37 vols. New York, Gabriel Wells, Definitive Edition, 1922–25.

8. DeVoto, *Mark Twain in Eruption*, p. xvii.

infinitely more effective. Its object is not a generalized hypo-
thesis about humanity but a social situation that is given a
local habitation and a name. Likewise, its instrument is not
the stale device of a "stranger"—a distant and detached
observer—but the deeply engaged moral consciousness of a
native son. The result is a concrete vitality which makes
Huck's rejection of civilization the repudiation not of mankind but of a particular social order: a world of senseless
feuds, needless cruelty, and deceitful cupidity masquerading
under a false front of honor, piety, and gentility.

This is the world of actuality from which Huck returns to
the raft invariably with a sense of relief. It constitutes the
negative half of Twain's theme. But to say that Twain had
"nothing solid" to put in its place is simply to overlook the
moral and structural significance of the other half of *Huckleberry Finn*. Opposed to the established creed in this novel are
the values represented by Jim's flight, and more than that, by
Huck Finn, and still more, the community that Huck and Jim
create on the raft. The raft, in Marx's own words, functions as
"the symbolic locus of the novel's central affirmations."[9] It is
not often given to serious satirists to portray concretely the
positive side of a vision that constitutes the basis of their
satire. The fact that Twain succeeds in doing so is one of the
great features of his achievement. As such portrayals in
fiction go, his richly evoked community aboard the raft is
solid enough. Notwithstanding the charge of its impracticality
in a given type of society, it embodies serious values of social
ethics: simple fellowship, mutual kindness and consideration,
and a general harmony in human relationships: "what you
want, above all things, on a raft, is for everybody to be satis-
fied, and feel right and kind towards the others."

Here one has to realize that the raft is a created symbol, an
imagined social construct, rather than a faithful transcript

9. Marx, p. 438.

from some idyllic and bygone days. As described by Twain himself elsewhere, life on the Mississippi rafts was in reality as little immune from stupidity, ugliness, brutality, and knavery as that of the steamboats or the banks of the river. Even the raft in *Huckleberry Finn* is eventually invaded by the representatives of the surrounding world. The affirmation that it stands for thus derives not so much from its romantic picturesqueness as from the harmonious community for which it provides a symbolic locus. It is true that such harmony in human relationships presupposes a radically different social organization. That, however, is precisely the point. Of course Twain does not go into the question of how the change can be effected. But that is an irrelevant consideration, since no artist can be held accountable for not drawing up a program adequately suited to the practical realization of his vision. Artists usually work on a different plane of effectiveness. Twain's concern here is with an alternative concept of human society, and it is a concept that derives its power from the emotively charged concreteness of the presented image as well as from its projection against the background of the established order.

Stated in abstract terms, the values that govern the community on the raft sound ridiculously simple-minded. But it is not as moral abstractions that they function in the context. Their seriousness is validated in terms of the contrast, enforced at every step, with the norms and sanctions of actual society. All this is done with the insistence of a profoundly experienced vision rather than the obvious and superficial deliberateness of virtuosity. Thus in the realm of domestic relationships, where the world at large presents a picture of dislocated natural ties, Huck and Jim form a family united by spontaneous affection. Deserted and in a sense murdered by his real father, Huck finds on the raft the paternal care unknown to him previously. Jim's relatively undemonstrative but genuine concern for this orphan is thrown into further relief by the conduct of the scheming King and Duke toward their "wards" in the Wilks episode, their hypocritical effusiveness making Huck observe, "It was enough to make a body ashamed of the human race." The plot of these two confidence men to rob the orphaned girls is itself an echo of Pap's designs on Huck's money earlier in the novel; while the systematic brutality to which Huck is subjected by his father, in its turn, stands in sharp contrast with Jim's remorseful recollection of having once thoughtlessly hit his deaf and dumb daughter.

As a microcosmic civil community, the raft stands likewise for simple decency and humanity. It is only here that Jim can acquire the dignity of a human being. In opposition to the mutual respect and consideration upon which the bond between Huck and Jim is based, we have, on the other hand, the thieves' honor that unites the King and the Duke: the incorporated frauds who begin by supporting each other for mutual profit and end by each trying to outwit and defraud the other. Equally spurious is the code of honor—of lynching, feuding, and bloodshed—that governs the larger social world. While Huck and Jim, members of two different races, symbolize the possibility of human harmony, the Grangerfords and Shepherdsons enact in real life the internecine feud of the Capulets and the Montagues, and the King and the Duke soon follow up the performance by actually rehearsing the balcony scene of *Romeo and Juliet*, thereby parodying the affirmative part of the play. Thus it is not surprising that at each return from this world of hatred and violence Huck should recognize and reaffirm the contrasted values of the raft community:

I was powerful glad to get away from the feuds, and so was Jim to get away from the swamp. We said there warn't no home like a raft, after all. Other places do seem so cramped up and smothery, but a raft don't. You feel mighty free and easy and comfortable on a raft.

The community of Huck and Jim represents the positive half of the meaning of *Huckleberry Finn*, the half that is complementary to its satire. The keystone of this social structure is the loyal fellowship of two persons who are akin in their humanity as well as in their opposition to the inhuman established order. While it assumes the existence of democratic equality, such a community aims at a social condition beyond democracy. Its relation to equality is not unlike the relation between friendship and equality as Jacques Maritain, paraphrasing St. Thomas Aquinas' commentary on Aristotle's *Ethics*, defines it:

> Friendship supposes that beings are close to each other and that they have arrived at equality among themselves. It is up to friendship to put to work, in an equal manner, the equality which already exists among men. But it is up to justice to draw to equality those who are unequal: the work of justice is fulfilled when this equality has been achieved. Thus equality comes at the terminus of justice, and lies at the base and origin of friendship.[10]

When Twain wrote *Huckleberry Finn*, justice had already done its share of the work by proclaiming the legal freedom and equality of the slave. Whether or not it was a part of Twain's literary purpose to endorse this accomplished fact, he certainly looked beyond it. Insofar as he saw the freeing of the slave as the necessary but not the sufficient condition for the realization of the true community, his vision can provide a commentary on the development of American history since

10. Jacques Maritain, *The Rights of Man and Natural Law* (New York, Scribner's, 1943), p. 37.

the Civil War. It is a vision which American democracy is still very far from having achieved.

Huck's commitment to Jim's freedom is a part of this deeper and more comprehensive creed. It is true that he often expresses a preference for being alone. But this avowed propensity to solitude, like his distaste for being civilized, is not a sign of misanthropy or irresponsible individualism. It is rather a reflection on the "cramped up and smothery"society which he has repudiated. These attitudes are of a piece with the general mode of satire by which Twain redefines many concepts in the pattern of our sympathies—concepts of right and wrong, home and wilderness, education and ignorance, gentility and moral uncouthness—often reversing their meaning completely. T. S. Eliot has described Huck as the most solitary character in fiction.[11] But he is also the most desirous of human fellowship and most willing for its sake to put up with many things of which his moral sensibility disapproves, including the King and the Duke until their part in the Wilks episode and, later, their treacherous sale of Jim.

It is worth while to recall here that in the first chapters of the novel, where we are still in the world of *Tom Sawyer*, Huck returns to the house of Widow Douglas only because Tom has made this step a condition for his admission into Tom's latest band of respectable robbers—a band in whose fantastic rituals and activities Huck participates with characteristic reservations. One may thus see Huck's later development in terms of his deepening awareness of the meaning, the true necessity, and the real dangers of human fellowship. From the secret gang of Tom Sawyer he is plunged into the life of a community which must be kept equally secret' but which involves real-life issues and not the fantastic projections of a schoolboy's literary imagination. The change from

11. T. S. Eliot, *The Adventures of Huckleberry Finn* (London, Cresset Press, and New York, Chanticleer Press, 1950), p. ix.

Tom's to Jim's company thus represents the beginning of Huck's growth: his entry into a life of increasing maturity and responsibility.

Most of the novel's subsequent raft scenes are concerned with the exploration and establishment of the values that constitute the code of this community. To take one great example, such is the concern that lies behind the memorable chapter which is called "Fooling Poor Old Jim" and which describes Huck's separation from Jim in the fog followed by their reunion several hours later. Since the implications of this scene have been commented upon extensively, it is only necessary to point out that it has nothing to do with the issue of Jim's flight. Although that issue is in a critical stage on account of the raft's proximity to Cairo, even Jim himself rises above it in the face of a more important crisis. The scene resolves itself into three parts marked respectively by the threatened destruction of the community, the violation of its code by Huck's practical joke, and finally its reaffirmation on a higher plane of mutual respect and understanding. The often quoted and magnificent end, which gathers the threads into a single dramatic moment, can easily bear yet another quotation:

> "When I got all wore out wid work, en wid de callin' for you, en went to sleep, my heart wuz mos' broke bekase you wuz los', en I didn' k'yer no' mo' what become er me en de raf'. En when I wake up en fine you back ag'in, all safe en soun', de tears come, en I could 'a' got down on my knees en kiss yo' foot, I's so thankful. En all you wuz thinkin' 'bout wuz how you could make a fool uv ole Jim wid a lie. Dat truck dah is *trash;* en trash is what people is dat puts dirt on de head er dey fren's en makes 'em ashamed."

> Then he got up slow and walked to the wigwam, and

297

went in there without saying anything but that. But that was enough. It made me feel so mean I could almost kissed *his* foot to get him to take it back.

It was fifteen minutes before I could work myself up to go and humble myself to a nigger; but I done it, and I warn't ever sorry for it afterward, neither.

To understand the significance of this scene fully, one should bear in mind the similar trick that Tom Sawyer plays on Jim in one of the early chapters of the novel. The difference is not that Jim is no longer gullible—because he is, and Huck's signal success proves it. Nor is it that on the raft there is any reason for his being immune from a friendly joke. If it therefore turns out to be something worse than a practical joke, the reason lies in Huck's misunderstanding of the situation. He realizes of course that the accident has led each of them to give the other up for lost. Knowing this, he does not deliberately ignore Jim's feelings; he is simply unaware that the event of his own death can cause any such feelings at all. In view of his previous forsaken and loveless condition, this is quite understandable. But nevertheless it involves a certain blindness to his present situation, an obliviousness to the new bond that has grown up between him and Jim. What makes this lapse particularly callous is that he perseveres with his joke even after Jim has demonstrated the strength of the bond by bursting into a fit of spontaneous, incredulous, and grateful joy at seeing him alive again. Insofar as Huck's story is one of initiation into manhood, this point may be said to mark the consummation of the process. But it also marks his final attainment of equal membership in the short-lived and foredoomed community on the raft. This single moving scene gives us an idea of the distance Huck has traveled from the elaborately silly initiation rites of Tom Sawyer's gang.

The pattern of the journey is in this manner meaningfully

associated with the development of the theme of community. It is true, as Marx says, that "Huck knows that the journey will have been a failure unless it takes Jim to freedom."[12] But Huck also knows that it *is* freedom. The raft is not only a means of transportation to the promised land; in a symbolic sense it is the promised land itself. For Huck, who has rejected the social values of the great valley, it holds the only sort of society to which he can give unqualified allegiance. That Jim's primary loyalty also belongs to this community is obvious from the first sentence of his speech quoted above. Against this aspect of the novel's theme, escape from slavery is an issue that becomes, especially after they have missed Cairo, somewhat unreal to Huck and Jim themselves. For one thing, as has been pointed out, the river is against them. When they discover that they have floated below Cairo, however, they decide to buy a canoe and go back up the river. But they make no attempt to execute this scheme; and when Huck does "borrow" canoes subsequently, it is for the usual purpose of reconnoitering the shores. Indeed, considered in its entirety, the journey affirms the value of their community more than it indicates any definite goal ahead of them. This fact seems to me to help in raising the theme of *Huckleberry Finn* above the particularities of its time and place. The book remains an abiding document of human fellowship in a world perverted by selfishness, religious cant, hypocrisy, greed, and violence.

To sum up: the banks of the Mississippi river present the picture of the repudiated social order; the river itself, with its magnificently evoked majesty, power, and capriciousness, represents the amoral physical forces of Mark Twain's deterministic universe; while the raft, which Huck and Jim can control only partially, embodies the image of the most

12. Marx, p. 426.

humane community possible in such a universe. This is the sociomoral geography of the world as projected in *Huckleberry Finn*. And this is the novel's essential form. That the universe is far from being wholly friendly to the human beings who live in it only enhances the tragic folly of their treatment of each other. Even in *The Mysterious Stranger*, where gods, like wanton boys, seem to watch indifferently the killing of human flies, the sport is carried on, not by the gods but by men themselves. In *Huckleberry Finn* the view is more hopeful and compassionate. It is not unlike Wordsworth's view, but with Wordsworth's conception of the relation between nature and man neutralized to heighten the indictment of man's relation to man:

> To her fair works did Nature link
> The human soul that through me ran;
> And much it grieved my heart to think
> What man has made of man.

Such an evaluation of the novel leaves out the question of its concluding chapters. It also sees the novel's central conflict spread out in space rather than worked out in time. This, it is worth recapitulating here, has been my approach to most of the fiction that I have discussed. It seems to me that such an approach is dictated by the works themselves, and that it helps one to understand their achievement as well as their weakness. Furthermore, it reveals the distinctive quality of their genius and suggests the nature of their relation to the culture from which they derive. Twain is not alone in distributing the meaning of his novel along the spatially disjunct areas of the river bank and the raft. Cooper's Leatherstocking Tales derive their thematic significance from a similar opposition between the settlements and the wilderness. In the same way, Hawthorne and Melville divide their world—to take two obvious examples—into Boston and Blithedale and into

Vivenza and Serenia. What we are dealing with here is a particular manifestation—a literary variation—of the general imaginative response to the sociomoral meaning of America. The idealism of the novelists is a part of the larger American idealistic tradition. One of the hallmarks of this tradition has been its emphasis on separate geography rather than continuing history. America has figured in it persistently as a place rather than a process: a place, moreover, where an ideal has only to declare itself in order to find instant embodiment in the world of reality.

Although the limitations and potentialities of this view in general are not my main concern, I shall have something further to say about it in the following chapter. Here it is my purpose to refer again in a summary way to its consequences for the work of the novelists. As I have repeatedly pointed out, the polarized projection of the actual and the ideal makes for the most emphatic affirmation of the values that inform such symbolic constructs as the raft community of *Huckleberry Finn*. Furthermore, such constructs come to be identified frankly for what they are: ideal possibilities and not segments of existing social reality. In each case, too, there is a more or less open recognition of defeat, but it is a defeat that affirms, rather than negates, the postulated alternative. Advancing civilization catches up with Natty Bumppo, but as it does so it only serves to make the hero increasingly sympathetic. Blithedale is discredited but not the serious values it embodies. In the same way the raft is taken over by the King and the Duke, and their machinations begin that process of inevitable destruction which is eventually consummated by the society whose marginal representatives they are. The destruction of the raft, however, only vindicates in our sympathies the value of what it stands for.

In this process of critical affirmation all these novelists achieve a remarkable degree of success. They are not, however, equally successful in meeting another problem also implicit in a theme one of whose poles represents a visionary construct while the other investigates solid reality. This is simply the problem of connecting the two parts of the action, or, in other words, suggesting the relation between their vision and history. The difficulty becomes increasingly apparent toward the end, when the necessity of providing some sort of a resolution becomes urgent. It is usually at this point that these novels become uncertain. A few of them leave the ends unrelated and open. But in a majority of cases the ideal is at length brought into contact with the actual and, in a physical sense, made to disappear. There is nothing wrong with this course except that the novelist himself seems unaware of the implications involved in what finally, and rightly, happens. This is a charge that can be brought against Cooper and Melville with only a little less force than against Twain, for it arises basically from a common weakness: the spatial rather than temporal apprehension of the connection between social problems and social possibilities. Only Hawthorne—the supposed day-dreamer—escapes it. Although he, too, divides the two poles of his theme in space, he does not wholly disregard the time of day. In presenting his ideal community in *The Blithedale Romance* he recognizes, with his acute historical understanding, that it is doomed to unreality because it is essentially a premature interpolation into the process of history. He can thus isolate from the defunct experiment its forward-looking social values and refer them explicitly to a possible future age.[13]

Having said all this, one can return to the ending of *Huckleberry Finn*. The final Tom Sawyer sequence, as Leo Marx has argued, is unsatisfactory in many ways. It is not only tedious but also quite unnecessary even as plot machinery. Unlike Hawthorne, Twain possessed no understanding

13. See above, pp. 211–13.

of the relation between his vision and history, between the community on the raft and the society on the banks. Moreover, he did not choose to leave the two sides of his theme physically apart, nor yet was he content to bring them together and terminate his action with the dissolution of the raft community. Instead he attempted to cover up "the problem of the ending" by relapsing into the sort of burlesque which is the bane of much of his writing. While all this is true, it is difficult to agree with Marx that the final episode represents a "compromise" with the discredited river-valley civilization and that it thus "betrays" the whole meaning of the novel. Although the bulk of the action in the concluding chapters bears scarcely any perceptible relation to Twain's central concern in *Huckleberry Finn*, they do not endanger at any point the critical affirmation made by his theme.

Since a basic question with regard to the thematic significance of imaginative works is involved here, it would be best to illustrate the point by a concrete example. In analyzing the meaning of a novel one ought to be guided by what I have called the pattern of aroused and redistributed sympathies, for it is at this level that a novel makes its essential impact.[14] The words "compromise" and "betrayal" belong properly to the judgment of works where there is a shift in the focus of sympathy itself. An example of this process that comes readily to mind is the series of Forsyte novels by John Galsworthy: a series in which the meaning is reversed to such a degree that Soames Forsyte, the central character, who begins as something of a villain in *The Man of Property*, ends by becoming the most sympathetic character in the concluding volumes of *The Modern Comedy;* the very things which he represents being seen now no longer as objects of satire but rather as solid moral virtues. Thus one can say of Galsworthy, as D. H. Lawrence did, that he was unable to see what lay

14. See above, p. 46.

beyond the Forsytes. Accordingly, after he had satirized their values, he turned to sentimentalizing them.

Surely there is neither such reversal of sympathies nor such limitation of vision in *Huckleberry Finn*. The community of Huck and Jim does not survive beyond the point at which it is finally overwhelmed by the massed power of the established order; but there is no repudiation of the values it embodies. Nor does Twain now accept the values of the society that has triumphed over it. As a matter of fact Tom Sawyer is nowhere else so unsympathetic, and his "heroism" nowhere so meretricious, as in the concluding chapters of this novel. It is true that Huck acquiesces in his nonsense, but he had done the same, it must be remembered, when the Duke painted Jim blue to pass him off as a combination of an Arab and King Lear. Just as Huck agrees to the Duke's strategem because it promises to protect Jim from capture, he goes along with Tom's schemes in the hope that they will eventually lead to Jim's escape. In both cases his justification lies in his concern for Jim, for one must not forget that he is kept ignorant until the end that Jim has been free all the time. In other words, he accepts the silly machinery for the sake of what he believes to be the serious underlying motive. Nor does such acceptance preclude characteristic reservations—reservations which, in the latter case, are directed quite effectively at the Sunday-school attributes of Tom and his proceedings. One must also remember that Huck's position in the Phelps household is so precarious that it makes his dependence upon Tom's assistance virtually indispensable. Thus his acquiescence does not represent a compromise with the society he has repudiated. His judgment of it, unwavering throughout, is reaffirmed resonantly in the very last words of the novel: "But I reckon I got to light out for the territory ahead of the rest, because Aunt Sally she's going to adopt me and sivilize me, and I can't stand it. I been there before."

7. Concluding Note:

SOCIAL REALITY
AND THE FORM OF AMERICAN FICTION

Every work of Art embodies an idea, and so confesses its distinctively human genesis. Art is nothing
more than the shadow of humanity. To make the
ideal actual in the sphere of production, in the
sphere of work, is the function of the Artist. To
make the ideal actual *in the sphere of life*, is the
function of Man.

—Henry James, Sr.,
"The Principle of Universality in Art"

The Adventures of Huckleberry Finn brings into sharp focus a
question with which I started: realism in the classic American
novel. In the light of the preceding discussions of Fenimore
Cooper, Hawthorne, Melville, and Mark Twain it may be
useful to revert to this and certain related questions. To a
greater degree than the others, or perhaps more simply than
the others, Mark Twain illustrates what Lionel Trilling means
when he says that American novelists have traditionally
sought a reality that "was only tangential to society." The
curve of the action in *Huckleberry Finn*, as we have seen,

305

rises from and eventually returns to the social reality of the Mississippi Valley civilization. But between the beginning and the end, though it makes intermittent contact with this society, it concerns itself most profoundly with the exploration of a possibility which is totally denied in the world of actuality and which therefore hovers precariously on its edges without touching it. In this sense the raft represents indeed a reality that is tangential to society. But this reality itself is fundamentally social in character. It is the reality of human community; and by invoking it, Twain opposes the established order with an image of what society can be or ought to be.

In *Huckleberry Finn* the two sides of the theme are perhaps more sharply divided than in some of the other novels that I have considered. But in all of them the action falls into the same basic rhythm: the movement away from a corrupt civilization and toward a more or less ideal community life. Of course the many individual works thus offhandedly brought under the cover of one generalization are in reality as varied as the distinctive characters of their different authors' genius. The two contrasted images interpenetrate in one novel while in another they are held sharply apart; the opposition between them is loud here and muted there; in one place the inspiring ideal is motivated by a certain religious feeling and in the other by a secular ethic; the repudiated civilization is more or less corrupt; in some instances it is shown as possessing an attractiveness of its own. The postulated community, on the other hand, is not always as ideally or as sympathetically conceived as it is in *Huckleberry Finn;* and if in some cases it is fully invested with a separate existence, in others its investigation is fleeting and fragmentary. These and other important variations of the theme I have already discussed at length in the previous chapters. Here it is my purpose to focus attention on a feature that is common to all the variants, that suggests their place in a unified tradition, and that has provided through the years a center of controversy on more than one score.

In the works of all these four novelists there comes undoubtedly a stage at which they diverge from what Trilling has called the "classic intention" of the novel. This intention Trilling describes as "the investigation of the problem of reality beginning in the social field." One must remark at the outset, however, that, taken in a certain sense, Trilling's description provides no difficulty; for the actions of most American novels, like that of *Huckleberry Finn*, begin in the field of existing society. We can think here of *The Pioneers*, in which Cooper explores realistically the problems and tensions of a historical situation before making the protagonist turn his back upon it at the end. Or we can take the whole of the Leatherstocking saga in its relation to the whole of the Littlepage Trilogy, and consider the investigation of real social issues in the latter as a background for the projection of an ideal myth in the former. In Hawthorne's case we can leave aside *The House of the Seven Gables*, about whose status as a regular novel there is no disagreement. But even in the romances the action begins invariably in the solid world of actuality before it moves into a divergent region. We arrive at the forest scenes in *The Scarlet Letter* only after a long stay in the richly evoked Puritan settlement; and in *The Blithedale Romance* Boston provides a substantial preface to the investigation of the communitarian colony. Nor must we forget that even *Mardi*, the most fanciful of Melville's novels—a deliberate romance, as a matter of fact—starts as an ordinary voyage and goes on to present an allegory of the real world before turning to the allegory of an ideal Christian republic.

But this is not the point at issue. The distinctive characteristic of American fiction is not that it wholly disregards existing social reality but that it is not wholly preoccupied with it. Unlike European fiction, it is not confined within the limits

307

of the given social field. It often projects and examines an imagined alternative: a construct like Blithedale, Serenia, or the raft community of *Huckleberry Finn;* or simply a new human relationship, such as the one between Natty and Chingachgook, which the novel invests with significance as the nucleus of a new social order. These symbolic constructs and ideal relationships, as I have attempted to point out, are products of the American novelist's preoccupation with the theme of human community. They represent his response to one of the more intractable problems of a society based upon democratic individualism.

Stated in a nutshell, this is the argument that emerges from the preceding studies of nineteenth-century American fiction. Such an account, based as it is on the recognition that questions of theme and form are inseparably related, sees the novel elements in the structure of this fiction as determined by the new strains in its theme. Furthermore, it sees the newness of the theme itself as connected with certain distinctive characteristics of the broader cultural tradition. It is my purpose here to justify in theoretical terms such an approach to the formal problems of the American novel, and also to suggest a few further ideas concerning the relevance of its theme to the development of the culture that produced it.

Taken by itself, the formal problem is easy to delimit. It relates fundamentally to the manner in which the American novelist deals with the theme of community. Indeed one can argue that if the values which inform this theme had figured as unstated assumptions, or if they had been merely stated as ideas, this body of fiction would have passed muster without much controversy about its form. There would have been no complaint about its lack of realism and no urgent attempts at identifying and explaining the elements of romance in it. But as things are, it confronts us with these values in the form

308

of a concrete social image that is planted in the very center of the narrative; and it is this singular feature of its performance that has occasioned the greatest uncertainty about it. These pictures of ideal communities, communitarian experiments, and Christian republics have seemed to fail somehow in measuring up to any mature standard of artistic procedure. Since they diverge so obviously from the conventional field of fictional representation, the general response to them has tended to be apologetic. Some critics have charitably ignored them; others have sought to explain them away in terms of elaborate psychological theories; but even the most sympathetic ones have felt uneasy in their admiration.

Thus it is the point of divergence—the fork in the accustomed path—that constitutes the chief critical stumbling block. The reader usually follows the novelist into the region that lies beyond with one of two misguided attitudes. He either goes on to read this part of the novel as a literal narrative of everyday life, an account of what happened, and quite expectedly finds it implausible, or, alternatively, recognizing it as something that could not have happened, he takes it as a dream or a romance and concludes that it can have no possible relevance to real life and its issues. (There is a suggestion, perhaps unintended, of the latter attitude even in Trilling's image of tangential movement away from social reality.) In either case the novel seems to offend deeply his trained sense of fictional realism.

It can be admitted readily that with the exception of Hawthorne the novelists themselves can be blamed to some extent for the situation. As I indicated in the last chapter, a certain lack of comprehension on their part virtually invites a great deal of misunderstanding on ours. If we do not always feel compelled to take this aspect of their fiction seriously, it is partly because they themselves often abandon its implications in a manner remarkable for its casualness. Moreover, the

external forms with which they clothe the theme of community—the vehicles they choose for their positive values—
are at times ridiculous in their outlandishness. Nor does
everyone among them display Hawthorne's clear gift of ironic
insight—an insight that reaches through the patent absurdity
of Blithedale to its underlying seriousness.

Undoubtedly the bulk of nineteenth-century American
fiction reveals these somewhat obvious technical shortcom-
ings. But the inability to face up to the problem of its distinctive form is not wholly explained by them. It arises from a
more basic failure: the failure to recognize the intimate
relation between the theme of this novel and the means and
materials it employs. So far from attempting such a correlation, however, criticism has tended to deny to the social
theme of the classic American novel any serious consideration
beyond the point where it breaks away from the realism of the
European novel. The assumption seems to be that at this
point the novelist, otherwise so alert to the problems of his
society, more or less abandons his concern with social
questions. It is such an attitude, for instance, that lies behind
the fact that *The Blithedale Romance* has not received the
critical attention that it deserves. Although it is a novel with
a serious sociopolitical theme, a masterpiece of incomparable
poetic richness and profound psychological wisdom, it has
been treated as a fanciful exercise, and its central issue of
community has been dismissed as a matter of no consequence.

In reality, however, the preoccupation with an ideal society
constitutes an integral part of the American novelist's work,
a part that must be taken fully into account in any appraisal
of his achievement. One cannot ignore it charitably while one
goes on to acclaim his penetrating exploration of the existing
social order. The two are inseparably connected with each
other in a single theme. Moreover, a charitable or apologetic
attitude is plainly unnecessary, since, however uncouth in

their externalities, these evocations of an ideal social condition provide only too often the vital center of the novels.
How significant, to take a concrete example, would the
Leatherstocking Tales be without the myth embodied in the
career of Natty Bumppo and in the "immortal friendship"
(to use Lawrence's words) between him and Chingachgook?
Or how much would *Huckleberry Finn* lose if it lost the raft?
This aspect of nineteenth-century American fiction is not
important simply because it is distinctive, nor because we
suppose the novelist to have hung up here a sign announcing:
"Positive Affirmations." In the last analysis both the distinction and the affirmation come through successfully because
here the novelist's imagination is so profoundly at work that
it has produced some of the most powerful and enduringly
effective portions of his fiction.

This is the fact of paramount importance for the literary
critic, the fact that must be accounted for by his theory. If
there is no place for it in the given theory of the novel, the task
of criticism should be to revise the established assumptions in
order to accommodate the new achievement, and not the
other way round. Obviously these symbolic constructs and
ideal relationships of American masterpieces are not fictional
transcripts from existing reality. They are avowedly presented
as something else. But they are not for this reason idle
fantasies or dreams. They embody social ideals and concepts
which are situationally transcendent but not unreal. They can
be called unreal only if by reality we mean the status quo. On
that assumption we can even call them products of a utopian
imagination, using the term "utopia" in the sense in which
Karl Mannheim uses it, or, better still, defining it, in David
Riesman's words, as "a belief, not in existing reality, but in
a potential reality"—a belief which, as Riesman goes on to say,
does not "violate what we know of nature, including human
nature, though it may extrapolate our present technology

and must transcend our present social organization."[1]

Thus if the American novelists of the nineteenth century did not follow the techniques of their English contemporaries, it is not because they were less concerned with the perfection of human society but because they were more so. By and large the social purpose of the English novel of this period reflected the radical drives of contemporary society itself. The English novelists kept abreast of widespread movements and prodded them forward in their humanitarian direction. They publicized known facts and strengthened existing attitudes, thereby widening the awareness of the one and the effectiveness of the other. The contrivances they used for this purpose were as artificial as the contrivances of a good deal of other literature, including American literature, but in their case the artificiality was legitimized and made meaningful by what one could observe all around in the actual world.

No similar corroborative reference to contemporary social movements was available to the ideals of the American novelist. Just as his criticism of society was directed against more fundamental issues, the attitudes and values he championed diverged more radically from the main current of history. Accordingly, the fictional situations necessary for the presentation, the critical examination, or the affirmation of these values could not be related to the social field within the framework of conventional realism. Since the positive part of his theme was concerned with a social vision that had no firm roots in contemporary developments, it could hardly be represented in the ordinary literary sense of the term. In this respect the only possible aid that life provided to the novelist consisted of such marginal phenomena as vestigial survivals

---

1. David Riesman, "Some Observations on Community Plans and Utopia," in *Individualism Reconsidered* (Glencoe, Illinois, Free Press, 1954), p. 72. The essay was originally published in *Yale Law Journal*, 57 (1947).

of older societies and supposedly forward-looking social experiments. By and large, however, in projecting this vision he had to depart more radically from the imitation of existing reality and rely more heavily instead on the plastic power of his imagination.

The tenacious habit of judging American fiction in terms of formal assumptions derived from another body of fiction with a different thematic purpose has resulted in certain curiously inadequate theories of the development of the novel in America. Consider, for instance, the exclusive reliance with which several critics have put forward two widely cited reasons for the divergence between the American and the European novel: paucity of raw materials in the new country and the immaturity or technical incompetence of the new novelists themselves. If American writers were unable to create the social novel, so the argument goes, the explanation lies in the fact that, apart from their own failings, America could boast no social scenes subtle or picturesque enough to tempt the artist's palette.

This view is neither accurate nor wholly satisfactory. As I have already indicated, the American novelists were quite capable of writing in the best manner of European fiction. They have left considerable proof of this ability, as well as of the availability of necessary materials, in such portions of their work as the Albany scenes of *Satanstoe*, the Boston scenes of *The Blithedale Romance* (not to mention the Salem of *The Seven Gables*), and the urban descriptions in *Pierre*. As for Twain, leaving aside the masterful evocation of a well-defined regional milieu in *Tom Sawyer*, *Huckleberry Finn*, and *Pudd'nhead Wilson*, we have the whole of *The Gilded Age*—or at least Twain's contribution to it.

Henry James himself, from whom the view derives its current ascendancy, believed the American scene to be poor

313

but not wholly devoid of possibilities for the social novelist. While he bewailed its deficiencies, he also found occasion to suggest how much Hawthorne could have made out of it by simply turning to such things as "portraits of actual types," the "Yankee of comedy," and the New-World "variations of colloquial English." To this one can add that these novelists enjoyed the same opportunity for supplementing their native situation that young James was to make use of later in the century. With their own European experience, the Jamesian way was wide open to them.

The truth of the matter is that, unlike James, they did not *choose* to explore or develop these possibilities. James himself recognized this fact in his study of Hawthorne. In commenting upon the absence "of that quality of realism which is so much in fashion," he was careful to say that Hawthorne had "not *proposed* to himself" (italics mine) to utilize the themes which he mentions and which I have cited above.[2] This is a point worth noting, since it reinstates an idea whose absence has vitiated discussion of the relation between American society and the American novel. The emphasis on raw materials and artistic maturity in current theory makes it seem indeed as though the American novelist was seeking to reproduce the form of the European novel but was altogether too handicapped to succeed in such an objective. This view thus overlooks an important factor that enters into the production of art, a factor which Wilhelm Worringer, following Alois Riegl, has defined as will-to-art or will-to-form (*Kunstwollen*). It is a factor that relates to the artist's conception of the function of his art, and that is related in its turn to certain decisive characteristics of the culture which produces it.

As a matter of fact, Worringer's whole thesis, as presented in *Abstraction and Empathy* (first published in 1908), is of

2. See above, pp. 140–41.

particular relevance to the problem of form in the nineteenth-century American novel. Although his theory is concerned with the history of the plastic arts, it is also directed against the general idea that "approximation to the natural model" or "approximation to reality" has been the one unchanged objective of artists through the ages and that it provides the sole criterion for judging the value of artistic creation.[3] The literary applicability of Worringer's argument derives from the parallel significance of the concepts of naturalism and realism, from the fact that, as he puts it himself, if he has chosen the term "naturalism," it is "because it seems to us more appropriate to the province of the plastic arts than the expression realism, which is reminiscent of literature."[4]

Worringer makes it clear that, in disputing the view that regards art and truth to nature as inseparable concepts, his purpose "is only discrimination, and not disparagement of the one art in the interests of the other." What he questions basically is "the habit of approaching them all with the same apparatus of artistic terms and epithets of value. As though each one of these . . . forms of artistic expression did not demand its own terminology, which leads to absurdities when applied to the others."[5] The standards of a naturalistic style—derived from the classical age of Greek sculpture, the Italian Renaissance, the art of Western Europe to the end of the nineteenth century—cause gross misunderstanding when applied to non-naturalistic art. On the basis of such standards Egyptian monumental sculpture and Oriental art, for example, appear to be barbarous distortions—incompetent attempts to reproduce natural forms. To people who make such evaluations art is essentially the product of factors like

3. Wilhelm Worringer, *Abstraction and Empathy: A Contribution to the Psychology of Style*, tr. Michael Bullock (New York, International Universities Press, 1953), p. 10.

4. Ibid., p. 27.

5. Ibid., p. 30.

"raw material" and "technics," and the history of art "a history of *ability*."[6] And yet, as Worringer observes, in ancient Egypt the startling realism of popular statues like the Scribe or the Village Magistrate could exist side by side with a style that eschewed all realism. Thus he concludes: "The stylistic peculiarities of past epochs are, therefore, not to be explained by lack of ability, but by a differently directed volition. . . . What seems to us to-day a strange and extreme distortion is not the fault of insufficient ability, but the consequence of differently directed volition. Its creators could *do* no otherwise because they *willed* no otherwise."[7]

Rejecting the idea that all art is per se naturalistic, Worringer sees human artistic experience as tending toward two antithetical poles, "empathy" and "abstraction," neither of which can be set up as a norm to which the other must conform. Although mutually exclusive in theory, in actual fact, as Worringer is careful to point out, the two tendencies can be found in the artistic styles of all periods, the history of art itself representing "an unceasing disputation" between them.[8] The question is one of degree, and the most illuminating part of Worringer's book is devoted to identifying the connection between the spiritual conditions and cultural climate of particular periods and the dominance of the one or the other artistic tendency in them. The urge to empathy, which results in the representation of the objective world of organic nature and ordinary experience, has ascendancy when between man and the universe there exists a relationship of friendly confidence (*Vertraulichkeitsverhältnis*). When, on the other hand, the relationship between man and the external world is one of disharmony, art tends toward abstract form: "the urge to abstraction is the outcome of a great inner unrest inspired in

6. Ibid., p. 9.
7. Ibid., pp. 9, 124.
8. Ibid., p. 45.

man by the phenomena of the outside world; in a religious respect it corresponds to a strongly transcendental tinge to all notions."[9] The function of abstraction in art is "to wrest the object of the external world out of its natural context" and thus "to render it necessary and irrefragable, to approximate it to its *absolute* value."[10]

It is relatively simple to transfer these observations to the field of literature. If we consider that the novel deals with man in society as the plastic arts deal with natural organic objects, and if accordingly we substitute the term realism for naturalism and idealization for abstraction, we will find in Worringer's account a theoretical framework for the view of American fiction that I have argued in this study. We will discover as a matter of fact how the two tendencies of empathy and abstraction can operate side by side in a body of literature that sought not only to represent the existing social order, but also to confront it with the image of an ideal society. Of course the American novelist's urge toward idealization was partly the outcome of a condition that Worringer describes as a fundamental sense of disharmony between man and the external world, the sort of disharmony of which Hawthorne's "The Artist of the Beautiful" can be considered an exemplary parable. But it was also connected with, and accentuated by, a whole imaginative tradition that was constantly preoccupied with the problematic relationship between the culture's postulated ideals and its actual development.

Finally, Worringer's theory contains a hint that is useful in illuminating a question to which I referred in the last chapter: the spatial rather than temporal conception of the connection between social problems and social ideals in several American novels. In the course of his argument Worringer observes that the urge to abstraction, seeking as it does to resolve the

9. Ibid., p. 15.
10. Ibid., p. 17.

317

disquieting phenomena of the outside world, impels the artist "to approximate the representation to a plane."[11] With the help of this insight Joseph Frank has recently demonstrated in a brilliant essay that under certain cultural conditions, a similar process of abstraction can give rise to what he calls "spatial form" in literature. Although literature is a time art, the dimension of historical time tends to vanish from the content of literary works as the dimension of depth vanishes from the plastic arts in abstract style.[12]

Where such spatialization occurs in the American novels of the nineteenth century, it relates not to the whole content of the work but only to that part of it in which the novelist seeks to project the image of his ideal social construct. It is here that he tends to eliminate the temporal factor. By working in terms of timeless myths and archetypes and by using past epochs and future possibilities without too much concern for their historicity, he attempts to invest his vision with the value of a social absolute. Partly, as noted above, such spatialization is the inevitable function of idealization or abstraction. But it is also once again a question of cultural tradition. As I indicated in the previous chapter, it is related to the oldest and most persistent of American beliefs: that faith in America itself which associated the fulfillment of ideals with the promise of separate geography rather than the process of continuing history.

If such is the relation between these works of fiction and the culture in which they were produced, the question that I should like to turn to finally, and briefly, is whether they can be said to possess any relevance to that culture's present reality. Since, however, this question involves the large and

11. Ibid., p. 21.
12. Joseph Frank, "Spatial Form in Modern Literature," *Sewanee Review*, *53* (1945), 221–40, 433–56, 643–53.

complex issue of literature's re-entry into history, a good way to approach it would be to ask how far the writers themselves recognized any connection between their ideals on the one hand and historical reality on the other.

Hawthorne, as I have attempted to show, worked out the two in close relation to each other. By virtue of remarkable artistic penetration he made the two sides of the theme act themselves out in a mutual critique: new social ideals challenging history and history in its turn testing the new ideals. In this respect, as in so many others, his achievement represents the high-water mark of American literature, and one can refer to it profitably for judging the relative failures of the other writers who belonged with him in the same tradition and who shared some of his themes.

In their various ways, Cooper, Melville, and Twain also recognized—perhaps more acutely than Hawthorne—that American history had intended more than it had accomplished, that, in fact, its development had betrayed its promise. But with regard to this promise itself they tended to be comparatively uncritical. They understood history and they felt the conviction of their ideals, but unlike Hawthorne they did not intuitively apprehend or deliberately think out the relation between the two. Because they begin by being more hopeful than Hawthorne, they end almost inevitably by becoming less so. The actions of their novels eventually return into, even as they arise from, the field of existing society, and to this extent they bow as unreservedly as Hawthorne does to the claims of historical necessity. But the sense of bewilderment, the note of bitterness, which accompanies the process almost invariably suggests an attitude of betrayed expectancy. It seems as though the novelist had very nearly hoped that things would turn out otherwise, as though he had expected to see his ideals materialize immediately and on the spot.

This attitude indicates a complex relationship between the

American novelist's sensibility and the experience of his culture that is best exemplified by Cooper. Cooper's criticism of America, as I have pointed out, was not confined to nineteenth-century developments. In both the Leatherstocking Tales and the Littlepage Trilogy he extended it backward to explore the moral and material foundations of the first settlements, and in both cases he demonstrated how the moral idealism of the experiment had been poisoned at the very source by the dubious character of the material drives behind it. Unprincipled cupidity, which he regarded as the primary source of all contemporary evils, had crossed the seas, as the upright Indian of the trilogy declares, in the first boats of the settlers. Thus, insofar as his criticism was based on the recognition of historical forces, he understood the futility of the belief that a new geographical region automatically promotes moral or social regeneration. In other words, he recognized the inadequacy of New World idealism. Yet it was an idealism that his imagination did not wholly transcend. His sensibility was so deeply committed to it that when he came to his own ideals they were projected uniformly in geographical rather than historical terms. When history caught up with them, he lost his earlier hopefulness and, with it, his belief in the distinctive destiny of America. He finally abandoned the implications of his own myth and in his last fragment denied that the New World would turn out to be in any way different from the Old. Melville and Twain, as I have pointed out, experienced a similar sense of bewilderment—a similar intellectual prostration—in the face of historical developments.

It is not likely that today many persons will repeat the nineteenth-century mistake of assuming an easy relation between ideals and reality. Indeed it is not likely that many persons would even remotely entertain such large-scale ideals as the earlier imagination delighted in. Emerson castigated reformers, especially American scholars or intellectual men, for making "a sally against evil by some single improvement, without supporting it by a total regeneration."[13] By and large, intellectuals would still prefer bearing the weight of the old philosopher's displeasure to facing the uncertain risk of believing in the imminence of paradise. Among other things, they can point to the story of nineteenth-century idealism itself to prove the futility of harboring admittedly noble but not readily attainable ideals.

Yet if certain prophets of the nineteenth century erred in assuming that paradisal possibilities are within easy grasp of anyone who but extends his hand to reach them, if they put too much reliance on the immediate realization of their visions, is it not equally erroneous to suppose that social ideals of such scope can have no relevance to the problems of existing reality? Because history defeated their hopes, is it fair to conclude that it also discredited them irrevocably? Did history not rather discredit itself in the process, and does not America need today, perhaps more than ever before, great myths and visions with which to support history and perhaps even shape it?

After all, the basic problem of democratic society which their bold imagination seized upon is still there, more accentuated today than it was in their time, more complexly entrenched, and increasingly more visible in diverse realms of human experience. To this extent the novelists' critical insights, born of a deeply engaged encounter with their culture's reality, remain as diagnostic and valid today as they were in the nineteenth century. Nor, if we conceive them rightly, are the answers they fathomed altogether wide of the mark. Of course, taken literally, some of their attitudes—as, for instance, the often celebrated idea of withdrawal from a corrupt society —possess all the attributes of quixotic absurdity. But even this ideal of heroic withdrawal is not a recommended

13. See above, pp. 37, 72.

course of action but rather the dramatization of an attitude of uncompromising integrity. In the same way, not everyone may agree today with Hawthorne's point of view—the conservative view that regards the moral transformation of the individual as the first step in any effective social change. We may be more inclined to accept the perspective of a novel like *White Jacket*, which refers the good and evil in man explicitly to the surrounding system, or *Huckleberry Finn*, where private morality, even individual conscience, is almost wholly the product of social forces and institutions. But this difference notwithstanding, Hawthorne also insisted—indeed more firmly than the others—on the ideal of fundamental regeneration. He held it to be not only possible but absolutely necessary for the full realization of the promise of human existence; and when all is said and done he was hopeful that such a transformation, among individuals and in society, would be accomplished.

What this fiction compels in us finally is a recognition of the underlying seriousness and continued validity of its vision. The challenge with which it confronts us is one of assimilating its ideals and values in and for our own time. That it possesses this quality of enduring effectiveness in the sphere of human thought and action must be counted among its chief claims to great literature. We may not wholly accept the elder James' cryptic observation that, while it is the function of the artist to make the ideal actual in his work, it is the function of man to do so in life.[14] Though naive in some ways, this statement of the relation between art, ideas, and reality is not essentially wrong. As Trilling has argued, "the extreme rationalist position ignores the simple fact that the life of reason, at least in its most extensive part, begins in the emotions. What comes into being when two contradictory emotions are made to confront each other and are required to

14. Henry James, *Lectures and Miscellanies*, p. 124.

322

have a relationship with each other is . . . quite properly called an idea. Ideas may also be said to be generated in the opposition of ideals."[15]

Of course, like any other body of serious literature, the classic American novel proposes no instrumentalities for the attainment of the social ideals it affirms. It works at a deeper and more effective level. Even if it fails to create a potential matrix for radical ideas and rational schemes of action, by arousing and redistributing our sympathies it builds a reservoir of moral energy to support such ideas and actions.

15. Lionel Trilling, "The Meaning of a Literary Idea," in *The Liberal Imagination*, p. 298.

References

General Critical Studies in the Field

Bewley, Marius, *The Eccentric Design: Form in the Classic American Novel*, New York, Columbia University Press, 1959.

Bowden, Edwin T., *The Dungeon of the Heart: Human Isolation and the American Novel*, New York, Macmillan, 1961.

Brownell, W. C., *American Prose Masters*, New York, Scribner's, 1909.

Chase, Richard, *The American Novel and Its Tradition*, New York, Doubleday, 1957.

Feidelson, Charles, Jr., *Symbolism and American Literature*, Chicago, University of Chicago Press, 1953.

Fiedler, Leslie A., *Love and Death in the American Novel*, New York, Criterion Books, 1960.

Lawrence, D. H., *Studies in Classic American Literature*, New York, Thomas Seltzer, 1923.

Levin, Harry, *The Power of Blackness: Hawthorne, Poe, Melville*, New York, Knopf, 1958.

Lewis, R. W. B., *The American Adam: Innocence, Tragedy, and Tradition in the Nineteenth Century*, Chicago, University of Chicago Press, 1955.

Matthiessen, F. O., *American Renaissance, Art and Expression in the Age of Emerson and Whitman*, New York, Oxford University Press, 1941.

Parrington, Vernon Louis, *The Romantic Revolution in America 1800–1860*, New York, Harcourt, Brace, 1927. Vol. 2 of *Main Currents in American Thought*.

Rourke, Constance, *American Humor*, New York, Harcourt, Brace, 1931.

Shapiro, Charles, ed., *Twelve Original Essays on Great American Novels*, Detroit, Wayne State University Press, 1958.

Smith, Henry Nash, *Virgin Land: The American West as Symbol and Myth*, Cambridge, Harvard University Press, 1950.

Winters, Yvor, *Maule's Curse, Seven Studies in the History of American Obscurantism*, Norfolk, New Directions, 1938.

CHAPTERS 1 AND 7

Primary Works

Bradford, William, *Of Plymouth Plantation 1620–1647*, ed. Samuel Eliot Morison, New York, Knopf, 1959.

Brisbane, Albert, *Social Destiny of Man*, Philadelphia, C. F. Stollmeyer, 1840.

Crèvecoeur, Hector St. John de, *Letters from an American Farmer*, New York, Dutton, Everyman's Library, 1951.

Dickens, Charles, *American Notes*, in *American Notes and Pictures from Italy*, intro. Sacheverell Sitwell, London, Oxford University Press, 1957.

Emerson, Ralph Waldo, *Emerson's Complete Works*, 12 vols. Boston, Houghton, Mifflin, Riverside Edition, 1888–93.

Franklin, Benjamin, *The Autobiography of Benjamin Franklin*, New York, Holt, 1916.

James, Henry, Sr.:

  What Constitutes the State, New York, John Allen, 1846.

  Letter to *The Harbinger*, May 23, 1846.

  Tracts for the New Times. No. 1. Letter to a Swedenborgian, New York, John Allen, 1847.

  Moralism and Christianity, New York, Redfield, 1850.

  Lectures and Miscellanies, New York, Redfield, 1852.

  "An American in Europe . . . III," *New York Daily Tribune*, Sept. 22, 1855.

  The Social Significance of Our Institutions, Boston, Ticknor and Fields, 1861.

  Society the Redeemed Form of Man, Boston, Houghton, Osgood, 1879.

Mather, Cotton, *Magnalia Christi Americana*, 2 vols. Hartford, Silas Andrus, 1855.

Miller, Perry, ed., *The American Puritans*, New York, Doubleday, 1956.

REFERENCES

Miller, Perry, and Johnson, Thomas H., eds., *The Puritans*, New York, American Book Company, 1938.

Tocqueville, Alexis de, *Democracy in America*, ed. Phillips Bradley, 2 vols. New York, Knopf, 1956.

Whitman, Walt, *Walt Whitman's Workshop*, ed. C. J. Furness, Cambridge, Harvard University Press, 1928.

Secondary Works

Aaron, Daniel, *Men of Good Hope: A Story of American Progressives*, New York, Oxford University Press, 1951.

Adams, Henry, *History of the United States of America*, 9 vols. New York, Scribner's, 1890–91.

Bestor, Arthur Eugene, Jr., *Backwoods Utopias: The Sectarian and Owenite Phases of Communitarian Socialism in America: 1663–1829*, Philadelphia, University of Pennsylvania Press, 1950.

Burke, Kenneth, "Ideology and Myth," *Accent*, 7 (1947), 195–205.

Frank, Joseph, "Spatial Form in Modern Literature," *Sewanee Review*, 53 (1945), 221–40, 433–56, 643–53.

Gabriel, Ralph Henry, *The Course of American Democratic Thought*, New York, Ronald Press, 1956.

Mannheim, Karl, *Ideology and Utopia*, tr. Louis Wirth and Edward Shils, London, Kegan Paul, Trench, Trübner, 1936.

Maritain, Jacques, *The Rights of Man and Natural Law*, tr. Doris C. Anson, New York, Scribner's, 1943.

Miller, Perry, Introduction to Jonathan Edwards, *Images or Shadows of Divine Things* (New Haven, Yale University Press, 1948), pp. 1–41.

Morgan, Edmund S., *The Puritan Dilemma: The Story of John Winthrop*, Boston, Little, Brown, 1958.

Mumford, Lewis, *The Story of Utopias*, New York, Boni and Liveright, 1922.

Murdock, Kenneth B., *Literature and Theology in Colonial New England*, Cambridge, Harvard University Press, 1949.

Nisbet, Robert A., *The Quest for Community*, New York, Oxford University Press, 1953.

Parrington, Vernon Louis, *The Colonial Mind 1620–1800*, New York, Harcourt, Brace, 1927. Vol. 1 of *Main Currents in American Thought*.

Riesman, David, "Some Observations on Community Plans and Utopia," *Yale Law Journal*, 57, 1947. Reprinted in the author's *Individualism Reconsidered*, Glencoe, Illinois, Free Press, 1954.

Trilling, Lionel, *The Liberal Imagination*, New York, Viking Press, 1950.

REFERENCES

Warren, Austin, *The Elder Henry James*, New York, Macmillan, 1934.

Worringer, Wilhelm, *Abstraction and Empathy: A Contribution to the Psychology of Style*, tr. Michael Bullock, New York, International Universities Press, 1953.

CHAPTER 2

Bewley, Marius, *The Complex Fate*, London, Chatto and Windus, 1952.

Chesterton, G. K., *Charles Dickens*, New York, Dodd, Mead, 1929.

Dorfman, Joseph, *Thorstein Veblen and His America*, New York, Viking Press, 1934.

Fuller, Margaret S., *Papers on Literature and Art*, New York, Wiley and Putnam, 1846.

George, Henry, *Progress and Poverty*, New York, Modern Library, 1929.

Gissing, George, *Charles Dickens*, New York, Dodd, Mead, 1898.

Goldman, Eric F., *Rendezvous with Destiny*, New York, Knopf, 1953.

House, Humphry, *The Dickens World*, London, New York, Oxford University Press, 1941.

Jones, Howard Mumford, *The Theory of American Literature*, Ithaca, New York, Cornell University Press, 1948.

Parkes, Henry Bamford, "Metamorphosis of Leatherstocking," in *Modern Writing*, No. 3, ed. William Phillips and Philip Rahv, New York, Berkeley Publishing Company, 1956. Reprinted in *Literature in America*, ed. Philip Rahv, New York, Meridian Books, 1957.

Rahv, Philip, "Paleface and Redskin" and "The Cult of Experience in American Writing," in *Image and Idea*, New York, New Directions, 1949.

Simms, William Gilmore, *Views and Reviews in American Literature*, First Series, New York, Wiley and Putnam, 1845.

Tillotson, Kathleen, *Novels of the Eighteen-Forties*, Oxford, Clarendon Press, 1954.

Young, G. M., *Victorian England, Portrait of an Age*, London, Oxford University Press, 1936.

CHAPTER 3

Primary Works

Cooper, James Fenimore:
  The Complete Works of J. Fenimore Cooper, 32 vols. New York,
    Putnam's, Leather-Stocking Edition, ca. 1893.
  Gleanings in Europe, ed. Robert E. Spiller, 2 vols. New York, Oxford
    University Press, 1928, 1930.
  New York, ed. Dixon Ryan Fox, New York, William Farquhar
    Payson, 1930.
  James Fenimore Cooper, Representative Selections, ed. Robert E.
    Spiller, New York, American Book Company, 1936.
  The Letters and Journals of James Fenimore Cooper, ed. James Frank-
    lin Beard, 2 vols. Cambridge, Harvard University Press, 1960.

Secondary Works

Brady, Charles A., "James Fenimore Cooper, Myth-Maker and
  Christian Romancer," in *American Classics Reconsidered*, ed. Harold
  C. Gardiner, S.J., New York, Scribner's, 1958.
Christman, Henry, *Tin Horns and Calico*, New York, Holt, 1945.
Conrad, Joseph, "Tales of the Sea," in *Notes on Life and Letters*, New
  York, Doubleday, Page, 1927.
Fox, Dixon Ryan, *The Decline of Aristocracy in the Politics of New
  York*, New York, Columbia University Press, 1919.
Grossman, James, *James Fenimore Cooper*, American Men of Letters
  Series, New York, William Sloane Associates, 1949.
Jones, Howard Mumford, *The Pursuit of Happiness* (Cambridge, Har-
  vard University Press) 1953, pp. 104–13.
Melville, Herman, review of *The Sea Lions*, in *The Literary World*, April
  28, 1849.
Parkman, Francis, "James Fenimore Cooper," *North American Review*,
  74 (Jan. 1852), 147–61.
Pearce, Roy Harvey, "The Leatherstocking Tales Re-examined," *South
  Atlantic Quarterly*, *46* (1947), 524–36.
Poe, Edgar Allan, Review of *Wyandotté*, *Graham's Magazine*, Nov.
  1843.
Ringe, Donald A., "Cooper's Littlepage Novels: Change and Stability
  in American Society," *American Literature*, *32* (Nov. 1960), 280–90.
Ringe, Donald A., "Cooper's Last Novels," *PMLA*, *75* (1960), 583–90.

Ross, John F., *The Social Criticism of Fenimore Cooper*, Berkeley, Calif., University of California Press, 1933.

Shulenberger, Arvid, *Cooper's Theory of Fiction*, Lawrence, University of Kansas Press, 1955.

Spiller, Robert E., *Fenimore Cooper, Critic of His Times*, New York, Minton, Balch, 1931.

Twain, Mark, "Fenimore Cooper's Literary Offenses," *North American Review*, July 1895. Available in Vol. 1 of *The Shock of Recognition*, ed. Edmund Wilson, New York, Doubleday, Doran, 1943. Later editions of the book include the second part of the essay discovered by Bernard DeVoto and published as "Fenimore Cooper's Further Literary Offenses" in *New England Quarterly*, Sept. 1946.

Waples, Dorothy, *The Whig Myth of Fenimore Cooper*, New Haven, Yale University Press, 1938.

CHAPTER 4

Primary Works

Hawthorne, Nathaniel:

> *The Complete Works of Nathaniel Hawthorne*, ed. George Parsons Lathrop, 12 vols. Boston, Houghton, Mifflin, Riverside Edition, ca. 1882–99.

> *The American Notebooks*, ed. Randall Stewart, New Haven, Yale University Press, 1932.

> *The English Notebooks*, ed. Randall Stewart, New York, Modern Language Association, London, Oxford University Press, 1941.

Secondary Works

Arvin, Newton, *Hawthorne*, Boston, Little, Brown, 1929.

Cowley, Malcolm, "Hawthorne in the Looking-Glass," *Sewanee Review*, 56 (1948), 545–63.

Dichman, Mary E., "Hawthorne's 'Prophetic Pictures,'" *American Literature*, 23 (1951), 188–202.

Fick, Leonard J., *The Light Beyond: A Study of Hawthorne's Theology*, Westminster, Maryland, Newman Press, 1955.

Fogle, Richard Harter, "The World and the Artist: A Study of Hawthorne's 'The Artist of the Beautiful,'" *Tulane Studies in English*, 1 (1949), 31–52.

REFERENCES

Hall, Lawrence S., *Hawthorne, Critic of Society*, New Haven, Yale University Press, 1944.

Howe, M. A. DeWolfe, *Memories of a Hostess*, Boston, Atlantic Monthly Press, 1922.

James, Henry, *Hawthorne*, London, Macmillan, English Men of Letters Series, 1879.

James, Henry, "Nathaniel Hawthorne," *Library of the World's Best Literature*, ed. Charles Dudley Warner, New York, R. S. Peale and J. A. Hill, 1897, *12*, 7053–61.

Leavis, Q. D., "Hawthorne as Poet," *Sewanee Review*, *59* (1951), 179–205, 426–58.

Melville, Herman, "Hawthorne and His Mosses," published pseudonymously in *The Literary World*, August 17, 24, 1850. Available in *The Shock of Recognition*, ed. Edmund Wilson.

More, Paul Elmer, "The Solitude of Nathaniel Hawthorne" and "The Origins of Hawthorne and Poe," *Shelbourne Essays*, First Series, New York, Putnam's, 1904.

More, Paul Elmer, "Hawthorne: Looking Before and After," *Shelbourne Essays*, Second Series, New York, Putnam's, 1905.

Pearson, Norman Holmes, Introduction to *The Complete Novels and Selected Tales of Nathaniel Hawthorne* (New York, Modern Library, 1937), pp. vii–xv.

Trollope, Anthony, "The Genius of Nathaniel Hawthorne," *North American Review*, *129* (Sept. 1879), 203–22.

Turner, Arlin, "Hawthorne and Reform," *New England Quarterly*, *15* (1942), 700–14.

Turner, Arlin, *Nathaniel Hawthorne: An Introduction and Interpretation*, New York, Barnes and Noble, 1961.

Van Doren, Mark, *Nathaniel Hawthorne*, American Men of Letters Series, New York, William Sloane Associates, 1949.

Wagenknecht, Edward Charles, *Nathaniel Hawthorne, Man and Writer*, New York, Oxford University Press, 1961.

Waggoner, H. H., *Hawthorne*, Cambridge, Harvard University Press, 1955.

CHAPTER 5

Primary Works

Melville, Herman:
   The Works of Herman Melville, 16 vols. London, Constable, Standard Edition, 1922–24.

REFERENCES

The Letters of Herman Melville, ed. Merrell R. Davis and William H. Gilman, New Haven, Yale University Press, 1960.

Secondary Works

Anderson, Charles R., *Melville in the South Seas*, New York, Columbia University Press, 1939.

Arvin, Newton, *Herman Melville*, American Men of Letters Series, New York, William Sloane Associates, 1950.

Auden, W. H., "Herman Melville" in *Another Time*, New York, Random House, ca. 1940.

Baird, James, *Ishmael*, Baltimore, Johns Hopkins Press, 1956.

Bezanson, Walter E., Introduction to *Clarel: A Poem and Pilgrimage in the Holy Land* (New York, Hendricks House, 1960), pp. ix–cxvii.

Blackmur, R. P., "The Craft of Herman Melville: A Putative Statement" in *The Expense of Greatness*, New York, Arrow Editions, 1940.

Bowen, Merlin, *The Long Encounter: Sex and Experience in the Writings of Herman Melville*, Chicago, University of Chicago Press, 1960.

Chase, Richard, *Herman Melville: A Critical Study*, New York, Macmillan, 1949.

Davis, Merrell R., *Melville's Mardi: A Chartless Voyage*, New Haven, Yale University Press, 1952.

Fogle, Richard Harter, *Melville's Shorter Tales*, Norman, University of Oklahoma Press, 1960.

Gilman, William H., *Melville's Early Life and Redburn*, New York, New York University Press, and London, Oxford University Press, 1951.

Hetherington, Hugh W., *Melville's Reviewers, British and American, 1846–1891*, Chapel Hill, University of North Carolina Press, 1961.

Howard, Leon, *Herman Melville: A Biography*, Berkeley, University of California Press, 1951.

Leyda, Jay, *The Melville Log: A Documentary Life of Herman Melville 1819–1891*, 2 vols. New York, Harcourt, Brace, 1951.

Mumford, Lewis, *Herman Melville*, New York, Literary Guild of America, 1929.

Olson, Charles, *Call Me Ishmael*, New York, Reynal and Hitchcock, 1947.

Pearson, Norman Holmes, "Billy Budd: 'The King's Yarn,'" *American Quarterly*, *3* (1951), 99–114.

Sedgwick, William Ellery, *Herman Melville: The Tragedy of Mind*, Cambridge, Harvard University Press, 1944.

REFERENCES

Short, R. W., "Melville as Symbolist," *University of Kansas City Review, 15* (1948), 38–46.

Thorp, Willard, Introduction to *Herman Melville: Representative Selections* (New York, American Book Company, 1938), pp. xi–cxxix.

Vincent, Howard P., *The Trying-Out of Moby-Dick*, Boston, Houghton, Mifflin, 1949.

Vincent, Howard P., "'White Jacket': An Essay in Interpretation," *New England Quarterly, 22* (1949), 304–15.

Watters, R. E., "Herman Melville's Metaphysics of Evil," *University of Toronto Quarterly, 9* (1940), 170–82.

Watters, R. E., "Melville's 'Sociality,'" *American Literature, 17* (1945), 33–49.

Watters, R. E., "Melville's 'Isolatoes,'" *PMLA, 60* (1945), 1138–48.

Watters, R. E., "The Meanings of the White Whale," *University of Toronto Quarterly, 20* (1951), 155–68.

Weaver, Raymond, *Herman Melville, Mariner and Mystic*, New York, Doran, 1921.

CHAPTER 6

Primary Works

Twain, Mark:
  The Writings of Mark Twain, 37 vols. New York, Gabriel Wells, Definitive Edition, 1922–25.
  Mark Twain in Eruption, ed. Bernard DeVoto, New York, Harper, 1922.

Secondary Works

Adams, Richard P., "The Unity and Coherence of *Huckleberry Finn*," *Tulane Studies in English, 6* (1956), 87–103.

Blair, Walter, *Mark Twain and Huck Finn*, Berkeley and Los Angeles, University of California Press, 1960.

Brooks, Van Wyck, *The Ordeal of Mark Twain*, New York, Dutton, 1920.

Cox, James M., "Remarks on the Sad Initiation of Huckleberry Finn," *Sewanee Review, 62* (1954), 389–405.

DeVoto, Bernard, *Mark Twain at Work*, Cambridge, Harvard University Press, 1942.

Dyson, A. E., "Huck Finn and the Whole Truth," *Critical Quarterly, 3* (1961), 29–40.

REFERENCES

Eliot, T. S., Introduction to *The Adventures of Huckleberry Finn* (London, Cresset Press, New York, Chanticleer Press, 1950), pp. vii–xvi.

Foner, Philip S., *Mark Twain Social Critic*, New York, International Publishers, 1958.

Leary, Lewis, "Tom and Huck: Innocence on Trial," *Virginia Quarterly Review*, *30* (1954), 417–30.

Lynn, Kenneth S., *Mark Twain and Southwestern Humor*, Boston, Little, Brown, 1959.

Marx, Leo, "Mr. Eliot, Mr. Trilling, and *Huckleberry Finn*," *American Scholar*, *22* (1953), 423–40.

Marx, Leo, "The Pilot and the Passenger: Landscape Conventions and the Style of *Huckleberry Finn*," *American Literature*, *28* (1956), 129–46.

Salomon, Roger B., *Twain and the Image of History*, New Haven, Yale University Press, 1961.

Stone, Albert E., Jr., *The Innocent Eye: Childhood in Mark Twain's Imagination*, New Haven, Yale University Press, 1961.

Trilling, Lionel, Introduction to *The Adventures of Huckleberry Finn*, New York, Rinehart, 1948. Reprinted as "Huckleberry Finn" in *The Liberal Imagination*, New York, Viking Press, 1950.

Index

Aaron, Daniel, 33
Abercrombie, Lascelles, 215, 259
Adams, Henry, 29–30, 34, 81–82, 89;
  Democracy, 81–82
Alcott, Bronson, 37, 52
Americans: two important
  characteristics, 8; Crèvecoeur's
  definition, 19–20, 22; sense of
  mission, 20–21; Dickens' view of,
  30–31; myth of America, 7, 34, 43,
  56, 84; reason for pride of country,
  42; society, actual vs. ideal, 43;
  imagination, 60
Anti-Rent Movement, 85, 106, 108,
  109
Arvin, Newton, 240
Austen, Jane, 98–99, 112, 141

Baird, James, 221
Balzac, Honoré de, 2, 4, 50, 57, 141
Bellamy, Edward, 81
Bestor, Arthur Eugene, Jr., 35, 36–37
Bewley, Marius, 68, 130, 152, 163,
  165
Bezanson, Walter E., 276–77
Bowden, Edwin T., 13, 151
Bradford, William, 10–11, 12–13,
  14–17, 20–21, 114, 120, 197, 200,
  265, 281; *Of Plymouth Plantation
  1620–1647*, 10–11, 12–13, 14–17,
  20–21

Brady, Charles A., 87, 96, 100, 117
Brisbane, Albert, 37–38, 45; *Social
  Destiny of Man*, 38
Brontë, Emily, 57, 58–59; *Wuthering
  Heights*, 58–59, 60
Brook Farm, 36, 37, 45, 145
Bulwer. *See* Lytton
Butler, Samuel, 223–24; *Erewhon*,
  223–24

Chase, Richard, 84
Chaucer, Geoffrey, *Canterbury Tales*,
  72
Chesterton, G. K., 54
Children, use of, 55–56
Christian social ideals vs. individual
  self-interest, 11
Christianity, true, 40
Communitarian experiments, 11–12,
  14, 35–43
Community life: concept, 9; ideal, 28
Conrad, Joseph, 154
Cooper, James Fenimore, 1–6 passim,
  18, 25, 45, 53, 63 ff., 68, 71, 76,
  84–138, 139, 144, 173 f., 181, 191 ff.,
  196, 211, 213, 218–22, 225, 233,
  237, 244, 280 ff., 286, 300–07
  passim, 319–20; *The American
  Democrat*, 115; *The Chainbearer*,
  86, 89, 91, 92–93, 100, 105–06,
  108–09, 111, 117–18; *The Crater*,

88, 112–13, 138; *The Deerslayer*, 2, 119 ff., 122–24, 128–31, 132; *Home as Found*, 94, 96, 114–15; *The Last of the Mohicans*, 88, 118–19, 127–28, 135, 136; Leatherstocking Tales, 118–37, 219; Littlepage Trilogy, 86–111, 191; Littlepage Trilogy and Leatherstocking Tales, relation between, 84–86, 111–19, 133; *New York*, 112 f.; *Notions of the Americans*, 63; *The Pathfinder*, 124, 128, 132, 220; *The Pioneers*, 96, 118–22, 123–24, 125–27, 130, 132, 136, 307; *The Prairie*, 124 f., 128–29, 135; *The Redskins*, 86, 89, 93, 99–100, 106–07, 108, 109–11; *Satanstoe*, 65, 86, 89–92, 95, 99, 100–05, 107–08, 118, 313; *The Water-Witch*, 68; *Ways of the Hour*, 85
Cotton, John, 115
Cowley, Malcolm, 153
Crane, Hart, *The Bridge*, 137, 243
Crane, Stephen, 81
Crèvecoeur, Hector St. John de, 18–28, 32, 62–63, 68, 135, 216, 221 f.; *Letters from an American Farmer*, 18–28, 221

Daudet, Alphonse, 50
Davis, David Brion, 130
Defoe, Daniel, 17, 70; *Moll Flanders*, 70; *Robinson Crusoe*, 70
Democracy: vision of New Jerusalem defeated by, 34; accomplishment, 42; a step toward perfect fellow-ship, 42; essential function, 43; portrait of democratic man in, 70–71
DeVoto, Bernard, 282, 291
Dickens, Charles, 4, 30–31, 32, 47–58 passim, 80, 89, 257, 289; *American Notes*, 30–31, 32, 52; *Bleak House*, 48; *David Copperfield*, 48; *Dombey and Son*, 57–58; *Nicholas Nickleby*, 49; *The Old Curiosity Shop*, 48, 54; *Oliver Twist*, 48 f., 54
Disraeli, Benjamin, 47 f., 50, 81; *Sybil*, 50
Dorfman, Joseph, 79
Dostoevsky, Fyodor, 2, 50, 57
Dreiser, Theodore, 81; *Sister Carrie*, 205

Economic aspect of Plymouth colony, 12
Eliot, T. S., 296
Emerson, Ralph Waldo, 13, 31 f., 33–34, 37, 40, 51, 72–76 passim, 89, 139, 144 f., 174, 176, 186, 189, 207, 320–21; "The American Scholar," 189; "Friendship," 33, 76; "Love," 76; "Man the Reformer," 31, 34, 72–75, 176; "New England Reformers," 31–37, 51, 207; "Society and Solitude," 33–34
Experience, three dimensions of, 60

Faulkner, William, 91, 102, 112, 140; *The Bear*, 102
Feidelson, Charles, Jr., 239
Fick, Reverend Leonard J., 169
Fielding, Henry, 70
Fitzgerald, F. Scott, 115, 243; *The Great Gatsby*, 243
Flaubert, Gustave, 141
Forster, E. M., 60
Fourier, François M. C., 36–38, 40; Fourierists, 37, 41
Frank, Joseph, 318
Franklin, Benjamin, 17 ff.
Friendship, 76–77
Frontier, social influence of, 13, 14
Frost, Robert, "Mending Wall," 117
Fruitlands, 52
Fuller, S. Margaret, 47

Gabriel, Ralph Henry, 28–29

Galsworthy, John, 303; *The Man of Property*, 303; *The Modern Comedy*, 303

Gaskell, Mrs Elizabeth Cleghorn, 47 f., 50, 52; *Mary Barton*, 48, 50; *North and South*, 48, 50

George, Henry, 79–80; *Progress and Poverty*, 79–80

Gissing, George, 50, 54 f.

God and Satan, drama of, 15–16

Goldsmith, Oliver, *The Vicar of Wakefield*, 100

Hardy, Thomas, 265

Hawthorne, Nathaniel, 1–6 passim, 32, 36 f., 45, 53, 55, 59, 63 ff., 68 ff., 73–74, 79 f., 139–213, 214 f., 218 f., 221, 244, 270, 284, 300–22 passim; "The Artist of the Beautiful," 32, 166–68, 317; *The Blithedale Romance*, 65, 71, 80, 140, 142, 145–46, 150, 177, 194, 196–213, 214, 302–13 passim; "The Christmas Banquet," 165, 170; "The Devil in Manuscript," 151, 167; "Drowne's Wooden Image," 166; "Earth's Holocaust," 171–72, 198–99; "Egotism; or, The Bosom Serpent," 150, 157 f., 165, 186; "Ethan Brand," 150, 154, 159 160–64, 165; "The Gentle Boy," 55; *The House of the Seven Gables*, 140, 142, 150, 190–96, 204–05, 208–09, 307, 313; "Lady Eleanore's Mantle," 170–71; "Little Annie's Ramble," 55; "Main Street," 174; "The Man of Adamant," 150, 156–57; *The Marble Faun*, 59, 63, 150; "The Minister's Black Veil," 150, 157–58, 186; "Mrs. Bullfrog," 73–74; "The New Adam and Eve," 172–73, 175–76, 177, 179; "The Prophetic Pictures," 164–65, 167 f.; "Rappaccini's Daughter," 150,

159–60, 165; "Roger Malvin's Burial," 151; *The Scarlet Letter*, 2, 142 f., 147–48, 150, 173–89, 190, 194, 196, 199, 307; *The Snow-Image*, 163–64; *Twice-Told Tales*, 168; "Wakefield," 150, 155–56, 158; "Young Goodman Brown," 70, 170, 177

Hazlitt, William, 69

Hemingway, Ernest, 280

Hofstadter, Richard, 21, 112

House, Humphry, 49

Howells, William Dean, 79, 81, 282; *A Hazard of New Fortunes*, 81; *Annie Kilburn*, 81

Hugo, Victor, 50

I'll Take My Stand, 7–8

Individualism: as factor in American social life, 8, 11, 13, 14; Franklin representative of shift to, 17–18; economic, 21; dominant force of nineteenth century, 28–29; individuals isolated by products of, 33; Emerson's position, 33; moral regeneration of individual, 34; at the heart of civilization, 39; positive aspects, 40–41; individual the moral key to democracy, 44; Americans required neither to conform nor to reform, 53; individual freedom, 70–71; freedom vs. social life, 77–78. *See also names of novelists*

Jackson, Andrew, 87

James, Henry, 55, 61–62, 63, 65–66, 81 f., 140–42, 144, 154, 167, 184, 211, 313–14; *The Bostonians*, 81; *The Princess Casamassima*, 81

James, Henry, Sr., 37, 38–44, 45, 57, 67, 71, 76, 79, 112, 137, 139, 144, 148, 153, 171, 196 f., 204, 244, 261–68, 322; *Lectures and Miscel-*

lanies, 42–43; *Letter to a Swedenborgian*, 40; *Moralism and Christianity*, 40–41; "Property as a Symbol," 261–68; *The Social Significance of Our Institutions*, 42; *Society the Redeemed Form of Man*, 39 ff., 43; *What Constitutes the State*, 38–39

James, William, 80

Jeffersonian Republicanism, 87

Jones, Howard Mumford, 86

Judd, Sylvester, *Margaret: A Tale of the Real and Ideal*, *Blight and Bloom*, 6

Kingsley, Charles, 47 f., 50, 81; *Alton Locke*, 48, 50; *Yeast*, 48, 50

Koestler, Arthur, *Darkness at Noon*, 175

Land, focus of Cooper on, 86, 103–11

Lawrence, D. H., 96 f., 122, 128, 137, 217, 234, 275, 303, 311

Leavis, Mrs. Q. D., 144, 147, 198

Levin, Harry, 260

Lewis, R. W. B., 121

Love, in American novels, 73–76

Loyalty, 78

Lytton, Edward G. E. L. Bulwer-, 48; *Eugene Aram*, 48; *Paul Clifford*, 48

Manners, American novel not concerned with, 64

Mannheim, Karl, 5, 6, 11, 53, 311

Maritain, Jacques, 76–77, 113, 295

Marlowe, Christopher, 265

Marryat, Captain Frederick, 229, 249

Marx, Leo, 284–85, 287–88, 292, 299, 302 f.

Mather, Cotton, 11–12, 15, 17

Matthesseni, F. O., 150, 164, 194–95

Melville, Herman, 1–6 passim, 22, 45, 53, 64 f., 68, 71, 76, 82–83, 136, 147, 200, 214–79, 280–86 passim, 290, 300, 302, 305, 307, 319 f.; "Bartleby the Scrivener," 215; "Benito Cereno," 215, 276; *Billy Budd*, 277–79; *Clarel*, 82–83, 276–77; *The Confidence-Man*, 215, 283; "The Encantadas," 215, 216–17, 275 f.; *Israel Potter*, 215; *Mardi*, 238–47, 252, 257, 307; *Moby-Dick*, 2, 64, 218 f., 221, 239, 251, 258, 259–75; *Omoo*, 217, 222, 234, 235–38; "The Paradise of Bachelors and The Tartarus of Maids," 275–76; *Pierre*, 65, 215, 313; *Redburn*, 218, 247–52, 255 ff.; *Typee*, 6, 136, 216 ff., 222–35, 236 ff., 243, 246, 252, 254, 257, 290; *White Jacket*, 252–58, 270, 277 f., 322

Mencken, H. L., 173–74

Mennonites, 35

Mill, J. S., 51–52

Moral regeneration, 34. *See also* Hawthorne

Moravians, 35, 36

Negroes, 19, 22

Nisbet, Robert A., 149 n.

Norris, Frank, 81

Novel: aim and content, 46; truth or falsity judged by "pattern of aroused and redistributed sympathies," 46; difference between English and American, 47–48, 51–52, 55–63; social, in England, 48–50; deals with three dimensions of experience, 59–60; vindication of individual freedom, 71.

IN AMERICA: diverges from "classic intention" of investigating social reality, 2–3, 307; concerned with both actual society and ideal social relationships, 4–5; theme of ideal community life, 5, 308 ff.;

metaphysical dimension, 15; difference between English novel and, 47–48, 51–52, 55–63; conception of social reality in, 52–53, 305–19; visionary, not reformist, 53 ff.; addressed to needs of idea! community life, 57; absence of institutionalized relations, 64; not concerned with manners, 64; archetypal, not social, characters, 64; stylistic devices, 64–65; heroes, 66–67; pattern of journey in, 72; love in, 73–76; friendship in, 76–77; the "social" novel, 81; failure of, 310; theories of development of, 313. *See also names of novelists*

Olson, Charles, 271
Owen, Robert, 36, 40; Owenites, 37

Parker, Theodore, 52
Parkman, Francis, 219
Pearson, Norman Holmes, 277
Plymouth colony, 10–12
Pope, Alexander, 163

Ransom, John Crowe, 8
Rappites, 36
Realism, 52–53, 305–19
Reform: movements, 51; American novelists not reformers, 53; reformist intention of English novels, 57; Emerson's view of, 72; man the reformer 72.
Richardson, Samuel, 70; *Clarissa Harlowe*, 70
Riegl, Alois, 314
Riesman, David, 311–12
Ripley, George, 36, 199, 225
Royce, Josiah, 78

Saint-Simon, Claude, Henri de Rouvroy, Comte de, 40

Santayana, George, 288
Scott, Sir Walter, 3, 51, 114, 144
Sedgwick, William Ellery, 224, 226–27, 231
Self-interest: as economic motivation, 12, 21; principle of, 31–32
Selfishness, 39; man a creature of, 41
Shakers, 35, 36
Shakespeare, William, 69, 165, 200, 238
Simms, William Gilmore, 47
Sin, original, 69–70
Smith, Henry Nash, 131
Smith, John E., 78
Socialism, 40
Society: as evil invention, 8; governed by laws of mutual destructiveness, 24; the ultimate state of man, 42; relation between American literature and, 64
Solitude, 13. *See also* Hawthorne
Spiller, Robert E., 94
Swedenborg, 38, 43

Tennyson, Lord Alfred, 247
Tillotson, Kathleen, 54–55, 57–58
Tocqueville, Alexis de, 28, 30, 33, 60–62, 63–65, 152–53
Trilling, Lionel, 2–3, 281, 305, 307, 309, 322–23
Trollope, Anthony, 3
Twain, Mark, 1–6 passim, 45, 53, 56, 68, 71, 76, 82 f., 114, 204, 219, 280–304, 305–06, 313, 319 f.; *The Gilded Age*, 4, 82 f., 282, 313; *Huckleberry Finn*, 2, 4, 51, 71, 83, 130, 204, 280–304, 305–06, 307 f., 311, 313, 322; *Life on the Mississippi*, 283; *The Mysterious Stranger*, 68, 282, 290–91, 300; *Pudd'nhead Wilson*, 313; *Tom Sawyer*, 296, 313; *What is Man?*, 282

Utopian. *See* Communitarian
Values: social, of twelve southerners, 7–8; search for, 71
Van Doren, Mark, 210
Vincent, Howard P., 252

Warner, Charles Dudley, *The Gilded Age*. *See* Twain
Warren, Austin, 44
Watters, R. E., 235 n., 274
Whitman, Walt, 34–35, 39, 82, 219, 255; *Democratic Vistas*, 82; *Song of Myself*, 255
Winters, Yvor, 98

Winthrop, John, 9 ff., 21, 45, 281; "A Model of Christian Charity," 9
Wordsworth, William, 19, 300
Worringer, Wilhelm, *Abstraction and Empathy*, 314–18

Yankees, 89. *See also* Cooper
Yeats, William Butler: "Among School Children," 189; "The Second Coming," 130 f.

Zoar, community at, 36
Zola, Emile, 141